Measuring College Learning Responsibly

Measuring College Learning Responsibly

Accountability in a New Era

Richard J. Shavelson

Stanford University Press
Stanford, California

To Ali, Amy, Justin, Karin, Patti, Potter, and Remy

Stanford University Press

Stanford, California

©2010 by the Board of Trustees of the Leland Stanford Junior University. All rights reserved.

Printed in the United States of America on acid-free, archival-quality paper

Library of Congress Cataloging-in-Publication Data

Shavelson, Richard J.
   Measuring college learning responsibly : accountability in a new era / Richard J. Shavelson.
     p. cm.
   Includes bibliographical references and index.
   ISBN 978-0-8047-6120-8 (cloth : alk. paper)
   ISBN 978-0-8047-6121-5 (pbk. : alk. paper)
   1. Universities and colleges—United States—Examinations.   2. Educational tests and measurements—United States.   3. Educational accountability—United States.
   4. Education, Higher—United States—Evaluation.   I. Title.
   LB2366.2.S53 2010
   378.1'664—dc22   2009019665

Typeset by Westchester Book Group in 10/14 Minion

Contents

Figures and Tables   vi

Preface   viii

Abbreviations   xv

1   Assessment and Accountability Policy Context   1

2   Framework for Assessing Student Learning   8

3   Brief History of Student Learning Assessment   21

4   The Collegiate Learning Assessment   44

5   Exemplary Campus Learning Assessment Programs   70

6   The Centrality of Information in the Demand
for Accountability   102

7   Accountability: A Delicate Instrument   121

8   State Higher-Education Accountability
and Learning Assessment   133

9   Higher-Education Accountability Outside the United States   161

10   Learning Assessment and Accountability for American
Higher Education   183

Notes   211

References   217

Index   231

Figures and Tables

Figures

2.1 Framework for student learning outcomes   13

3.1 Sampling of questions on the Pennsylvania
Senior Examination   25

3.2 Relationship between mean SAT/ACT scores
and CLA scores   36

3.3 Collegiate Learning Assessment performance task   38

4.1 Collegiate Learning Assessment structure   48

4.2 CLA in-basket items from the "Crime" performance task   51

4.3 Faculty perceptions of the CLA's performance tasks   59

4.4 Relationship between academic domain
and performance task type   63

6.1 Accountable to whom?   115

7.1 Standard organizational production model   126

8.1 State-by-state report card   137

8.2 National Center for Public Policy and Higher Education's
"Learning Model"   139

8.3 State profiles of performance on learning assessment measures   140

8.4 State-by-state performance by white and nonwhite
students on the Collegiate Learning Assessment   141

8.5   Value-added performance on Collegiate Learning Assessment   151

10.1   Learning outcomes   187

Tables

3.1   Summary of Tests and Testing Programs by Era   22

3.2   Characteristics of the Collegiate Learning Assessment   35

3.3   Critique an Argument   37

4.1   Criterion Sampling Approach and the Collegiate Learning
Assessment   49

4.2   Scoring Criteria for Performance Tasks   52

4.3   Criteria for Scoring Responses to Analytic Writing Prompts   53

4.4   Students' Mean (Standard Deviation) Perceptions
of CLA Performance Tasks   60

5.1   Cross-Campus Comparison on Dimensions
of Development, Philosophy, Operation, and Impact   81

6.1   Competing "Cultural" Views of Accountability   113

8.1   Most Frequent Indicators in State Higher-Education
Performance Reports by Type   143

8.2   Early State Learning Assessment Programs   145

8.3   Direct Measures of Learning Found in State Report Cards   149

8.4   State Higher-Education Report Cards Database:
Information Collected   159

8.5   State Higher-Education Report Cards   160

Preface

THIS BOOK HAS BEEN GESTATING for almost twenty years. It was conceived, unbeknownst to me at the time, when a program officer at the National Science Foundation asked if I thought that a collegiate version of NAEP could be built.[1] I wondered why the government would want a one-size-fits-all, largely multiple-choice test for all colleges and universities in their full diversity. What good might come of information provided by a collegiate NAEP with scores reported publically in league tables? Why adopt wholesale for higher education an assessment built to monitor mandatory precollegiate education?

I paused then and said that that wasn't a good idea, and, if it was tried, I would oppose it. I didn't see how a single, narrowly gauged achievement test of basic skills could be developed in a manner sensitive to the diversity of education and missions in the nation's institutions of higher education, including the development of higher-order cognitive abilities and personal and interpersonal skills. I didn't see how information provided by a single, general test could be used to improve teaching and learning in higher education. And I didn't see why it would be appropriate to adopt a solution to mandatory precollegiate education for elective higher education, knowing the strengths and limitations of large-scale assessments in an accountability context, as well as the political uses and misuses that have been made of such tests.

I then lost sight of the question of higher-education accountability for a couple of years until a friend, a music professor at a small midwestern liberal arts college, phoned. He had been appointed to a campus-wide committee charged with responding to the North Central Accreditation and School Improvement Association's mandate to assess student learning. He wondered if I thought it appropriate that his college replace its current system of assessing students with an on-demand, multiple-choice test of largely factual and procedural knowledge in the humanities, social sciences, and sciences to meet accreditation demands. He explained that currently all seniors completed a capstone course with high performance expectations; for example, his opera students had to stage an opera, among other requirements. This, he thought, was more relevant to his students' achievement than a humanities multiple-choice test. He asked if I saw something wrong in his thinking. I told him that I didn't think so and suggested that perhaps his committee and his college were overreacting to the accreditation mandate. The questions raised about a collegiate NAEP returned in a new context.

A few years later, learning assessment and accountability came to my attention again, this time in a newspaper article. On Sunday, September 27, 1998, the *New York Times* alerted readers to the New York State Education Department's plan to evaluate public and private colleges and publish the findings as early as 2001. The department planned to convene a higher-education advisory council of college presidents to guide its efforts to produce a "report card" based on a mandatory test for the state's higher-education institutions, public and private. New York was following a trend in the United States (and other countries, such as Britain and Australia) toward increased higher-education accountability. The State University of New York, for one, demurred; the proposal needed further study; a system-wide committee was appointed to do the review.

The New York situation weighed on me. What alternatives were there to one-size-fits-all assessment? What alternatives were there to U.S.-style accountability? Is the K-12 vision embodied in the No Child Left Behind federal legislation the only reasonable option?

These questions were on my mind when a program officer from the Atlantic Philanthropic Service Company (APS), Myra Strober, invited me to lunch to talk about trends in higher education, especially the push for accountability. Myra had just taken a leave from Stanford to direct APS's higher-education grants program and was in the process of framing a portfolio of new projects. When I told her my concerns about accountability trends, she, too, became concerned about the possible unintended negative consequences for higher education.

My discussion with Myra ultimately led to support for the work contained herein, in large part a grant from APS (now called Atlantic Philanthropies). Once Myra asked for a proposal, she turned everything over to Jim Spencer, her predecessor, to avoid any conflict of interest, she and I both being from Stanford.

In this text I examine current practice in assessment of learning and higher-education accountability. By "assessment of learning" I mean the use of both direct measures of achievement (e.g., certification examinations) and ability (e.g., Graduate Record Examination, Collegiate Learning Assessment) and indirect measures (graduation and retention rates, time to degree, job placement and employer satisfaction, and student surveys of engagement). By "accountability" I mean the collection, provision, and interpretation of information on higher-education quality sought by educators and policy makers who have responsibility for assuring the public and "clients"—students, parents, businesses, and government—that invest in education, training, or research.

The goal of this text is to provide education policy makers—in the academy, in government, and in the public—with an overview and critical analysis of options for crafting learning assessment and accountability systems that meet needs for campus teaching and learning improvement and external accountability. Along the way, I identify alternative conceptions of and procedures for assessment and accountability systems, some of which may substantively improve college teaching and learning, both in general education and in the disciplines, while at the same time informing external audiences.

The book begins by introducing the higher-education policy context in the United States and the current demand for learning assessment and external accountability (Chapter 1). A number of tensions emerge, not the least of which is between the formative (institutional improvement) and summative (comparative) functions of accountability and who controls that agenda. A second, related tension is whether and to what extent campuses' performances are publicly compared with one another.

Chapters 2 through 5 address the quest to assess student learning. Chapter 2 distinguishes among direct and indirect measures of learning, arguing that indirect measures do not measure learning, and distinguishes learning (relatively permanent change in behavior over time) from achievement (level of academic performance at one time point) and propensity to learn (level of achievement within a student's reach with minimal scaffolding). A framework is then presented for considering assessment of learning and achievement, ranging from knowledge and reasoning within a domain (e.g., quadratic equations) or major (e.g., mathematics) to broad reasoning, decision making, and communicating within the sciences, social sciences, and humanities; to quantitative, verbal, and spatial reasoning; to general ability. The framework locates current learning assessments and provides a crosswalk among different notions and recommendations for measuring learning outcomes.

In Chapter 3, the 100-year history of learning assessment in higher education is sketched, drawing lessons to be learned from the past for the design of learning assessment and showing that the current debate is not new. I then turn to currently available, externally provided learning assessments and what they attempt to do, concluding that the recent Collegiate Learning Assessment (CLA) offers a great deal of promise. Chapter 4 provides detailed information about the CLA, as it is, arguably, the newest, most innovative assessment of college learning today and relatively little is known about its philosophy and technical qualities.

The last chapter of the learning assessment sequence (Chapter 5) examines undergraduate learning assessment as practiced on campuses; campus-based assessment efforts are essential to meet both formative and summative accountability demands. External assessments signal areas in need of improvement by benchmarking campus performance against the performance of campuses viewed as peers; local campus information is needed to pinpoint challenges and to conjecture and test out possible ways of improving learning. The variability among even exemplary campus assessment programs becomes immediately apparent—in how they were started and are sustained, in what they did (do), and in their intended and unintended consequences for student learning and teaching. The goal here is to identify programs and their implementation and operation that appear to have salutary effects on teaching and learning and draw lessons for the design of learning assessment and accountability systems.

Chapters 6 through 9 focus on accountability. Chapter 6 addresses the centrality of information in accountability and the "cultural conflict" among academe, government, and clients. Although conflict is inevitable, it can nevertheless be productive when cool heads prevail; given the politics of higher-education accountability, the assumption of cool heads is tenuous. Rather, there is considerable room for mischief on all sides.

Chapter 7 examines the role of accountability in a democracy, drawing implications for the role of accountability in higher education. There is a tension between accountability for formative (improvement) and summative (external informative) purposes, as well as between accounting for actions and accounting for outcomes. Moreover, the application of accountability to higher education gives rise to issues such as the presumption of control and causality, the role of sanctions, and the power of whoever controls the stories or accounts that that provide interpretations of accountability information for the public. What becomes clear is that accountability is a powerful policy instrument but a delicate one, one that, if misapplied, may lead to as much mischief as good.

Chapter 8 explores current state-level accountability practices in the United States. How many states have such practices? What do these practices look like? How do they vary? What consequences, intended and unintended, do they appear to have? Performance reporting of some kind dominates in a wide variety of forms. While myriad indicators are published, few states actually report direct measures of learning. And states report so many indicators that performance reports lack focus; the public and policy makers are overwhelmed by data.

In Chapter 9 I analyze accountability systems in different parts of the world, including the European Community generally, especially England and Scandinavia, and Australia, New Zealand, and Hong Kong. Clear alternatives to current practice in the United States (although that is changing) exist. Outside the United States, quality assurance has taken hold. Accreditation, assessment of learning for cognitive and responsibility outcomes, and quality assurance are, in a certain combination, shown to be viable alternatives to current practice in the United States.

The book concludes (in Chapter 10) by setting forth a vision of an assessment and accountability "system" that integrates the findings from the previous chapters. I envision a multifaceted approach to the assessment of learning that includes cognitive outcomes in the majors and in broad abilities, including critical thinking, analytic reasoning, problem solving, and communicating. This vision of learning assessment also encompasses individual and social responsibility outcomes, including the development of personal identity, emotional competence, resilience, and perspective taking (interpersonal, moral, and civic). Learning assessment, both internal and external to colleges and universities, is a centerpiece for a quality assurance system of accountability that incorporates accreditation and assessment. Such a system provides both formative and summative information to higher educators, policy makers, clients, and the public while addressing the tension of conflicting policy and education cultures.

Inevitably, some readers will find some topics of little or no interest. For example, I have not distinguished between public and private four-year institutions or distinguished institutions by Carnegie classification. I believe that because I have been a faculty member and dean at both public (University of California at Los Angeles and University of California at Santa Barbara) and private (Stanford) universities, what I say here can be applied fruitfully across these institutional types (although perhaps more to some types, such as liberal arts colleges, than to, say, research universities). Setting clear goals, building programs to reach them, monitoring progress, and feeding back findings that provide a basis for improvement and experimentation would seem to be beneficial across the spectrum.

Moreover, community colleges and for-profit institutions are not addressed specifically. To be sure, what is said about four-year public and private colleges and universities here may be informative for community colleges and for-profit institutions. However, none of the examples or case studies presented draw on these institutions. Nor was consideration given to their differences and what might be said about them that would differ from what is said about four-year campuses. Simply put, they were beyond the scope of this work.

I am indebted to many colleagues, not the least of whom were program officers at APS overseeing this work—Myra Strober, Jim Spencer, Ted Hullar, and Ray Handlan. I have already described Myra's role. Jim Spencer, in his review of my proposal, said it all sounded academic and why didn't I immerse myself in practice? (Jim's an engineer.) His advice led to my involvement in the creation of the Collegiate Learning Assessment. The responsibility for guiding my grant, however, largely fell on the shoulders of Ted Hullar, who replaced Myra as higher-education program director for APS. His strong support for the project and his patience in the face of slow progress were motivating and greatly appreciated. Ultimately, as the APS higher-education program was phased out, Ted saw to it that I had the resources needed to complete the work and write this text; Ray Handlan did the same, following Ted as my contact.

I am also deeply indebted to Maria Araceli Ruiz-Primo, formerly of Stanford University and now at the University of Colorado–Denver. She helped design, analyze, and report the empirical research conducted for the book. And she patiently read and critiqued a number of chapters. I am also indebted to Blake Naughton, who, as a graduate student at Stanford, helped conceive and design the study of state accountability systems; to Anita Suen, who assisted with research reported in Chapter 8; and to Gayle Christensen, now at the University of Pennsylvania, who as a graduate student and then a Humboldt Fellow at the Max Planck Institute in Berlin provided research support for the chapter on international approaches to accountability (Chapter 9). Finally, a debt of gratitude goes to Lee Shulman, who provided support, advice, wisdom, and encouragement throughout the project.

My colleagues at the Council for Aid to Education—Roger Benjamin, Roger Bolus, and Steve Klein—provided invaluable support for the chapter on the Collegiate Learning Assessment (Chapter 4). My experiences with them in the development and now the use of the CLA proved formative in my thinking about the assessment of learning and its role in higher-education accountability.

Abbreviations

AAC&U	Association of American Colleges and Universities
AACC	American Association of Community Colleges
AASCU	American Association of State Colleges and Universities
AAU	Association of American Universities
ACT	ACT (formerly American College Testing program)
ACU	Assessment Centered University
AP or APS	Atlantic Philanthropic or Atlantic Philanthropic Service
ACE	American Council on Education
CAAP	Collegiate Assessment of Academic Proficiency
CAE	Council for Aid to Education
CIRP	Cooperative Institutional Research Project
CLA	Collegiate Learning Assessment
CNE	Comité National d'Evaluation (France)
College BASE	College Basic Academic Subjects Examination
COMP	College Outcomes Measures Project
CRS	College Results Survey
EAQAHE	European Association for Quality Assurance in Higher Education
ECTS	European Credit Transfer System
ENQA	European Network for Quality Assurance in Higher Education
ETS	Educational Testing Service
EVA	Danish Evaluation Institute
EU	European Union

FU	Flexible University
GPA	grade point average
GPRA	Government Performance and Results Act
GRE	Graduate Record Examination
K-12	kindergarten through 12th grade
LSAT	Law School Admissions Test
LOU	Learning Outcomes University
MAPP	Measure of Academic Proficiency and Performance
NAALS	National Assessment of Adult Literacy Survey
NAEP	National Assessment of Educational Progress
NAICU	National Association of Independent Colleges and Universities
NASULGC	National Association of State Universities and Land-Grant Colleges
NCLB	No Child Left Behind Act
NCPPHE	National Center for Public Policy and Higher Education
NGA	National Governors Association
NCPI	National Center for Postsecondary Improvement
NPEC	National Postsecondary Education Cooperative
NSSE	National Survey of Student Engagement
OECD	Organization of Economic Cooperation and Development
PEA	Progressive Education Association
RAE	Research Assessment Exercise
SAT	SAT (College Admissions Test)
SCLU	Student Centered Learning University
SHEEO	State Higher Education Executive Officers
TIAA/CREF	Teachers Insurance and Annuity Association / College Retirement Equities Fund
UAP	Undergraduate Assessment Program
UK	United Kingdom
VSA	Voluntary System of Accountability
VSNU	Association of Dutch Universities
WTO	World Trade Organization

Measuring College Learning Responsibly

1 Assessment and Accountability Policy Context

ONE MEASURE OF THE IMPACT of a National Commission Report is that it stirs debate and changes behavior. Most such reports, however, come with great fanfare and exit, almost immediately, leaving hardly a trace. The report of former U.S. Secretary of Education Margaret Spellings' Commission on the Future of Higher Education—*A Test of Leadership: Charting the Future of U.S. Higher Education*—is an exception to this rule (www.ed.gov/about/bdscomm/list/hiedfuture/reports/final-report.pdf). It spurred and continues to spur debate; it has demonstrably changed behavior.

This chapter sets the policy context for the quest to assess undergraduates' learning and hold higher education accountable. What follows is a characterization of the Spellings Commission's recommendations and those of professional associations for a new era of accountability, along with academics' critiques of the proposals. The chapter then sketches some of the major issues underlying assessment and accountability and concludes with a vision of a new era in which learning is assessed responsibly within the context of an accountability system focused on teaching and learning improvement, while at the same informing higher education's various audiences.

Spellings Commission Findings and Recommendations

While praising the accomplishments of American higher education, the Spellings Commission said that the "system" had become complacent. "To meet the challenges of the 21st century, higher education must change from a system primarily based on reputation to one based on performance. We urge the creation of a robust culture of accountability and transparency throughout higher education"

1

(p. 21). The Commission considered "improved accountability" (p. 4) the best instrument for change, with colleges and universities becoming "more transparent about cost, price and student success outcomes" and "willingly shar[ing] this information with students and families" (p. 4).

The Commission found fault with higher education in six areas; the three most pertinent here are:

- Learning: "The quality of student learning at U.S. colleges and universities is inadequate and, in some cases, declining" (p. 3).
- Transparency and accountability: There is "a remarkable shortage of clear, accessible information about crucial aspects of American colleges and universities, from financial aid to graduation rates" (p. 4).
- Innovation: "Numerous barriers to investment in innovation risk hampering the ability of postsecondary institutions to address national workforce needs and compete in the global marketplace" (p. 4).

Student learning was at the heart of the Commission's vision of a transparent, consumer-oriented, comparative accountability system. Such a system would put faculty "at the forefront of defining educational objectives . . . and developing meaningful, evidence-based measures" (p. 40) of the value added by a college education. The goal was to provide information to students, parents, and policy makers so they could judge quality among colleges and universities. In the Commission's words (p. 4):

> Student achievement, which is inextricably connected to institutional success, must be measured by institutions on a "value-added" basis that takes into account students' academic baseline when assessing their results. This information should be made available to students, and reported publicly in aggregate form to provide consumers and policymakers an accessible, understandable way to measure the relative effectiveness of different colleges and universities.

The Commission was particularly tough on the current method of holding higher education accountable: accreditation. "Accreditation agencies should make performance outcomes, including completion rates and student learning, the core of their assessment as a priority over inputs or processes" (p. 41). The Commission recommended that accreditation agencies (1) provide comparisons among institutions on learning outcomes, (2) encourage progress and continual improvement, (3) increase quality relative to specific institutional missions, and (4) make this information readily available to the public.

Higher Education Responds to the Commission's Report

At about the same time that the Commission released its report, higher-education associations, anticipating the Commission's findings and recommendations and wanting to maintain control of their constituent institutions' destinies, announced their take on the challenges confronting higher education. In a "Letter to Our Members: Next Steps," the American Council on Education (ACE), American Association of State Colleges and Universities (AASCU), American Association of Community Colleges (AACC), Association of American Universities (AAU), National Association of Independent Colleges and Universities (NAICU), and the National Association of State Universities and Land-Grant Colleges (NASULGC) enumerated seven challenges confronting higher education (www.acenet.edu/AM/Template.cfm?Section=Home&CONTENTID=18309 &TEMPLATE=/CM/ContentDisplay.cfm):

- Expanding college access to low-income and minority students
- Keeping college affordable
- Improving learning by utilizing new knowledge and instructional techniques
- Preparing secondary students for higher education
- Increasing accountability for educational outcomes
- Internationalizing the student experience
- Increasing opportunities for lifelong education and workforce training

Perhaps the most astonishing "behavior change" came from AASCU and NASULGC. These organizations announced the creation of the Voluntary System of Accountability (VSA). Agreeing with the Spellings Commission on the matter of transparency, these organizations created the VSA to communicate information on the undergraduate student experience through a common web reporting template or indicator system, the College Portrait. The VSA, a voluntary system focused on four-year public colleges and universities (www.voluntarysystem.org/index.cfm), is designed to do the following:

- Demonstrate accountability and stewardship to the public
- Measure educational outcomes to identify effective educational practices
- Assemble information that is accessible, understandable, and comparable

Of course, not all responses to the Commission's report and the associations' letter were positive in nature or reflective of behavior change. The report, as well as the letter, was roundly criticized. Critics rightly pointed out that the proposals did not directly address the improvement of teaching and learning but focused almost exclusively on the external or summative function of accountability.

The recommendation for what appeared to be a one-size-fits-all standardized assessment of student learning by external agencies drew particular ire (but see Graff & Birkenstein, 2008). To academics any measure that assessed learning of all undergraduates simply was not feasible or would merely tap general ability, and the SAT and GRE were available to do that. Moreover, it was not possible to reliably measure a campus's value added. Finally, cross-institutional comparisons amounted to comparing apples and oranges; such comparisons were nonsensical and useless for improving teaching and learning.

The critics, moreover, pointed out that learning outcomes in academic majors varied, and measures were needed at the department level. If outcomes in the majors were to be measured, these measures should be constructed internally by faculty to reflect the campus's curriculum. A sole focus on so-called cognitive outcomes would leave out important personal and social responsibility outcomes such as identity, moral development, resilience, interpersonal and inter-cultural relations, and civic engagement.

The report had failed, in the critics' view, to recognize the diversity of higher-education missions and students served. It had not recognized but intruded upon the culture of academe in which faculty members are responsible for curriculum, assessment, teaching, and learning. The higher-education system was just too complex for simple accountability fixes. Horse-race comparisons of institutions at best would be misleading to the public and policy makers, and at worse would have perverse effects on teaching and learning at diverse American college and university campuses.

Assessment and Accountability in Higher Education

The Commission report and the multiple and continuing responses to it set the stage for examining assessment and accountability in higher education in this text. The focus here is on accountability—in particular, the assessment of student learning in accountability. This is not to trivialize the other challenges identified by the Commission or by the professional higher-education organizations. Rather, the intent is to tackle what is one of the three bottom lines of higher education: student learning, which is the hardest outcome of all to get a good handle on. (The other two are research and service.)

As we saw, there is a tug-of-war going on today as in the past among three forces: policy makers, "clients," and colleges and universities. The tug-of-war reflects a conflict among these "cultures." The academic culture traditionally focuses on assessment and accountability for organizational and instructional improvement through accreditation, eschewing external scrutiny. "Clients"— students and their parents and governmental agencies and businesses—rely on colleges and universities for education, training, and research. They want comparative information about the relative strengths and weakness among institutions in order to decide where to invest their time and economic resources. And policy makers are held responsible by their constituencies to ensure high-quality education. Consequently, policy makers have a need to know how well campuses are meeting their stated missions in order to assure the public. Reputation, input, and process information is no longer adequate for this purpose. As the Commission noted, "Higher education must change from a system primarily based on reputation to one based on performance" (p. 21).

All of this raises questions such as, "What do we mean by student learning?" "What kinds of student learning should higher education be held accountable for?" "How should that learning be measured?" "Who should measure it?" And "How should it be reported, by whom, to whom, and with what consequences?"

The Commission's report and its respondents also raised questions about the nature of accountability. The Commission took a client-centered perspective— transparency of performance indicators, with intercampus comparative information for students and parents. Four-year public colleges and universities have, in the most extreme response, in the VSA, embraced this perspective.

The Commission's vision is shared by the policy community. The policy community's compact with higher education has been rocked by rising costs, decreasing graduation rates, and a lack of transparency about student learning and value added. No longer are policy makers willing to provide resources to colleges and universities on a "trust me" or reputational basis; increased transparency of outcomes and accountability are demanded.

In contrast, most higher-education professional organizations view accountability as the responsibility of colleges and universities and their accrediting agencies. External comparisons are eschewed (with exceptions noted above); internal diagnostic information for the improvement of the organization and teaching and learning is sought. This is not to say colleges and universities do not recognize the challenges presented to them in the 21st century, as we saw in the open letter issued by the major higher-education organizations in the United States. They do, and they want to control accountability rather than be controlled by it.

These varying views of accountability lead back to first principles and questions. "What is accountability?" "What should campus leaders be held accountable for—valued educational processes? Valued outcomes? Both?" "How should accountability be carried out?" "Who should carry it out?" "Who should get to report findings?" "What sanctions should be meted out if campuses fail to measure up?" "Should there be sanctions and, if not, what?" "What are states currently doing to hold their colleges and universities accountable?" "How do other nations hold their higher-education systems accountable?" "What seems to be a reasonable and effective approach to accountability for the United States going forward into the 21st century?"

A Vision of Higher-Education Assessment and Accountability in a New Era

The vision of assessment and accountability presented in this text is one of continuous improvement of teaching and learning by campuses evolving into learning organizations, with progress based on an iterative cycle of evidence, experimentation, action, and reflection. The vision, in part, is one of direct assessment of student learning on cognitive outcomes in the major and in general or liberal education (measured by the Collegiate Learning Assessment). However, the vision of learning outcomes goes beyond the cognitive to individual and social responsibility outcomes, including, for example, the development of one's identity, emotional competence, perspective taking (moral, civic, interpersonal, intercultural), and resilience.

Colleges and universities would be held accountable by regional agencies governed by boards composed of higher-education leaders, policy makers, and clients. These agencies would be accountable to a national agency of similar composition. Agencies would conduct academic audits and report findings publicly, in readily accessible form, to various interested audiences.

The audit would focus on the *processes* a campus has in place to ensure teaching and learning quality and improvement. To do this, the audit would rely on and evaluate the campus's assessment program. The campus assessment program would be expected to collect, analyze, and interpret data and feed back findings into campus structures that function to take action in the form of experiments aimed at testing ideas about how to improve teaching and learning. Over time, subsequent assessments would monitor progress made in the majors, in general or liberal education, and by individual students. In addition to providing data on student learning outcomes, the audit program would include other indicators of quality—for example, admission, retention, and graduation rates and consumer quality surveys.

The audit findings—not the learning assessment findings per se—would be made public. The report, based on data from the campus assessment program and a report by an external expert visiting panel, would include appraisals as to how rigorous the institution's goals were, how rigorous the assessment of those goals was, how well the institution had embedded quality assurance mechanisms throughout the organization (including delving deeply into a sample of departments and their quality assurance processes), and how well the institution was progressing toward those goals. The report would also include a summary of the general strengths and weaknesses of the campus and its quality assurance mechanisms. In this way such published academic audits would "have teeth" and would inform both educators within the institution and policy makers and clients outside.

2 Framework for Assessing Student Learning

OVER THE PAST TWENTY-FIVE YEARS the public, along with state and federal policy makers, has increasingly pressured colleges and universities to account for student outcomes. More recently the mantra has been to create a "culture of evidence" to guide improvement (e.g., Shavelson, 2007b). As part of the move to greater accountability than in past, states today have some form of performance reporting, and about half (Naughton, Shavelson & Suen, 2003; see Chapter 7) have what Gormley and Weimar (1999, p. 3) call report cards: "a regular effort by an organization [in our case, a state] to collect data on two or more *other* organizations [public colleges and universities in the state], transform the data into information relevant to assessing performance ["indicators"], and transmit the information to some audience external to the organizations themselves [public, parents, students, policy makers]." (Italics in original.)

Although virtually all state reports provide indicators of student "learning," these indicators are typically proxies—for example, graduation rates or student surveys. Today, states and campuses are being pressured to measure learning directly. The Spellings Commission (U.S. Department of Education, 2006), for example, has called for standardized tests of students' critical thinking, problem solving, and communication skills (see Chapter 1).

While most agree that colleges should track student learning, they may frequently have in mind different outcomes (e.g., knowledge in the majors vs. broad abilities like critical thinking), different ways of measuring these outcomes (indirect vs. direct measures), and different notions about what learning is—it is often confused with achievement. This chapter begins by clarifying what is meant by direct and indirect learning measures and argues that the latter do *not* measure learning: Direct measures of learning should be used. The chapter then distinguishes among learning, achievement, and propensity to learn and describes the kinds of data collection designs needed to measure each. By the very definition of *learning* as a permanent change in observable behavior over time, so-called indirect measures cannot measure learning. In order to clarify what we mean by "assessing learning outcomes," a framework is presented for conceiving and displaying these outcomes. The chapter concludes by using that framework to justify a recommendation to focus on three main learning outcomes: (1) knowledge and reasoning in the majors; (2) broad abilities such as critical thinking, analytic reasoning, and problem solving; and (3) individual and social responsibility.

Direct and Indirect Measures of Learning

Until quite recently indicators of student learning have been based largely on indirect measures, including graduation rates; progress or retention rates; employment rates; student, employer, and alumni satisfaction (Naughton, Shavelson & Suen, 2003; e.g., College Results Survey, see Zemsky, 2000; or NCPI, 2002); and student reports of the campus academic environment (e.g., National Survey of Student Engagement [NSSE]; Kuh, 2003). These measures are considered to be indirect because there is a big gap between, for example, graduation rates or students' reports of their learning and their actual learning as a relatively permanent change in *observed behavior* over a period of time.

Indirect measures of learning are not actual measures of learning because they do not directly tap observable behavior change. For example, even though NSSE has been developed to measure those indicators that past research has shown to be correlated with performance on direct measures of learning, student self-reports on this survey are uncorrelated (typically correlations of less than 0.15) with direct learning measures (Carini, Kuh & Klein, 2006; Pascarella, Seifert & Blaich, 2008). To reiterate, indirect measures of learning aren't. That said, such measures (e.g., of persistence, graduation rates) may be important indicators of campus performance in themselves or for improving educational processes. For example, NSSE may provide valuable insights into campus *processes* that support learning and might become the focus of experimentation to improve learning and teaching and surrounding support structures.

Direct measures of learning provide concrete observable evidence of behavior change. Such measures typically include scores on licensure (e.g., teacher or nurse certification) and graduate school admissions examinations (GRE; e.g., Callan & Finney, 2002; Naughton, Shavelson & Suen, 2003; Shavelson & Huang,

2003; see also National Center for Public Policy and Higher Education, 2002, 2004, 2006, 2008). Increasingly, broad measures of critical thinking, communication, and decision making have been used. Examples of these assessments include the Collegiate Learning Assessment (Klein et al., 2005; Klein et al., 2007; Miller, 2006; Shavelson, 2007a,b; Shavelson, 2008a,c), the Collegiate Assessment of Academic Proficiency, and the Measure of Academic Proficiency and Progress (Dwyer, Millett & Payne, 2006). Chapters 3 and 4 provide details on direct measures of learning, especially the Collegiate Learning Assessment.

On Learning, Achievement, and Propensity to Learn

Assessment of learning is a catch phrase that includes "indirect" and "direct" "measures of learning." The phrase is understood vaguely by the public and policy makers; but it communicates its intent—to focus on important outcomes, student learning being the most important, not simply on college inputs and processes as a basis for holding higher education accountable. However, this phrase is technically incorrect. Learning is defined as a relatively permanent change in a person's behavior (e.g., knowledge, problem solving ability, civic engagement, personal responsibility) over time that is due to experience rather than maturation. In order to measure students' cognitive learning, tasks are developed in which "correct or appropriate processing of mental information is critical to successful performance" (Carroll, 1993, p. 10). Moreover, we need to measure students' performance at two or more time points and to be able to interpret the change in their behavior as learning due to environmental factors (e.g., experience, instruction, or self-study). While this argument may seem picky, it turns out to be an important consideration in designing student learning assessments and in interpreting learning indicators in state report cards and elsewhere (e.g., Astin, 1993a).

This definition of learning rules out indirect measures of such factors as graduation rates, time to degree, and surveys of satisfaction (e.g., Zemsky, 2000) and student engagement (e.g., National Survey of Student Engagement; Kuh, 2001, 2003) as bearing directly on learning. These output measures do not tap the student-learning outcomes that include cognition (knowledge, reasoning, problem solving, writing), personal growth (ability to accept responsibility, manage on one's own), social engagement, and civic engagement (described in Chapter 3). Moreover, indirect measures refer to groups of students, not individual students; yet learning, in the last analysis, is a within-individual phenomenon. Finally, indirect measures do not focus on change over time but on rates at one point in time.

The phrase *direct measures of learning* is typically a misnomer, as well. For the most part, what gets measured by direct measures of learning is *not* learning but *achievement*. Achievement is the accumulation or amount of learning in (1) formal and informal instructional settings, (2) a period of self-study on a particular topic, or (3) a period of practice *up to a point in time when student performance is measured* (see Carroll, 1993, p. 17). That is, learning is about change in behavior. Most direct measures of learning that get reported to the public do not measure change. Rather, they measure the status of a group of students (e.g., seniors) at a particular point in time. What is measured when students sit for a certification examination or for a graduate admissions examination is achievement, not learning. Moreover, in interpreting that achievement, higher education alone cannot be said to be the "cause" of learning, as students may have learned outside of college while attending college. Attributing causality to one or another agent is problematic for learning assessment and accountability (see Chapters 6 and 7).

Finally, learning and achievement need to be distinguished from *propensity to learn,* which is perhaps what we would ideally like to know about students. Propensity to learn may be defined as a student's *achievement* under conditions of scaffolding (Vygotsky, 1986/1934), the provision of sequential hints or supports as the student attempts to perform a task or solve a problem ("dynamic assessment" is an exemplar; e.g., Campione & Brown, 1984; Feuerstein, Rand & Hoffman, 1979). That is, with a little assistance, how well can a student perform? And by implication, how much is she likely to learn from further instruction? Or, put another way, is the student able to apply what she has learned in college (and elsewhere) successfully in new learning situations?

Most direct measures of students' learning are actually measures of their achievement at a particular point in time. Attribution of causality for learning— e.g., solely to a college education—is not warranted, although the college most likely was a major part of the cause. To examine learning, individual students need to be tracked over time. Although ultimately we may want to know a student's propensity to learn, we do know that prior achievement is the best predictor of future achievement (e.g., Carroll, 1993), so the achievement indicator of "learning" seems a good proxy.[1]

Framework for Assessing Achievement and Learning

Having distinguished learning, achievement, and propensity to learn and argued that most assessment of learning in the current accountability context is actually assessment of achievement, I ask you to consider now the question of what achievement and learning should be measured. Should students' factual and conceptual knowledge in a domain such as economics be measured? Should their ability to reason analytically and write critically be measured? Should their ability to adapt to and learn in novel situations be measured? Should achievement be limited to the so-called cognitive domain and not the personal, social, and moral? As will be seen in the next chapter, answers to these questions have differed over the past one hundred years.

Currently, however, the answer seems to be "all of these." Americans hold diverse goals for their colleges and universities as Immerwahl (2000, table 3—national sample information) reported in a national survey. The public wanted graduates with:

- sense of maturity and ability to manage on own (71 percent of respondents)
- ability to get along with people different from self (68 percent)
- improved problem solving and thinking ability (63 percent)
- high-tech skills (61 percent)
- specific expertise and knowledge in chosen career (60 percent)
- top-notch writing and speaking skills (57 percent)
- responsibilities of citizenship (44 percent)

A conceptual framework, then, is needed to help answer the question of what might or should be measured to "assess learning." To this end research on cognition (e.g., Bransford, Brown & Cocking, 1999) and cognitive abilities (e.g., Martinez, 2000; Messick, 1984) has been integrated to create a framework for considering cognitive outcomes of higher education (Shavelson & Huang, 2003; Shavelson, 2007a,b). Cognitive outcomes range from domain-specific knowledge acquisition (e.g., Immerwahr's questionnaire item "Specific expertise and knowledge in chosen career") to the most general of reasoning and problem-solving abilities (Immerwahr's questionnaire item "Improved problem solving and thinking ability").

One caveat is in order before proceeding to the framework. Learning is highly situated and bounded by the context in which initial learning occurred. Only through extensive engagement, deliberative practice, and informative feedback in a domain such as "quadratic equations" does this knowledge become increasingly decontextualized for a learner. At this point knowledge transfers to similar situations in general and so enhances general reasoning, problem solving, and decision making in a broad domain (in this case, mathematics) and later to multiple domains as general quantitative reasoning (e.g., Bransford, Brown & Cocking, 1999; Messick, 1984; Shavelson, 2008b). Moreover,

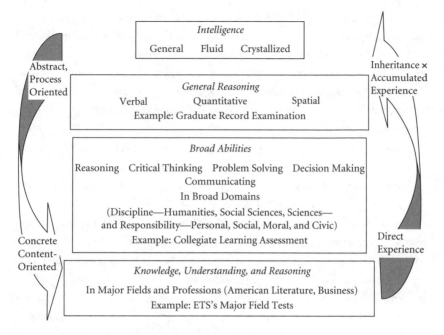

Figure 2.1 Framework for student learning outcomes.
SOURCE: Adapted from Shavelson, 2007a.

what is learned and how well it transfers to new situations depends on the natural endowments, aptitudes, and abilities that students bring with them. These aptitudes and abilities are a product of their education (in and out of school) in combination with their natural endowments (e.g., Shavelson et al., 2002).

A useful framework for distinguishing higher-education outcomes, then, must capture this recursive complexity. Moreover, it must allow us to see what cognitive outcomes different tests of learning attempt to measure. One possible framework for capturing knowledge and reasoning outcomes is presented in Figure 2.1 (from Shavelson, 2007a,b; Shavelson & Huang, 2003; see also Cronbach, 2002, p. 61, table 3.1; Martinez, 2000, p. 24, figure 3.2). The framework ranges from domain-specific knowledge, such as knowledge of chemistry, to what Charles Spearman called general ability or simply G. (G is used in the framework to denote general ability and to avoid the antiquated interpretation of G as genetically determined; see Cronbach, 2002; Kyllonen & Shute, 1989; Messick, 1984; Snow & Lohman, 1984.)[2]

Working from domain-specific knowledge toward general ability, we find increasingly general abilities, such as verbal, quantitative, and visual-spatial reasoning (and more; see Carroll, 1993), that build on inherited capacities and are typically developed over many years in formal and informal education settings. These general reasoning abilities, in turn, contribute to fluid intelligence and crystallized intelligence. "Fluid intelligence is functionally manifest in novel situations in which prior experience does not provide sufficient direction; crystallized intelligence is the precipitate of prior experience and represents the massive contribution of culture to the intellect" (Martinez, 2000, p. 19).

Of course, what has been presented is an oversimplification. Knowledge and abilities are interdependent. Learning and achievement depend not only on instruction but also on the knowledge and abilities that students bring to college instruction. Indeed, instruction and abilities most likely combine or interact to produce learning. This interaction evolves so that different abilities are called forth over time. Moreover, different and progressively more challenging learning tasks are needed in this evolution (Snow, 1994; Shavelson et al., 2002). Consequently, what is sketched in Figure 2.1 does not behave in strict, orderly fashion. (The figure could have been flipped 90 or 180 degrees!) The intent is heuristic: to provide a conceptual framework for discussing learning outcomes and their measures.

Domain-Specific Knowledge and Reasoning

By domain-specific knowledge and reasoning is meant knowledge in the domain of, for example, physics, sociology, or music, and its use to reason through a task or problem. This is the kind of knowledge that would be assessed to gauge students' learning in an academic major. Domain-specific knowledge corresponds to such valued higher-education outcomes as "high-tech skills" or "specific expertise and knowledge in chosen career."

Domain-specific knowledge and reasoning can be divided into four types (e.g., Li, Ruiz-Primo, & Shavelson, 2006):

- *Declarative* (knowing that)—knowing and reasoning with facts and concepts (e.g., the Earth circles the sun in a slightly elliptical orbit)
- *Procedural* (knowing how)—knowing and reasoning with simple and complicated routines (e.g., how to get the mass of an object with a balance scale)
- *Schematic* (knowing why)—knowing and reasoning with a system of procedural and declarative knowledge (predicting, explaining, modeling;

for example, knowing why San Francisco has a change of seasons over the course of a year)

• *Strategic* (knowing when, where, and how to apply these other types of knowledge)—so-called meta-cognitive knowledge and reasoning (e.g., knowing and reasoning when to apply the quadratic equation to solve a problem)

Conceptual and empirical support for these distinctions comes from diverse areas. Brain imaging studies have found that different types of knowledge, especially declarative knowledge and procedural knowledge, are localized in different areas of the brain (for a short summary, see Bransford, Brown & Cocking, 1999). Cognitive science research (Bransford, Brown & Cocking, 1999; Pellegrino, Chudowsky & Glaser, 2001) has provided evidence not only of declarative, procedural, and strategic knowledge, but also of what we have called schematic knowledge (Gentner & Stevens, 1983). Distinctions among these various types of knowledge have been made in K-12 content standards (e.g., Bybee, 1996) and in test-development frameworks for large-scale assessments such as the 2009 NAEP Science Assessment Framework. In practice, most tests of domain-specific knowledge still focus on declarative knowledge, as exemplified by, for example, ETS's Major Field Tests.

Disciplinary and Broad Abilities

Disciplinary and Broad Abilities[3] are complex combinations of cognitive and motivational processes ("thinking"). They come closest to what is implied when we hear that the cognitive outcomes of higher education include critical thinking, problem solving, and communicating. They differ in their specificity. Disciplinary abilities are developed within a discipline—e.g., historians use historiography to disentangle events; statisticians use randomized trials as an "ideal" for modeling nonexperimental data; and physicists reason with diagrams to resolve forces. Disciplinary abilities are typically developed within a major and are closely linked to disciplinary knowledge.

Broad abilities are generalized from specific, related disciplines. For example, reasoning in the behavioral and social sciences—as developed in anthropology, political science, psychology, sociology—is generalized from the discipline across common disciplinary reasoning features, such as the use of experimentally generated empirical evidence for arguing knowledge claims. These abilities are organized broadly into areas such as the humanities, social sciences, and sciences.

These reasoning processes underlie verbal, quantitative and spatial reasoning, comprehending, problem solving, and decision making. They can be called upon within a discipline (e.g., physics) and more generally across domains as situations demand, hence their name. Broad abilities are developed well into adulthood through learning in and transfer from nonschool and school experiences and repeated exercise of domain-specific knowledge. Knowledge development, of course, occurs in conjunction with prior learning interacting with previously established general reasoning abilities. Consequently, these developed abilities are not innate or fixed in capacity (e.g., Messick, 1984).

Disciplinary and Broad Abilities, along with different types of knowledge, play out in achievement situations: "In educational achievement, cognitive abilities and ability structures are engaged with knowledge structures in the performance of subject-area tasks. Abilities and knowledge combine in ways guided by and consistent with knowledge structure to form patterned complexes for application and action" (Messick, 1984, p. 226; see also Shavelson et al., 2002).

As tasks become increasingly broad—moving from a knowledge domain (discipline) to a field such as social science and then to broad everyday problems—general abilities exercise greater influence over performance than do knowledge structures and domain-specific abilities. Many of the valued outcomes of higher education are associated with the development of these broad abilities. For example, two important higher-education outcomes are "improved problem solving and thinking ability" and "top-notch writing and speaking."

Assessments of learning currently in vogue, as well as some developed in the mid 20th century, tap into these broad abilities. Most have focused primarily at the level of areas—sciences, social sciences, and humanities.[4] Nevertheless, many of the area tests (e.g., Collegiate Assessment of Academic Proficiency [CAAP], Undergraduate Assessment Program [UAP]) divide an area such as science into questions on physics, biology, and chemistry. Because too few questions are available in each discipline to produce reliable domain-knowledge scores, an aggregate, broader science area score is provided, even though the questions focus on knowledge at the level of a discipline (see Figure 2.1). The science area score falls between domain-specific knowledge and general reasoning abilities.

Other tests are more generic, focusing on critical thinking, writing, and reasoning. Some examples are the GRE's Issues and Analytic Writing prompts, the College BASE (Basic Academic Subjects Examination), the Academic Profile (recently replaced by the Measure of Academic Proficiency and Performance [MAPP]), CAAP, and what was ETS's Undergraduate Assessment Program Field

Tests. Indeed, many tests of broad abilities contain both area (e.g., sciences) and general reasoning and writing tests.

Intelligence: Crystallized, Fluid, and General

General reasoning abilities occupy the upper parts of Figure 2.1. These abilities have developed over significant periods of time through experience (e.g., school) in combination with one's inheritance. They are the most general of abilities and account for consistent levels of performance across heterogeneous situations. Cattell (1963) argued that intelligence involves both fluid and crystallized abilities. "Both these dimensions reflect the capacity for abstraction, concept formation, and perception and eduction [sic; Spearman's term] of relations" (Gustafsson & Undheim, 1996, p. 196). The fluid dimension of intelligence "is thought to reflect effects of biological and neurological factors" (p. 196) and includes speed of processing, visualization, induction, sequential reasoning, and quantitative reasoning. It is most strongly associated with performance on novel tasks. The crystallized dimension reflects acculturation (especially education) and involves language and reading skills (e.g., verbal comprehension, language development, as well as school-related numeracy) and school achievement (see Carroll, 1993).

These reasoning abilities are distal from current college instruction. They typically are interpreted as verbal ("crystallized") and quantitative ("fluid") reasoning and are measured by tests such as the SAT or GRE. They are developed over a long period of time, *in school and out*. Nevertheless, there is some evidence of short-term college impact on these abilities (e.g., Pascarella & Terenzini, 2005).

The most general of all abilities is general intelligence—the stuff that fuels thinking, reasoning, decision making, and problem solving—and accounts for consistency of performance across vastly different novel and not-so-novel situations. General intelligence involves induction "and other factors involving complex reasoning tasks" (Gustafsson & Undheim, 1996, p. 198). Although education might ultimately be aimed at cultivating intelligence (Martinez, 2000), changes in intelligence due to learning in college would be expected to be quite small and distal from the curriculum in higher-education institutions.

What to Assess When Assessing Learning?

The question of what to assess when we assess learning, then, is much more complex than thought at first. It seems that domain knowledge and reasoning in a broad domain (e.g., natural sciences) falls well within the purview of academic disciplines and liberal-arts programs. Here students are expected to delve deeply into a subject matter and develop considerable declarative, procedural, and schematic knowledge. Moreover, the strategic knowledge they develop includes planning and goal setting, strategies for reaching goals, and monitoring progress toward those goals that are known to be effective in that domain. For example, in physics, one strategy for solving force and motion problems is the use of force diagrams. Such diagrams help students know when, where, and how to apply their knowledge of mechanics.

Similarly, broad abilities that include verbal, quantitative, and spatial reasoning; decision making; problem solving; and communicating fall within the purview of liberal or general education. Here students are expected to draw broadly on what they have learned to address everyday practical problems that do not necessarily have convergent answers but involve trade-offs, moral issues, and social relations in addition to domain specific knowledge. As Shavelson and Huang (2003) noted, it is curious that these more complex abilities fall early in the college curriculum, whereas the domain-specific abilities fall later in the major; perhaps the two should be reversed.

Throughout the history of assessing learning in American higher education, the pendulum has swung between a focus on domain knowledge and on broad abilities. However, this is not an either-or situation. The two should be balanced in assessing learning—although today the pendulum has shifted to the broad ability part of Figure 2.1, as we shall see in the next chapter.

Finally, and not typically thought of when learning outcomes are discussed, although they should be (e.g., Shavelson & Huang, 2003; Shavelson 2007a), are the so-called soft skills (creativity, teamwork, and persistence; Dwyer, Millett & Payne, 2006) or "individual and social responsibility" skills (personal, civic, moral, social, and intercultural knowledge and actions; AAC&U, 2005). To a large extent, this neglect grows out of limitations in measurement technology, lack of research (funding), and suspicion. As Dwyer, Millett and Payne (2006, p. 20) pointed out, "At the present state of the art in assessing soft skills, the assessments are, unfortunately, susceptible to . . . undesirable coaching effects." Nevertheless, such "soft" outcomes are important and should be measured; not to measure them would mean they would likely be ignored.

Reprise

The design of any higher-education accountability system will, as one of its most important outputs, include an assessment of student learning. While there seems to be unanimity as to the importance of this student learning, there is disagreement as to how learning might be defined and measured. Learning indicators can be distinguished as to whether they are indirect (reflecting the consequences of learning) or direct (tapping into what and how much has been learned). Indirect measures of learning are not and cannot be such measures. Learning is a relatively permanent change in behavior over time that results from the interaction of an individual with the environment. To gauge learning, student performance needs to be measured at two points in time; indirect measures typically reflect a single time point. Moreover, most accountability systems that profess to measure learning directly actually measure achievement—the relative or absolute level of students' performance at a particular point in time. Finally, perhaps the best possible measure of learning, but one that would be problematic for large-scale accountability, would be a measure of students' propensity to learn in new situations.

The important consequences of this definitional hieroglyphics are twofold. First, accountability designers need to be clear on what student performance outcome is intended to be measured—achievement or learning. Second, if an accountability system intends to measure student learning, student performance should be measured at least at two points in time. This might be accomplished by following up students upon entry and exit from college. The importance of measuring the performance of all or a representative sample of students longitudinally cannot be overemphasized. Or learning might be measured cross-sectionally by comparing the performance of freshmen and, say, seniors. If the cross-sectional tack is taken, the system would have to provide measures on all or a representative sample of students in their freshman and senior years, adjusting for any change of demographics in the two classes over that time period (e.g., Klein et al., 2007; Klein et al., 2008).

This still leaves open the question of *what to assess*. On the basis of the framework for cognitive learning outcomes, knowledge and reasoning in the disciplines and broader abilities that include critical reasoning, decision making, problem solving, and communicating in the areas of the humanities, social sciences, and sciences should be the focus of learning and assessment of learning. Consequently, a single measure of learning is unlikely to fill the bill; multiple measures—some standardized to benchmark performance and some institutionally built to diagnose curricular strengths and weaknesses—are needed. That is, a balance is needed between external ("standardized") learning assessments for benchmarking and signaling purposes and internally developed assessments closely reflecting a campus's mission for improvement.

Finally, any assessment of learning should include the so-called soft skills (a preferred term, following the American Association of Colleges and Universities, is "individual and social responsibility"). At present, widespread agreement has not been reached upon what set of such knowledge and skills should be measured or how to measure them, but there are currently a number of efforts under way to move this agenda forward.

One possible idea for measuring these skills goes like this (Shavelson, 2007a,b). Consider a performance task involving the local environment. Students might be given an "in basket" of information (scientific reports, newspaper articles, opinion editorials, statistical and economic information) and be asked to review arguments made by local environmentalists and the business community for and against removing an old dam. In reviewing material from the in basket, students would find that environmentalists wanted to return the land to its prior state, supporting the natural streams and rivers, flora and fauna that once thrived there and providing hiking, camping, and fishing recreation with personal and commercial benefits. Students also would find that the environmentalists were pitted against other community members who use the manmade lake for fishing, boating, and swimming. Moreover, students would find that homes, restaurants, and other commercial establishments had been built up around the lake since the dam was constructed, that the dam is used to generate the county's power, and that excess energy is sold to other counties. On the basis of their review and analysis, students would be asked to outline the economic, political, social, and ethical pros and cons of removing the county's dam and to arrive at a recommendation for a course of action. While there would be no single correct answer, the quality of their reasoning—the application of their social responsibility skills—could be judged.

3 Brief History of Student Learning Assessment

YOU MIGHT CONCLUDE, reading policy documents, newspapers, or even the first chapter of this book that the current focus on learning outcomes is something new. But that's not so. For well over the past one hundred years, assessment-of-learning "movements"—which usually measured achievement and assumed that reflected college learning—have come and gone. However, there are excellent examples of learning being assessed intentionally, as we shall see, and plenty of good models of assessment that could and probably should inform today's practice (for details, see Shavelson, 2007b).

Four periods in the history of learning assessment can be distinguished: (1) origins of standardized testing of learning in higher education (1900–1933), (2) assessment of learning for general and graduate education (1933–47), (3) rise of the test providers (1948–78), and (4) era of external accountability (1979–present). For ease of reference, the tests and testing programs are summarized by each of these periods in Table 3.1.

Origins of Standardized Testing of Learning in Higher Education: 1900–1933

The first third of the 20th century marked the beginning of standardized, objective testing to assess learning in higher education, spurred by the success of standardized "objective" mental testing in World War I. In 1916 the Carnegie Foundation for the Advancement of Teaching led the testing movement when five graduate students and William S. Learned, Carnegie staff member and learning-assessment visionary, tested students "in the experimental school at the University of Missouri in arithmetic, spelling, penmanship, reading, and

Table 3.1. Summary of Tests and Testing Programs by Era

Era	Study, Program, or Test Provider	Test
Origins of standardized testing of learning: 1900–1933	Missouri Experimental School Study	Objective tests of arithmetic, spelling, penmanship, reading, English, and composition
	Thorndike MIT Engineers Study	Objective tests of mathematics, English, and physics
	Pennsylvania Study	Objective tests of general culture (literature, fine arts, history and social studies, general science), English (e.g., spelling, grammar, vocabulary), mathematics, and intelligence
Assessment of learning for general and graduate education: 1933–47	Chicago College General Education	Constructed response and objective tests focusing on analysis, interpretation, and synthesis
	Cooperative Study of General Education	Objective tests of general culture, mathematics, and English (based on the Pennsylvania Study) and inventories of general life goals, satisfaction in reading fiction, social understanding, and health
	Graduate Record Examination (GRE) Program	1936: Objective Profile Tests of content (e.g., mathematics, physical sciences, social studies, literature, and fine arts) and verbal ability (cf. Pennsylvania Study)
		1939: Above plus 16 advanced tests in major fields (e.g., biology, economics, French, philosophy, sociology) for academic majors
		1946: General Education Tests that included the Profile Tests plus "effectiveness of expression" and a "general education index"
		1949: Verbal and Quantitative Aptitude Tests created as stand-alone tests to replace the Verbal Factor Test and the Mathematics Test in the Profile Tests
		1954: Area Tests, "entirely new measures of unusual scope . . . [providing] a comprehensive appraisal of the college student's orientation in three principal areas of human culture: social science, humanities, and natural science" (ETS, 1954, p. 3); replaced the Profile and General Education Tests
Rise of the test providers: 1948–78	ETS	Undergraduate Assessment Program that included the GRE tests
	ACT	College Outcomes Measures Project evolved from constructed-response tests to objective tests to save time and cost
	New Jersey	Tasks in Critical Thinking constructed-response tests

Table 3.1. (*continued*)

Era	Study, Program, or Test Provider	Test
Era of external accountability: 1979–present	ETS	Academic Profile and Measure of Academic Proficiency and Progress (MAPP), largely objective tests
	ACT	College Assessment of Academic Proficiency (CAAP), largely objective tests
	CAE	Collegiate Learning Assessment, constructed-response tests

SOURCE: R. J. Shavelson, 2007b, table in the appendix of monograph.

English composition, using recognized tests, procedures, and scales, and a statistical treatment that though comparatively crude was indicative" (Savage, 1953, p. 284). E. L. Thorndike's study of engineering students followed, testing MIT, University of Cincinnati, and Columbia students on "all or parts of several objective tests in mathematics, English and physics" (Savage, 1953, p. 285). These tests focused on content knowledge, largely tapping facts and concepts (declarative knowledge) and arithmetic routines (procedural knowledge; see Figure 2.1). The early tests were "objective" in the sense that students responded by selecting an answer (e.g., in a multiple choice test) where there was one correct answer. These tests gained reliability in scoring and content coverage per unit of time over the theretofore widely used essay examination.

The monumental Pennsylvania Study (1928–32)—published tellingly as *The Student and His Knowledge*—emerged from this start; it tested thousands of high school seniors, college students, and even some college faculty members on extensive objective tests of largely declarative and procedural content knowledge. The study was conducted by Learned—"a man who had clear and certain opinions about what education ought to be . . . [with] transmission of knowledge as the *sine qua non*" (Lagemann, 1983, p. 101)—and Ben D. Wood, director of collegiate educational research at Columbia College and former E. L. Thorndike student who held the view, as did Learned, "that thinking was dependent upon knowledge and knowledge dependent upon facts" (Lagemann, 1983, p. 104). In many ways, the Pennsylvania study was extraordinary and exemplary with its clear conception of what students should achieve and how to measure learning; in other ways, it clearly reflected its time with its focus on factual and procedural knowledge and compliant students sitting for hours of testing.[1]

In the 1928 pilot study no less than 70 percent of all Pennsylvania college seniors, or 4,580 students, took the assessment, as did about 75 percent of high school seniors, or 26,500 high school students. Of the high school seniors, 3,859 entered a cooperating Pennsylvania college, and 2,355 of those students remained through their sophomore year (1930) and 1,187 through their senior year (1932) (Learned & Wood, 1938, p. 211).

The assessment itself was a whopping twelve hours and 3,200 items long—yet the examiners expressed regret at not being more comprehensive in scope! It covered nearly all areas of the college curriculum, contained selected-response questions (e.g., multiple-choice, matching, true-false), focusing mostly on declarative knowledge and procedural knowledge (see Chapter 2 and Figure 2.1)—that is, factual recall and recognition of content and application of mathematical routines (see Figure 3.1). The main study focused on student *learning* and not simply on knowledge (achievement) in the senior year. To examine student learning, Learned and Wood (1938) followed high school seniors and tested them as college sophomores in 1930 and again as seniors in 1932.

The Pennsylvania Study is noteworthy for at least four reasons. First, it laid out a conception of what was meant by undergraduate achievement *and* learning.[2] That is, the study focused on the nature, needs, and achievements of individual students, assuming "the educational performance of school and college as a single cumulative process the parts of which, for any given student, should be complementary" (Learned & Wood, 1938, p. xvi). More specifically, achievement resulted from college learning, which the researchers defined as the accumulation of breadth and depth of content knowledge.

The second noteworthy aspect of the assessment was its span of coverage. In terms of the cognitive outcomes framework, it focused heavily and *comprehensively* at the knowledge level, especially on declarative and procedural knowledge (see Figure 2.1). Nevertheless, the assessment program included an intelligence test, so that it spanned the extremes of the cognitive outcomes framework—content knowledge and general ability (Chapter 2).

The third noteworthy aspect of the study was that the technology for assessing student learning and achievement followed directly from the researchers' study framework. That objective-testing technology, influenced by behavioral psychology and especially the work of E. L. Thorndike and spawned by the Army Alpha test developed for recruitment in World War I, created a revolution (Figure 3.1). If knowledge was the accumulation of learning content, objective testing—the new technology—could be used to verify, literally index, the accumulation of that knowledge. In Learned and Woods' words, "The question, instead of requiring

IV. GENERAL SCIENCE, Part II

Directions. In the parenthesis after each word or phrase in the right hand column, place the number of the word or phrase in the left-hand column of the same group which is associated with that word or phrase.

14. 1. Unit of work

1. Unit of work	Calorie	(4)
2. Unit of potential difference	Dyne	(6)
3. Unit of electrical current	Erg	(1)
4. Unit of heat quantity	H.P.	(5)
5. Unit of power	Volt	(2)
6. Unit of force	Ampere	(3)
7. Unit of pressure	B.T.U.	(4)
	Atmosphere	(7)
	Foot-pound	(1)
	Watt	(5)

V. FOREIGN LANGUAGE

. . .

Multiple Choice

9. Sophocles' Antigone is a depiction of 1. the introduction of laws into a barbarous state, 2. the prevailing of sisterly love over citicenly duty, 3. idyllic peasant life, 4. the perils of opposing oneself to Zeus

10. Of Corneille's plays, 1. Polyeucte, 2. Horace, 3. Cinna, 4. Le Cid, shows least the influence of classical restraint

VIII. MATHEMATICS

Directions. Each of the problems below is followed by several possible answers, only one of which is entirely correct. Calculate the answer for each problem; then select the printed answer which corresponds to yours and put its number in the parenthesis at the right.

5. If two sides of a triangle are equal, the opposite angles are

(1) equal   (2) complementary   (3) unequal   (4) right angles   (1)

Figure 3.1 Sampling of questions on the Pennsylvania Senior Examination (Learned & Woods, 1938, pp. 374–78).

written answers, will be of a sort to test memory, judgment, and reasoning ability through simple recognition. . . . By this method a large amount of ground can be covered in a short time" (1938, p. 372).

The fourth exemplary aspect of the study was that it did, unlike many accountability systems today, distinguish achievement from learning. It defined *achievement* as the accumulation of knowledge and reasoning capacity at a particular point in time and *learning* as change in knowledge and reasoning over the college years. In some cases, the comparison was across student cohorts ("cross-sectional"—high school seniors, college sophomores, and college seniors), and in other cases it was longitudinal (the same high school seniors in 1928, tested again as college sophomores in 1930 and then as seniors in 1932). These various designs presage current-day assessments of learning by, for example, the Council for Aid to Education's Collegiate Learning Assessment.

Assessment of Learning for General Education and Graduate Education: 1933–1947

The 1933–47 era saw the development of general education and general colleges in universities across the country and the evolution of the Graduate Record Examination (GRE). The Pennsylvania Study demonstrated that large-scale assessment of student learning could be carried out—a sort of existence proof—and individuals as well as consortia of institutions put together batteries of tests primarily to assess cognitive achievement. Perhaps most noteworthy of this progressive period in education was the attempt not only to measure cognitive outcomes across the spectrum shown in Figure 2.1 but also to assess personal, social, and moral outcomes of general education. Here I briefly treat the learning assessment in general education, because it was an alternative to rather than an adaptation of the Carnegie Foundation's view of education and learning assessment. I then focus attention on the GRE.

Evolution of General Education and General Colleges

The most notable examples of general-education learning assessment in this era were developed by the University of Chicago College and the Cooperative Study of General Education (for additional programs, see Shavelson & Huang, 2003). The former had its roots in the progressive era; the latter had its roots in the Carnegie Foundation's conception of learning but embraced some progressive notions of human development, as well.

In the Chicago program a central University Examiner's Office, not individual faculty in their courses, was responsible for developing, administering, and scoring tests of student achievement in the university's general education program (Present and Former Members of the Faculty, 1950). Whereas the Pennsylvania Study assessed declarative knowledge (recall and recognition of facts) and procedural knowledge (application of routines), the Chicago examinations tested a much broader range of knowledge and abilities (Figure 2.1): the use of knowledge in a variety of unfamiliar situations (strategic knowledge); the ability to apply principles to explain phenomena (schematic knowledge); and the ability to predict outcomes, determine courses of action, and interpret works of art (schematic and strategic knowledge). Open-ended essays and multiple-choice questions demanding interpretation, synthesis, and application of new texts (primary sources) characterized the comprehensive exams.[3]

The Cooperative Study of General Education, conducted by a consortium of higher-education institutions, stands out from individual institutional efforts such as that at Chicago for cooperative efforts to build an assessment system to improve students' achievement *and well-being*. These institutions initiated the study on the beliefs that several institutions could benefit from a cooperative attack on the improvement of general education; that by sharing costs of test development and use, more could be done cooperatively than singly; and that a formative (improvement) rather than summative (win-lose compared to others) assessment was likely to lead to this improvement (Executive Committee of the Cooperative Study in General Education, 1947; Dunkel, 1947; Levi, 1948; see Chapter 6). Accordingly, the consortium developed instruments such as the Inventory of General Goals in Life, the Inventory of Satisfactions Found in Reading Fiction, the Inventory of Social Understanding, and the Health Inventories.

The Evolution of the Graduate Record Examination

While assessment of undergraduate learning was in full swing, so were Learned and Wood, parlaying their experience with the Pennsylvania Study into an assessment for graduate education. In setting forth the purpose of the Co-operative Graduate Testing Program, as it was initially called, Learned noted that demand for graduate education had increased following the Depression, that the AB degree had "ceased to draw the line between the fit and the unfit" (Savage, 1953, p. 288), and that something more than number of college credits was needed on which to base decisions about admissions and graduate-student quality. In the initial stages of the GRE, students were tested only after they had gained admission to graduate school, but that changed three years later to an admission test for undergraduates seeking graduate work and was formalized by graduate school deans in 1942. The overall goal of the project, then, was improvement of graduate education.

In consort with the graduate schools at Columbia, Harvard, Princeton, and Yale in October 1937, Learned's team administered seven tests to index the quality of students in graduate education; this was the first administration of what was to be the GRE. A year later Brown University joined the ranks, followed by Rochester and Hamilton in 1939, and Wisconsin, Iowa, Michigan, and Minnesota in 1940. By 1940, the test battery had become a graduate-school entrance examination with increasing subscriptions. In 1945, 98 institutions had enlisted in the program, and in 1947 the number jumped to 175.

The program, then, was a success. But it was also a growing financial and logistical burden at a time when the Carnegie Foundation was struggling to keep its faculty retirement system (TIAA) afloat.[4] As we shall see, these stresses provided the stimulus for the foundation to pursue an independent national testing service.

The original GRE, like the Pennsylvania Study's examinations, was a comprehensive objective test focused largely on students' organized content knowledge, but it also tapped verbal reasoning (see Figure 2.1). The test was used to infer students' fitness for graduate study (Savage, 1953).

In 1936, a set of "Profile" Tests was developed on *content* intended to cover the areas of a typical undergraduate general education program (Educational Testing Service, 1953, 1954). To be completed in two half-day sessions totaling six hours, the tests measured knowledge in "mathematics, physical sciences [differentiated into physics and chemistry in the first revision of the examination], social studies [reduced to history, government, and economics], literature and fine arts [revised to "general literature" and the fine arts], one foreign language [dropped in the first revision], and the verbal factor" (Savage, 1953, p. 289). "The Verbal Factor Test was developed primarily as a measure of ability to discriminate word meanings" (Lannholm & Schrader, 1951, p. 7).

In 1939, the second revision of the GRE added sixteen Advanced Tests in subject major fields—biology, chemistry, economics, engineering, fine arts, French, geology, German, government, history, literature, mathematics, philosophy, physics, psychology, and sociology—to complement the Profile Tests (Lannholm & Schrader, 1951; Savage, 1953).[5] Combining the elementary and advanced tests, total testing time in 1940 was two periods of four hours each.[6]

In the spring of 1946, the general-education section of the GRE's Profile Tests became available. The general-education section overlapped the Profile Tests and added tests of "effectiveness of expression" and a "general education index" (Educational Testing Service, 1953). Consequently, for a short period of time the GRE offered both the Profile Tests and the General Education Test.

In spring 1947, the Graduate Record Office (GRO) launched an "ambitious program to involve 20,000 students at fifty-odd accepted colleges and universities in giving the revised examination" (Savage, 1953, p. 292) for the purpose of establishing norms. A second purpose of the Carnegie–Ivy League project was to assist institutions in assessing program effectiveness and individual student need as a means to improvement, much like the Cooperative Study of General Education. "Although scores were not published, they probably made their contribution to the solution of a variety of institutional problems . . . , and the G.R.O. got its new norms" (Savage, 1953, p. 292).

In the fall of 1949, the GRE Aptitude Test was introduced (Lannholm & Schrader, 1951), replacing the verbal and quantitative portions of the Profile Tests. This shift to aptitude testing was quite significant in the evolution of learning assessment in higher education. Operationally, in 1950 the mathematics and the verbal factor tests were discontinued as part of the Profile Tests (Educational Testing Service, 1953, p. 3), creating the basis of the current-day GRE with its quantitative and verbal sections. In 1952 the familiar standardized scale of the Educational Testing Service (ETS), with a mean of 500 and a standard deviation of 100, was introduced for the purpose of reporting GRE scores.

This change in the GRE marked the beginning of an important shift away from the measurement of content knowledge to the measurement of broad abilities, especially verbal and quantitative reasoning, as the basis for making admission and fellowship decisions (see Figure 2.1). Then, in 1954, ETS announced Area Tests, replacing the Profile Tests and the Tests of General Education with a means of "Assessing the Broad Outcomes of Education in the Liberal Arts" (Educational Testing Service, 1954). The Area Tests focused on academic majors in the social and natural sciences and the humanities. They were "intended to test the student's grasp of basic concepts and his ability to apply them to the variety of types of materials which are presented for his interpretation" (Educational Testing Service, 1954, p. 3) and were considered "important to the individual's effectiveness as a member of society" (Educational Testing Service, 1966, p. 3). The tests emphasized reading comprehension, and interpretation; the tests often provided the requisite content knowledge "because of the differences among institutions with regard to curriculum and the differences among students with regard to specific course selection" (Educational Testing Service, 1966, p. 3). This, then, was one more step away from the recall-based Pennsylvania Study and the GRE in earlier years to a test of broader reasoning abilities (Figure 2.1). And unlike the lengthy Pennsylvania tests and the extensive Chicago comprehensives, the "new" GRE Area Tests took 3.75 hours of testing time.

The Rise of the Test Providers: 1948–1978

During the period following World War II and with funding from the GI Bill, postsecondary education enrollments mushroomed, as did the number of colleges to accommodate the veterans and the number of testing companies to assist colleges in screening them. The most notable among those companies were the Educational Testing Service, which emerged in 1948, and the American College Testing program, which emerged in 1959 (becoming simply ACT in 1996).

By the time the Carnegie Foundation had moved the GRE to ETS and moved out of the testing business, it had left an extraordinarily strong legacy: objective, group-administered, cost-efficient testing using selected response—now solely multiple-choice—questions. Precursors to the major learning assessment programs today were developed by testing organizations in this era (e.g., Shavelson & Huang, 2003). These 1960s and 1970s testing programs included ETS's Undergraduate Assessment Program, which incorporated the GRE, and ACT's College Outcomes Measures Project (COMP). The former evolved via the Academic Profile into today's Measure of Academic Proficiency and Progress (MAPP), and the latter evolved into today's Collegiate Assessment of Academic Proficiency (CAAP). Simply put, the Carnegie Foundation's conception of learning assessment at the turn of the 20th century had an immense influence on what achievement has been tested in higher education and the nature of achievement tests today.

However, several developments in the late 1970s augured for a change in the course set by Learned and Wood. Faculty members were not entirely happy with multiple-choice tests. They wanted to get at broader abilities, such as the ability to communicate, think analytically, and solve problems, in a holistic manner. This led to several new developments including ETS's study of constructed response tests (Warren, 1978), ACT's open-ended assessments of learning, and the State of New Jersey's Tasks in Critical Thinking. These assessment programs embraced what college faculty considered as important learning measures. For a short period of time, these assessment programs set the mold; but due to time and cost limitations, as well as scoring issues, they either faded into distant memory or morphed into multiple-choice tests.

Warren (1978, p. 1) reported on an attempt to measure academic competence with "free-response questions." The examination tapped communication skill, analytic thinking, synthesizing ability, and social/cultural awareness. He encountered two consequential problems—scoring and interpretation. Scoring by faculty was complex and time consuming, especially for students from non-selective institutions. Interpretation was complicated because questions that fell conceptually into a common domain did not hang together empirically.

At about the same time, ACT was developing the College Outcomes Measures Project. The COMP began as an unusual performance-based assessment that sought to measure skills for effective functioning in adult life in social institutions, in using science and technology, and in using the arts (an area not often addressed by large-scale assessments at the time). The test's contents were sampled from materials culled from everyday experience, including film excerpts, taped discussions, advertisements, music recordings, stories, and newspaper articles. The test sought to measure three process skills—communication, problem solving, and values clarification—in a variety of item formats: multiple choice, short answer, essay, and oral response (an atypical format). COMP, then, was path breaking, bucking the trend toward multiple-choice tests of general abilities by directly observing performance in simulated, real-world situations.

The test was costly in time and scoring, however. In the 1977 field trials students were given six hours to complete it; testing time was reduced to 4.5 hours in the 1989 version. Raters were required to score much of the examination. As a consequence, and characteristic of trends in assessment of learning, a simplified Overall COMP was developed as a multiple-choice only test. In little more than a decade, however, this highly innovative assessment was discontinued due to the costliness of administration and scoring.

Roughly the same story can be told about Tasks in Critical Thinking (e.g., Erwin & Sebrell, 2003). The assessment grew out of the New Jersey Basic Skills Assessment Program (1977), New Jersey's effort to assess student learning in a manner consistent with faculty members' notion of what was important to assess—students' performance on holistic, meaningful tasks. Tasks in Critical Thinking was a "performance-based assessment of the critical thinking skills of college and university students . . . [that measured the] ability to use the skills of inquiry, analysis, and communication" (Educational Testing Service, 1994, p. 2) where the prompts "do not assess content or recall knowledge" (p. 2). "A task resembles what students are required to do in the classroom and the world of work" (p. 3). Each task took ninety minutes to complete; students and tasks were randomly matched so that each student received only one task. Local faculty scored students' performances based on extensive scoring guides. The New Jersey project ended due to the recession of the late 1980s and early 1990s; ETS took over marketing the examination but no longer supports it.

The influence of the Carnegie Foundation, then, waned in the mid 1970s. However, as we shall see, the foundation's vision of objective, selected-response testing remained in ETS's and ACT's learning assessment programs.

The Era of External Accountability: 1979–Present

By the end of the 1970s, political pressure to assess student learning and hold campuses accountable coalesced. While only a handful of states (e.g., Florida, Tennessee) had some form of mandatory standardized testing in the 1980s, public and political demand for such testing increased into the new millennium (Ewell, 2001). To meet this demand, some states (e.g., Missouri) created incentives for campuses to assess learning; campuses responded by creating learning assessment programs.

Tests of College Learning

ETS, ACT, and others were there to provide tests. By this time a wide array of college learning assessments was available, following in the Carnegie Foundation tradition of objective tests. ETS currently provides the Measure of Academic Proficiency and Progress; ACT provides the Collegiate Assessment of Academic Proficiency. MAPP, a multiple-choice test battery, measures college-level reading, mathematics, writing, and critical thinking in the context of the humanities, social sciences, and natural sciences. It was designed to enable colleges and universities to assess their general education outcomes with the goal of improving the quality of instruction and learning. CAAP, also multiple choice, measures the domains of reading, writing, mathematics, science, and critical thinking. It was designed to enable postsecondary institutions to measure, evaluate, and enhance the outcomes of their general education programs.

From 1979 onward significant contributions to object testing were realized, especially with the rapid evolution in computing capacity. ETS pioneered work in test-item scaling and equating (item response theory) and in computer adaptive testing.

However, as we shall see, it was up to a newcomer, the Council for Aid to Education (CAE), a spin-off of the RAND Corporation, to take the next step and marry open-ended assessment of real-world holistic tasks and computer technology to create the next generation of learning assessments for higher education.

Vision for Assessing Student Learning

As we saw at the end of the 1970s, objective testing did not fit with the way faculty members assessed student learning or wanted student learning to be assessed. For them, *life is not a multiple-choice test*. Life does not present itself as a clearly defined statement of a problem or task with a set of specific alternatives from which to choose. Rather, faculty members sought open-ended, holistic, problem-based assessment, something like that found in the COMP and in Tasks in Critical Thinking.

Intuitively, faculty members suspected that the kind of thinking and performing students exhibited on multiple-choice and other highly structured tests was different from what they exhibited on more open-ended tasks. Empirical evidence supports their intuition. While a multiple-choice test and a "constructed-response" test may produce scores that are positively correlated with each other, this correlation does not mean that the kind of thinking and reasoning involved is the same (e.g., Martinez, 2000; National Research Council, 2001). In a variety of domains student performance varies considerably when the same task is presented as a multiple-choice question, an open-ended question, or a concrete performance task. Lythcott (1990) and Sawyer (1990), for example, found that "it is possible . . . for [high school and college] students to produce right answers to chemistry problems without really understanding much of the chemistry involved" (Lythcott, 1990, p. 248). Moreover, Baxter and Shavelson (1994) found that middle school students who solved complex hands-on electric circuit problems could not solve the same problems represented abstractly in a multiple-choice test; these students did not make the same assumptions that the test developers made. Finally, using "think aloud" methods to tap into students' cognitive processing, Ruiz-Primo et al. (2001) found very different reasoning on highly structured and loosely structured assessments; in the former case the students "strategized" as to what alternative fit best, and in the latter case they reasoned through the problem.

To be concrete about the difference between multiple-choice and open-ended assessments and what is measured, consider the following example (described in a bit more detail below): College students are asked to pretend they work for DynaTech—a company that produces industrial instruments—and have been asked by their boss to evaluate the pros and cons of purchasing a SwiftAir 235 for the company. Concern about such a purchase has risen with the report of a recent SwiftAir 235 accident. When provided with an in-basket of information, some students, quite perceptively, recognized that there might be undesirable fallout if DynaTech's own airplane crashed while flying with DynaTech's instruments. Students were not prompted to discuss such implications; they had to recognize these consequences on their own. There is no way such insights could be picked up by a multiple-choice question.

Finally, consistent with the view of faculty, members of the secretary of education's Higher Education Commission and the Association of American Colleges and Universities (AAC&U) have a particular type of standardized learning assessment in mind—the Council for Aid to Education's Collegiate Learning Assessment. In the words of the American Association of State Colleges and Universities (AASCU) (2006, p. 4):

The best example of direct value-added assessment is the Collegiate Learning Assessment (CLA), an outgrowth of RAND's Value Added Assessment Initiative that has been available to colleges and universities since spring 2004. The test goes beyond a multiple-choice format and poses real-world performance tasks that require students to analyze complex material and provide written responses (such as preparing a memo or policy recommendation).

The AASCU (2006, p. 4) goes on to say, "Other instruments for direct assessment include ACT's Collegiate Assessment of Academic Proficiency (CAAP), the Educational Testing Services's [sic] Academic Profile and its successor, the Measure of Academic Proficiency and Progress (MAPP), introduced in January 2006. Around for more than a decade, these assessments offer tools for estimating student general education skills."

To complete this brief history, then, consider the new kid on the block, the Council for Aid to Education's Collegiate Learning Assessment, the successor of assessments such as COMP and Tasks (for details, see the next chapter).[7] Admittedly I am on shaky ground by presenting as history a current development—the CLA. Historians are a cautious lot. For them, history up to the current time stops no closer than twenty years from the present. Historians notwithstanding, the CLA just might provide a window into the future of standardized learning assessments.

The Collegiate Learning Assessment

Just as the new technology of objective testing revolutionized learning assessment at the turn of the 20th century, so has new information technology and statistical sampling technology ushered in a change in college learning assessment at the turn of the 21st century. And yet, in some ways, the "new" assessment technology is somewhat a return to the past; it moves away from selected-response, multiple-choice tests to realistic, complex, open-ended tasks. These new developments are best represented by the Collegiate Learning Assessment (e.g., Benjamin & Hersh, 2002; Klein et al., 2005; Shavelson, 2007a,b).

The CLA, whose roots can be traced to progressive notions of learning, focuses on critical thinking, analytic reasoning, problem solving, and written communication (see goals in Chapter 2). These capabilities are tapped in realistic "work-sample" tasks drawn from work, education, and everyday issues that are accessible to students from the wide variety of majors and general education programs found on college campuses (see Table 3.2). The capacity to provide these

Table 3.2. Characteristics of the Collegiate Learning Assessment

Characteristic	Attributes
Open-ended tasks	• Taps critical thinking, analytic reasoning, problem solving, and written communication • Provides realistic work samples • Features alluring task titles such as "Brain Boost," "Catfish," "Lakes to Rivers" • Applies to different academic majors
Computer technology	• Interactive Internet platform • Paperless administration • Natural language-processing software for scoring written communication • Online rater scoring and calibration of performance tasks • Reports institution's (and subdivision's) performance (and individual student's performance confidentially to student)
Focus	• Institution or divisions or programs within institutions • Not on individual students' performance (although their performance is reported to them confidentially)
Sampling	• Samples students so that not all students perform all tasks • Samples tasks for random subsets of students • Creates scores at institution or subdivision/program level as desired (depending on sample sizes)
Reporting	• Controls for students' ability so that "similarly situated" benchmark campuses can be compared • Provides value-added estimates—from freshman to senior year or with measures on a sample of freshmen and seniors • Provides percentiles • Provides benchmark institutions

SOURCE: R. J. Shavelson, 2007a, Chart 1 and Characteristics of the Collegiate Learning Assessment (p. 32).

rich tasks is afforded by recent developments in information technology. The assessment is delivered on an interactive Internet platform that produces a paperless, electronic administration. Written communication tasks have been scored using natural language–processing software, and performance tasks are scored by online raters whose scoring is monitored and calibrated. Reports are available online.

The CLA also uses sampling technology to move away from testing all students on all tasks as was done in the whopping twelve-hour and 3,200-item Pennsylvania Study in 1928. The focus then was on individual student development; CLA focuses on program improvement, with limited information provided to students confidentially (i.e., not available to the institution). Institutional (and subdivision) reports provide a number of indicators for interpreting performance. These include anonymous benchmark institution comparisons; percent of institutions scoring below a certain level; and value added over and above performance expected in the institution, based on admitted-student abilities (see

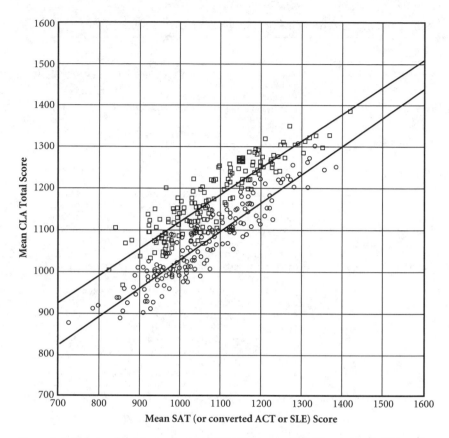

Figure 3.2 Relationship between mean SAT/ACT scores (in SAT units) and CLA scores for 176 schools tested in the fall of 2007 (freshmen) and spring of 2008 (seniors).

SOURCE: Council for Aid to Education (2008). 2007–2008 CLA Technical Appendices. New York: author (p. 2); www.cae.org/content/pdf/CLA.in.Context.pdf.

Figure 3.2), through cross-sectional comparisons, and through longitudinal co-hort studies or some combination.

For example, Figure 3.2 shows the performance of entering freshmen (fall 2007) and seniors (spring 2008) at a set of colleges participating in the CLA. Each point on the graph represents the average (mean) college performance on the SAT/ACT and the CLA; the swarm of points shows the relationship between colleges' mean SAT/ACT and CLA scores. A number of features in this are note-worthy. First, and perhaps most encouraging, the boxes and line (seniors) fall significantly (more than 1 standard deviation) above the circles and line (freshmen). This finding may be interpreted to mean that college does indeed

Table 3.3. Critique an Argument

A well-respected professional journal with a readership that includes elementary school principals recently published the results of a two-year study on childhood obesity. (Obese individuals are usually considered to be those who are 20 percent above their recommended weight for height and age.) This study sampled 50 schoolchildren, ages 5–11, from Smith Elementary School. A fast-food restaurant opened near the school just before the study began. After two years, students who remained in the sample group were more likely to be overweight relative to the national average. Based on this study, the principal of Jones Elementary School decided to confront her school's obesity problem by opposing any fast-food restaurant openings near her school.

SOURCE: www.cae.org/content/pdf/CLA.in.Context.pdf.

contribute to student learning (as do other life experiences). Second, most colleges (dots) fall along the straight ("regression") line of *expected performance based on ability* for both freshmen and seniors—but some fall well above and some well below. This means that by students' senior year, some colleges exceed expected performance compared to their peers, and some perform below expectation. So it matters not only *that* a student goes to college but also *where* that student goes.[8]

The assessment is divided into three parts—analytic writing, performance tasks, and biographical information; the first two are pertinent here. Two types of writing tasks are administered. The first, "Make an Argument," invites students to present an argument for or against a particular position. For example, the prompt might be: "In our time, specialists of all kinds are highly overrated. We need more generalists—people who can provide broad perspectives." Students are directed to indicate whether they agree or disagree and to explain the reasons for their position. In a similar vein, the second type of writing task asks students to "Critique an Argument" (see the example in Table 3.3). Students' responses have been scored by raters in some years and in other years by a computer with a natural language–processing program.

The performance tasks present real-life problems to students, providing an "in-basket" of information bearing on the problem (see Figure 3.3). Some of the information is relevant, some not; some is reliable, some not. Part of the problem is for the students to decide what information to use and what to ignore. Students integrate these multiple sources of information to arrive at a problem solution, decision, or recommendation.

Students respond in a real-life manner by, for example, writing a memorandum to their boss analyzing the pros and cons of alternative solutions and recommending what the company should do. In scoring performance, there are a set of recognized, alternative, justifiable solutions to the problem and alternative solution

You are the assistant to Pat Williams, the president of DynaTech, a company that makes precision electronic instruments and navigational equipment. Sally Evans, a member of DynaTech's sales force, recommended that DynaTech buy a small private plane (a SwiftAir 235) that she and other members of the sales force could use to visit customers. Pat was about to approve the purchase when there was an accident involving a SwiftAir 235. You are provided with the following documentation:

1. newspaper articles about the accident
2. federal accident report on in-flight breakups in single-engine planes
3. Pat's e-mail to you and Sally's e-mail to Pat
4. charts on SwiftAir's performance characteristics
5. amateur pilot article comparing SwiftAir 235 to similar planes
6. pictures and description of SwiftAir models 180 and 235

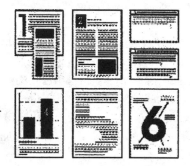

Please prepare a memo that addresses several questions, including what data support or refute the claim that the type of wing on the SwiftAir 235 leads to more in-flight breakups, what other factors might have contributed to the accident and should be taken into account, and your overall recommendation about whether or not DynaTech should purchase the plane.

Figure 3.3 Collegiate Learning Assessment performance task.
SOURCE: www.cae.org/content/pdf/CLA.in.Context.pdf.

paths. Currently, human judges score students' responses online, but by 2010, the expectation is that responses will be scored by computer.

The CLA does not pretend to be *the* measure of collegiate learning. Rather, as the Council for Aid to Education points out, there are many outcomes for college education; the CLA focuses on critical reasoning, problem solving, and communication. Moreover, with its institutional (or school/college) focus, it does not provide detailed, diagnostic information about particular courses or programs (unless the sampling is done at a program level). Rather, other institutional information, in conjunction with the CLA, is needed to diagnose problems. Moreover, campuses need to systematically test out possible solutions to those problems. (See Benjamin, Chun, & Shavelson, 2007, for a detailed explanation of how the CLA might be used for improvement.) The CLA, then, sends a strong signal to the campus to dig deeper.

Reprise

The assessment of student learning is a top priority today in the quest to hold campuses accountable. Although it is portrayed as the "new thing," student learning assessment has a long and distinguished history that can be traced to the Carnegie Foundation for the Advancement of Teaching at the turn of the last century. Over this time period, we have seen the following changes in learning assessment:

- from institutionally initiated to externally mandated
- from internally written to externally provided
- from content based to ability based, i.e. from assessing primarily declarative and procedural knowledge to assessing generic reasoning abilities
- from extensive coverage of many subjects toward narrower subject-specific coverage
- from an emphasis on an individual's level of competence (against some standard) to an emphasis on his relative standing (i.e., in comparison to others)
- from lengthy objective (e.g., multiple-choice) and constructed-response (e.g., essay) tests toward standardization, multiple-choice format, and short test lengths
- from multiple approaches to holistic assessment of broad abilities to largely admissions tests (most learning assessments failing to survive for long due to limited technology)

Nevertheless, there is much to be learned from the past in the design of an accountability system today. Over seventy-five years ago the Pennsylvania Study proved to be quite sophisticated and apropos for today in that it was built on (1) a well-articulated notion of achievement and learning, one that is prevalent today; (2) a comprehensive notion of what knowledge (across the college subjects of humanities, social science, and science) campuses should be developing in students; (3) a data collection design that indexed both *achievement* at one point of time for cohorts of high school seniors, college sophomores, and college seniors and *learning* of the same cohort of high school seniors throughout their college careers; and (4) state-of-the-art objective testing technology. Over time, especially in the progressive era, assessment of learning in areas other than cognitive outcomes came into vogue, signaling a broader conception of outcomes to be tested than is apparent today.

Philosophical differences emerged between the Carnegie vision of knowledge accumulation and the progressive movement's concern for practical application of and reasoning with knowledge. Disagreement emerged as to the relative value of the two and persists today. The Carnegie vision can be traced to the empiricist philosophers and their focus on internalization of regular patterns in the environment (e.g., Case, 1996). Learned and Wood (1938, pp. 7–8) state the position well when they say that content knowledge "must be a relatively permanent and available equipment of the student; that it must be so familiar and so sharply defined that it comes freely to mind when needed and can be depended upon as an effective cross-fertilizing element for producing fresh ideas; [and that] a student's knowledge, when used as adequate evidence of education . . . should represent as nearly as possible the complete individual."

One consequence of this concept is that knowledge can be divided into particular content areas, instruction proceeding step by step from one learning objective to the next. A second consequence is that assessment of learning should sample individual pieces of content from a knowledge domain (declarative and procedural knowledge) bit by bit in objective-test fashion, as did the tests developed for the Pennsylvania Study and as do many current learning assessments (e.g., the Measure of Academic Proficiency and Progress, and the Collegiate Assessment of Academic Proficiency).

In contrast, the progressive era notion of knowledge stemmed from a rationalist position. This position held that knowledge is built up by the student with its own internal structure. One consequence of this notion was that knowledge should be constructed in a guided-discovery fashion by engaging a student's natural curiosity and structuring abundant opportunities for exploration and reflection. A second consequence is that from a knowledge domain the assessment of learning should sample complex tasks that have embedded in them both knowledge and reasoning demands that multiple-choice tests are unable to tap adequately. This philosophy was implemented in the University of Chicago's Examiner's Office and can be seen most recently in the Collegiate Learning Assessment.

The relative emphasis on what should be learned in college has shifted between knowledge and broad abilities over the past hundred years. In the first half of the 20th century learning assessment emphasized declarative and procedural content knowledge; in the second half, assessments emphasized broad abilities and reasoning. The evolution of the current-day GRE reflects this trend nicely. In the end, some balance between outcomes seems reasonable such that learning assessments should tap the knowledge, broad abilities, and general reasoning levels reflected in the cognitive framework introduced in Chapter 2.

Assessment of learning in general education should focus on the last two levels; learning assessment in the majors should focus on the first two levels. Assessment of learning, then, should tap multiple cognitive outcomes ranging from declarative knowledge to broad domain abilities to verbal, quantitative, and spatial reasoning.

However, as noted in Chapter 2, emphasis on cognitive outcomes is insufficient for assessing learning.[9] Learning assessment needs to include what the AAC&U calls Individual and Social Responsibility Outcomes, such as civic engagement, ethical reasoning, intercultural knowledge and actions, and self-development. The current focus solely on cognitive outcomes is too narrow, judging by the outcomes the public expects from higher education and the mission statements of colleges and universities. Measurement problems in high-stakes accountability need to be addressed; these very problems affect indirect measures of student learning such as the National Assessment of Student Engagement and any high-stakes measures of cognitive outcomes. Simply put, a broader set of outcomes should be incorporated into learning assessments.

Just as the learning outcomes assessed have changed over the past hundred years, so have those organizations that provide learning assessments. In the first half of the 20th century, foundations and colleges provided the assessments; in the last half, external testing organizations provided the assessments. Testing organizations will continue to provide a wide array of assessments that campuses can use to assess students' learning. These assessments have mainly focused on cognitive outcomes and have varied in their emphasis on knowledge, abilities, and reasoning, reflecting the philosophical differences noted above.

If one assumes, as did Learned at Carnegie, that learning amounts to the accumulation of knowledge, and that the purpose of college education is to fill the student vessel full of that knowledge so that it is readily available for use, multiple-choice assessments of declarative and procedural knowledge would be appropriate for campuses to use to index performance in a major and in general education. Assessments such as MAPP and CAAP can be traced back to Learned's notion.

If, on the other hand, one assumes that learning amounts to the construction of knowledge and reasoning capacities within a knowledge domain or across domains in complex, meaningful, real-world tasks, as did the progressives and, apparently, as do today's faculty, a campus might seek assessments that employ constructed responses to tasks that are complex and require a variety of knowledge and reasoning types to complete them. Evidence that such assessments can be built and fielded come from the Chicago Examiner's Office examinations through the attempts in the 1980s to construct such examinations to the present-day Collegiate Learning Assessment.

Externally provided learning assessments, however, are not tied directly to any particular campus curriculum. They consequently strike a common denominator such that their content overlaps, generally, with most curricula. As a consequence, they tend to tap multiple content areas in assessing knowledge and reasoning. In doing so, they place considerable demand on *strategic knowledge,* both within a domain (e.g., psychology) and across domains (e.g., reasoning in social sciences). Strategic knowledge is closely related to general ability or "G." However as we pointed out, G is relatively stable by the time students get to college. Consequently, such measures as the SAT, which largely taps G, will be a good predictor of performance on these externally provided measures. Two implications follow:

1. Care must be taken in interpreting findings; externally provided measures may not be as sensitive to learning in the curriculum taught at the campus as might be desired and useful. Moreover, invidious comparisons that arise from the demand for summative accountability may lead to misinterpretation of learning assessment findings.
2. Externally provided measures are insufficient indices of student learning. They need to be supplemented with locally devised assessments that are sensitive to campus goals and curricula.

Regardless of the nature of the learning outcome measure, externally provided examinations largely serve a *signaling function.* They flag areas of strength and weakness that campuses might attend to. If MAPP or CLA, for example, signaled a problem with general education outcomes, it might not be sufficiently diagnostic to pinpoint, on a particular campus, what might be improved.

In attending to these signals, then, campuses inevitably need campus-contextualized information on student achievement and learning in order to formulate interventions (see Chapter 5). For this, more in-depth assessments of students' performances might be called for, in conjunction with an understanding of the particular program and its context. Consequently, these externally provided assessments need to be augmented by campus-specific measures.

The value of externally provided assessments, then, lies in their ability to benchmark performance (e.g., by norm data, by comparison sets of institutions, by value added) and signal that attention is needed. Assessment of learning should go beyond externally provided assessment and include context-sensitive indicators of learning. It should be combined with a campus's willingness to experiment with and study the effects of improvement alternatives. Some speak of this as building a "culture of evidence."

4 The Collegiate Learning Assessment

THE COLLEGIATE LEARNING ASSESSMENT (CLA) has a long, if relatively unknown, pedigree, as we saw in Chapter 3, stemming from the progressive era's conception of learning in the late 1930s. Yet it is also a newcomer in the sense that measures like the CLA, in their most recent incarnations, faded away about twenty years ago. There is, then, a bit of the unknown about the CLA, especially given its current prominence in higher-education assessment and policy circles. Hence, this chapter highlights one among several learning assessments.[1] It begins with background on the origin of the CLA and describes its underlying philosophy. This is followed by a description of the assessment tasks and criteria for scoring them. Then attention turns to score reliability and validity. The chapter concludes with a reprise that addresses published criticism of the assessment.

Background: A Personal Perspective

The CLA was conceived jointly by Roger Benjamin, Steve Klein, and me (for origins, see Benjamin & Hersh, 2002; Chun, 2002; Hersh & Benjamin, 2002; Klein 2002a,b). Benjamin came from a political economy background and as a former dean and provost was concerned that colleges and universities were making decisions in the absence of good information about student learning. To be sure, information about learning was available—in grades, pass rates, graduation rates, and the like. But there was no way to benchmark how good was good enough. From Benjamin's vast experience, he, along with colleague Dick Hersh, a former university president, felt and continues to feel that campuses could do more to improve student learning. Both Klein and I, as psychologists, shared Benjamin's belief but had come from backgrounds in assessment—traditional and especially alternative, nontraditional assessment. So we shared a vision of what such assessment of learning might look like. Klein did pioneering work on the Law Bar Examination (Klein, 2002b) and in science performance assessment (e.g., Klein et al., 1998), and I had done work in measurement of astronaut (Shavelson & Seminara, 1968) and military (Shavelson, 1991; Wigdor & Green, 1991) job performance, and in science performance assessment (Shavelson, Baxter & Pine, 1992).

We conceived of the CLA much as it has evolved today, as described in Chapter 3. Moreover, as Benjamin had recently become president of the Council for Aid to Education (CAE), we had an organizational structure for putting our ideas into practice. CAE is a national nonprofit organization based in New York City. Initially established in 1952 to advance corporate support of education and to conduct policy research on higher education, CAE today also focuses on improving quality in and access to higher education. CAE was an affiliate of the RAND Corporation from 1996 to 2005,[2] and that relationship fostered research and development of the CLA. The CLA is central to CAE's focus. (Incidentally, CAE is also the nation's sole source of empirical data on private giving to education, through the annual Voluntary Support of Education survey and its Data Miner interactive database.)

In conceiving the CLA, we were clear on several issues. First, none of us believed in "high-stakes" political use of assessment to improve institutional performance. Rather, our concern was and is with *signaling* to campuses how well they are doing in improving student learning compared to benchmark peers, as well as compared to their own goals over time. CAE and its board are on record about this matter, as follows:

> We support improving assessment, especially assessment of student learning outcomes in undergraduate education. The goal of undergraduate learning assessment should be to help faculty and administrators . . . use measures to improve teaching and learning. The Collegiate Learning Assessment (CLA) is one tool designed for this purpose. . . . We strongly believe that a national testing regime is not appropriate for America's higher education system. The greatness of American higher education rests in its independence, diversity of missions, and commitment to teaching, research, and service of the highest quality. A one-size-fits-all testing regime would run counter to the historical success of our postsecondary education sector, inject opportunities for inappropriate political intrusion, and weaken its future ability to innovate and compete in multiple ways. (www.ed.gov/about/bdscomm/list/hiedfuture/4th-meeting/benjamin.pdf)

Second, we do not believe the CLA provides all of the information campuses need to make informed improvement decisions (Benjamin, 2008). The CLA signals to campuses how well they are doing against what would be expected of their students' performance, against their own goals, and against benchmark campuses on broad abilities (Figure 3.2) of critical thinking, analytic reasoning, problem solving, and communication (e.g., Klein et al., 2008). At least two ingredients are missing to capture the overall picture for improvement: (1) External assessments of students' learning in the majors are needed, as are such assessments of students' learning in the areas of responsibility—personal, social, moral, and civic (Chapter 3). (2) Internal measures of student learning are needed (Shavelson, 2008a,b). Such measures would be sensitive to the particular curriculum and context of the campus and provide diagnostic information about where improvements in teaching and learning might be made. This is not to say the CLA cannot be used internally; it can be (see Benjamin, Chun & Shavelson, 2007). CLA-like tasks can be used as teaching tools, and classroom interchanges around these tasks can produce a wealth of diagnostic information. That said, the assessment of learning is broader and more deeply contextualized than CLA-type tasks can tap, and campus assessment programs can serve that function (see Chapter 5).

Finally, simply providing information about student learning and including this information in some kind of report card or balanced score card (Chapter 8) does not guarantee that that will do any good. A campus needs the will and capacity to make use of this information. In particular, as will be seen in Chapter 5, the campus needs its president on down to deans, department chairs, faculty, and students to be in the feedback loop; improvement needs to be highly valued, experimented on, and closely monitored.

Today, the CLA is run by about fifteen full-time CAE staff members and twelve to fourteen part-time consultants. Compared to that of most testing organizations, the staffing is lean. This means that a great deal of the attention given to the CLA is operational, as the assessment grew from fourteen participating campuses in 2005 to over three hundred in the spring of 2007. It also means that while the CLA is being researched at CAE, funding for that research—and producing, publishing, and otherwise publicizing it—has been slower than desired. Nevertheless, there is a substantial body of publications (see, for example, www.cae.org/content/pro_collegiate_reports_publications .htm). What is currently missing is a review summarizing this body of research (although Klein et al., 2007, and Klein et al., 2008, come close). This chapter attempts to bring this research and new analyses together in presenting much of what is known about the CLA.

Underpinnings of the CLA

The CLA, unlike other assessments of undergraduates' learning, which are primarily multiple-choice tests, is an assessment composed entirely of constructed-response tasks that are delivered and scored on an Internet platform (see Chapter 3). The CLA was developed to measure undergraduates' *learning*—in particular their ability to think critically, reason analytically, solve problems, and communicate clearly.

The assessment focuses on campuses or on programs within a campus—not on producing individual student scores. Campus- or program-level scores are reported, both in terms of observed performance and as value added beyond what would be expected from entering students' SAT scores. This said, the CLA also provides students their scores on a confidential basis so they can gauge their own performance.

The assessment consists of two major components: a set of performance tasks and a set of two different kinds of analytic writing prompts (see Figure 4.1 and see Chapter 3 for examples of tasks and prompts). The performance task component presents students with a problem and related information and asks them either to solve the problem or to recommend a course of action based on the evidence provided. The analytic writing prompts ask students to take a position on a topic, make an argument, or critique an argument.

As noted, the CLA differs substantially, both philosophically and theoretically, from most learning assessments, such as the Measure of Academic Proficiency and Progress (MAPP) and the Collegiate Assessment of Academic Progress (CAAP) (Chapter 3; Benjamin & Chun, 2003; Shavelson, 2008a,b). Such learning assessments grew out of an empiricist philosophy and a psychometric/behavioral tradition. From this tradition, everyday complex tasks are divided into component parts, and each is analyzed to identify the abilities required for successful performance. For example, suppose that components such as critical thinking, problem solving, analytic reasoning, and written communication were identified. Separate measures of each of these abilities would then be constructed, and students would take a test (typically multiple-choice) for each. At the end of testing, students' test scores would be added up to construct a total score. This total score would be used to describe, holistically, students' performance. This approach, then, assumes that the sum of component part test scores equals holistic performance.

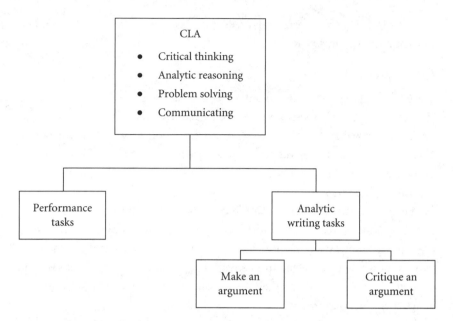

Figure 4.1 Collegiate Learning Assessment structure.
Source: R. Shavelson; www.cae.org/content/pdf/CLA.in.Context.pdf.

In contrast, the CLA is based on a combination of rationalist and sociohistorical philosophies in the cognitive-constructivist and situated-in-context traditions (e.g., Case, 1996; Shavelson, 2008b). The CLA's conceptual underpinnings are embodied in what has been called a *criterion sampling* approach to measurement (McClelland, 1973). This approach assumes that complex tasks cannot be divided into components and then summed. That is, it assumes that the whole is greater than the sum of the parts and that complex tasks require the integration of abilities that cannot be captured when divided into and measured as individual components.

The criterion-sampling notion goes like this: If you want to learn what a person knows and can do, sample tasks from the domain in which that person is to perform, observe her performance, and infer competence and learning from the performance. For example, if you want to find out not only whether a person knows the laws governing driving a car but also whether she can actually drive a car, don't judge her performance solely with a multiple-choice test. Rather, also administer a behind-the-wheel driving test. The task would include a "sample" of "real-life" driving conditions, such as starting a car, sig-

Table 4.1. Criterion Sampling Approach and the Collegiate Learning Assessment

Criterion Sampling Approach ⟹	*Collegiate Learning Assessment*
• Samples tasks from real-world domains	• Samples holistic, real-world tasks drawn from life experiences
• Samples "operant" as well as "respondent" responses	• Samples constructed responses (no multiple-choice)
• Elicits complex abstract thinking (operant thought patterns)	• Elicits critical thinking, analytic reasoning, problem solving, and communication
• Provides information on how to improve on tasks (cheating is not possible if student can actually perform the criterion task)	• Provides tasks for teaching as well as assessment

SOURCE: R. Shavelson; www.cae.org/content/pdf/CLA.in.Context.pdf.

naling and pulling into traffic, turning left and right into traffic, backing up, and parking. Based on this sample of performance, it would be possible to draw inferences about her driving performance more generally. Based on the combination of a multiple-choice test on driving laws and this performance assessment, it would be possible to draw inferences about her knowledge and performance.

The CLA follows the criterion-sampling approach by drawing from a domain of real-world tasks that are holistic and based on real-life situations (Table 4.1). It samples tasks and collects students' *operant responses*. That is, the task of, say, writing a memorandum corresponds to real-life tasks. Moreover, the initial operant responses students generate may be modified with feedback as they encounter new material in an "in-box" and cross-reference documents. These responses parallel those expected in the real world. There are no multiple-choice items in the assessment; indeed, life does not present itself as a set of alternatives with only one correct course of action. Finally, the CLA provides CLA-like tasks to college instructors so they can "teach to the test" (Benjamin, Chun & Shavelson, 2007). With the criterion-sampling approach, teaching to the test is not a bad thing. If a person "cheats" by learning and practicing to solve complex, holistic, real-world problems, she has demonstrated the knowledge and skills that educators seek to develop in students. That is, she has learned to think critically, reason analytically, solve problems, and communicate clearly. Note the contrast with traditional learning assessments, for which practicing isolated skills and learning strategies to improve performance may lead to higher scores but are unlikely to generalize to a broad, complex domain.

CLA Performance Tasks and Scoring

From Chapter 3 recall the DynaTech performance task (see Figure 3.3; see also Shavelson 2007a,b; 2008a,b), which exemplifies the type of performance tasks found on the CLA and their complex, real-world nature. In that task the company's president is about to approve the acquisition of a SwiftAir 235 for the sales force when the aircraft is involved in an accident. The president's assistant (the examinee) is asked to evaluate the contention that the SwiftAir is accident prone, given an in-basket of information. The examinee must weigh the evidence and use this evidence to support a recommendation to the president. The examinee is asked the following:

- Do the available data tend to support or refute the claim that the type of wing on the SwiftAir 235 leads to more in-flight breakups? What is the basis for your conclusion?
- What other factors might have contributed to the accident and should be taken into account?
- What is your preliminary recommendation about whether or not DynaTech should buy the plane, and what is the basis for this recommendation?

Consider another performance task, "Crime" (Shavelson 2007a,b; 2008a,b,c). The mayor of Jefferson is confronted with a rising number of crimes in the city and their association with drug trafficking. This issue arises just as the mayor is standing for reelection. He has proposed increasing the number of police. His opponent, a City Council member, has proposed an alternative to increasing the number of police—increased drug education. Her proposal, she argues, addresses the cause and is based on research studies. As an intern to the mayor, the examinee is given an in-basket of information regarding crime rates, drug usage, relationship between number of police and robberies, research studies, and newspaper articles (see Figure 4.2). The examinee's task is to advise the mayor, based on the evidence, as to whether his opponent is right about both drug education and her interpretation of the positive relationship between the number of police and the number of crimes.

Performance tasks are scored analytically and holistically (Table 4.2). Judges score specific components of each answer (typically 0 for incorrect or 1 for correct) and also provide holistic judgments of overall critical thinking and writing (on a Likert-type scale). Holistic and component scores are summed up to create a total score. A different analytic scoring system is developed for each performance task. This is necessary because tasks vary in the demands they

Crime Rate and Drug Use in Jefferson by Zip Code

Zip Code	Percent of Population Using Drugs	Number of Crimes in 1999
11510	1	10
11511	3	20
11512	5	90
11520	8	50
11522	10	55

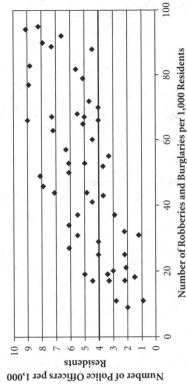

Crime Rates and Police Officers in Columbia's 53 Counties

(Chart: Number of Police Officers per 1,000 Residents vs. Number of Robberies and Burglaries per 1,000 Residents)

Jefferson Daily Press

Evening Edition   TUESDAY, September 21, 2001 $1.50

Smart-Shop Robbery Suspect Caught

Drug-Related Crime on the Rise in Jefferson

By PETRA SURIC

JEFFERSON TOWNSHIP – On Monday police arrested a man suspected of robbing the Smart-Shop grocery store of $125. The arrest came less than six hours after Ester Hong, the owner of the Smart-Shop store, reported the robbery.

The suspect, Chris Jackson, was found just a few blocks from the store, and he put up no resistance when police arrested him. He was apparently high on drugs he had purchased with some of the money taken from the store.

Ms. Hong told reporters that Mr. Jackson came into the store just after it opened and demanded all the money from the cash register. He threatened the owner with a knife, and Ms. Hong game him all the cash she had. The suspect fled, and Ms. Hong called the police. A few hours later police responded to a telephone complaint and found Mr. Jackson in an alley a few blocks from the store. The arresting officer said he appeared to be stoned and did not attempt to evade arrest. The officers found a syringe and other drug paraphernalia in Jackson's pocket. He was charged with armed robbery and possession of drugs.

This is the fifteenth drug-related arrest in Jefferson this month, and the police are calling it an epidemic. Sergeant Heather Kugelmass said, "Drugs are now the number one law enforcement problem in Jefferson. Half of our arrests involve drugs."

Mayor Stone has called for more money to hire more police officers to reduce the growing crime rate in Jefferson. But the Council is divided on what to do.

City Council members Alex Nemeth and LeighAnn Rodd called a press conference to demand that the rest of the council support an increase in the police budget. "If we put more cops on the street," they said, "we will show that criminals are not welcome in Jefferson."

Mayoral candidate Dr. Jamie Eager called for a different approach. "More police won't make a difference. We need more drug treatment programs," Eager said. "The problem is not crime, per se, but crimes committed by drug users to feed their habits. Treat the drug use, and the crime will go away."

The Council is slated to debate the proposed budget increase for police at its next meeting.

Figure 4.2 CLA in-basket items from the "Crime" performance task.

SOURCE: www.cae.or/content/pdf/CLA.in.Context.pdf.

Table 4.2. Scoring Criteria for Performance Tasks

Evaluation of evidence
How well does the student assess the quality and relevance of evidence, by doing the following?
• Determining what information is or is not pertinent to the task at hand
• Distinguishing between rational claims and emotional ones, fact from opinion
• Recognizing the ways in which the evidence might be limited or compromised
• Spotting deception and holes in the arguments of others
• Considering all sources of evidence

Analysis and synthesis of evidence
How well does the student analyze and synthesize data and information, by doing the following?
• Presenting his or her own analysis of the data or information (rather than accepting it as is)
• Avoiding and recognizing logical flaws (e.g., distinguishing correlation from causation)
• Breaking down the evidence into its component parts
• Drawing connections between discrete sources of data and information
• Attending to contradictory, inadequate, or ambiguous information

Drawing conclusions
How well does the student form a conclusion from his or her analysis, by doing the following?
• Constructing cogent arguments rooted in data or information rather than speculation or opinion
• Selecting the strongest set of supporting data
• Prioritizing components of the argument
• Avoiding overstated or understated conclusions
• Identifying holes in the evidence and suggesting additional information that might resolve the issue

Acknowledging alternative explanations and viewpoints
How well does the student consider other options and acknowledge that his or her answer is not the only perspective, by doing the following?
• Recognizing that the problem is complex and has no clear answer
• Proposing other options and weighing them in the decision
• Considering all stakeholders or affected parties in suggesting a course of action
• Qualifying responses and acknowledging the need for additional information in making an absolute determination

SOURCE: www.cae.org/content/pdf/CLA.in.Context.pdf.

make on and the weight given to critical thinking, analytic reasoning, problem solving, and communication to successfully carry out the task.[3]

Analytic Writing Tasks and Scoring

The CLA contains two types of analytic writing tasks, one asking students to make (build) an argument and the other asking them to critique an argument (see Chapter 3 for examples). Analytic writing invariably depends on clarity of thought in expressing the interrelated skill sets of critical thinking, analytic reasoning, and problem solving. Students' performances, then, depend on both writing and critical thinking as integrated rather than separate skills. Writing performance is evaluated using component and holistic scores that consider several aspects of writing, depending on the task. More specifically, both types of tasks are scored using criteria in Table 4.3, as appropriate to the particular task.

Table 4.3. Criteria for Scoring Responses to Analytic Writing Prompts

Analytic writing skills invariably depend on clarity of thought. Therefore, analytic writing and critical thinking, analytic reasoning, and problem solving are related skills sets. The CLA measures critical thinking performance by asking students to explain in writing their rationale for various conclusions. In doing so, their performance is dependent on both writing and critical thinking as integrated rather than separate skills. We evaluate writing performance using holistic scores that consider several aspects of writing depending on the task. The following are illustrations of the types of questions we address in scoring writing on the various tasks.

Presentation
How clear and concise is the argument? Does the student:
- Clearly articulate the argument and the context for that argument;
- Correctly and precisely use evidence to defend the argument; and
- Comprehensibly and coherently present evidence?

Development
How effective is the structure? Does the student:
- Logically and cohesively organize the argument;
- Avoid extraneous elements in the argument's development; and
- Present evidence in an order that contributes to a persuasive and coherent argument?

Persuasiveness
How well does the student defend the argument? Does the student:
- Effectively present evidence in support of the argument;
- Draw thoroughly and extensively from the available range of evidence;
- Analyze the evidence in addition to simply presenting it; and
- Consider counterarguments and address weaknesses in his/her own argument?

Technical Considerations: Reliability and Validity

Standardized assessments are obliged to provide information about the reliability of scores and the validity of score interpretations. Although considerable research on these technical considerations has been done with the CLA (e.g., Klein et al., 2005; Klein et al., 2007; Klein et al., 2008),[4] because it is a fairly new assessment, there are clearly missing pieces of information that in the near future need to be provided. Such pieces of information will be pointed out along the way.

Reliability

Reliability refers to the consistency of scores produced by a measurement procedure such as the CLA. If a test produces reliable scores, a person would be expected to get about the same score taking the test from one occasion to the next, assuming no intervening learning or maturation ("test-retest" reliability); about the same score from one form of the test to another form ("equivalent-forms" reliability); about the same score from one item to another on a single test ("internal-consistency" reliability); or about the same score from one rater to another rater ("inter-rater" reliability).[5] Each method for estimating reliability produces a reliability coefficient ranging from 0 (no consistency) to 1.00 (perfect consistency). Coefficients above .70 are useful for aggregates (e.g., campus scores); coefficients above .80 are useful when individual student scores are reported.

The CLA produces a variety of scores. It produces total "raw" scores and raw scores for performance and writing tasks. Moreover, it provides value-added scores for total, performance, and writing tasks.

Raw scores are produced by the scoring rubrics for each of the CLA tasks. For all tasks, a raw score is the sum of the analytic- and holistic-score components. As the number of components varies from one task to another, raw performance-task scores are scaled to an SAT standardized score. School-level scores are the average scores earned by students at a particular campus. For example, if a campus has a sample of one hundred students responding to a performance task, the school-level raw score would be the average of those one hundred students' performance-task raw scores (see Klein et al., 2007).

The CLA also reports "value-added" scores (Klein et al., 2008). Value-added scores reflect the extent to which a campus performed as expected, better than expected, or worse than expected on the CLA, based on the "quality" of its students upon matriculation as indexed by SAT or ACT scores (see Figure 3.2). Freshman CLA scores are predicted from the students' SAT scores. A better-than-expected score arises when a campus's raw CLA score is higher than its expected or predicted CLA score (above the regression line in Figure 3.2). An expected score arises when a campus's raw CLA score falls on or close to expected (represented by the line). And a below-expected score arises when a campus's raw CLA score falls below the regression line. That is, for each participating school, a "discrepancy" score is calculated that measures the distance the school's CLA score falls from what would be expected for a given level of SAT input. So a campus has a Freshman Discrepancy Score and a Senior Discrepancy Score. Each discrepancy score provides an estimate of above, at, or below expectation. In addition to discrepancy scores, the CLA reports a campus's Value-Added Score, which is its Senior Discrepancy Score minus the Freshman Discrepancy Score. To summarize,

- Freshman Discrepancy Score: CLA freshman raw score–expected score based on the SAT
- Senior Discrepancy Score: CLA senior raw score–expected score based on the SAT
- Value-Added Score: Senior Discrepancy Score–Freshman Discrepancy Score

Below, reliabilities are reported for raw scores, discrepancy scores, and value-added scores. This is done for performance-task and analytic-writing raw scores at both the individual and school levels and for discrepancy scores and value-added scores, which are defined only at the school (or program) level.

Performance Task Raw Scores.   Reliability data are available for seven performance tasks from spring 2006. The mean and median internal-consistency reliability of raw scores for individual students are .83 and .85, respectively, with a range from one performance task to another of .79–.88 (see Klein et al., 2005, for earlier, similar findings). School-level internal consistency reliabilities should be higher than individual-level reliabilities because average scores are typically more stable than individual scores (Klein et al., 2007). The mean and median internal consistencies for school-level performance-task scores are .90 and .91, respectively, with a range of .81–.93. The total performance-task score (aggregating over tasks as matrix sampled) internal consistency was .85 at the individual level and .93 at the school level.

Performance-task scores are based on raters' analytic evaluations of students' responses. A different type of reliability coefficient, the inter-rater reliability coefficient, is used to index the consistency of raters' ratings of student performance-task responses. It reflects the extent to which judges order students' performances from low to high consistently. In spring 2006, the mean and median inter-rater reliabilities for a single rater—the correlation between two raters' scores for a sample of students—were .79 and .81, respectively, with a range of .67–.84. In fall 2007, the mean and median inter-rater reliabilities were .86 and .86, respectively, with a range of .82–.98 (see Klein et al., 2005, for similar findings).

Critical Writing Raw Scores.   For four Make an Argument prompts, the mean and median internal-consistency reliabilities for individual level raw scores in fall 2007 were .94 and .95, respectively, with a range of .93–.95. The corresponding reliabilities for school-level scores were .97 and .97, with a range of .97–.98.

With respect to four Critique an Argument prompts given in fall 2007, the mean and median internal consistencies for individual-level scores were .70 and .71, respectively, with a range of .68–.72. At the school level, mean and median reliabilities were .84 and .84, respectively, with a range of .84–.84. These reliabilities are somewhat lower than other measures reported here but certainly acceptable at the school level.

Critical-writing raw scores, like performance-task raw scores, are based on raters' evaluations of students' responses. However, for critical writing prompts, students' performance might be rated by a human or a machine. Klein et al. (2007; see also Klein et al., 2005) reported inter-rater reliabilities for a single rater based on scores from two human raters to range from .80 to .85, while the human-machine inter-rater reliability was .78, based on data from 2005.

Discrepancy and Value-Added Scores.   Reliabilities for discrepancy and value-added scores are expected to be lower than those for raw scores (Klein et al., 2007; Klein et al., 2008). That is because measurement error is compounded by having two measurements involved: SAT and CLA. This has led some (e.g., Banta & Pike, 2007; Kuh, 2006) to conjecture that CLA total value-added scores were unreliable. It turns out that this is not the case. Klein et al. (2007) reported discrepancy-score reliabilities for freshmen and seniors to be .77 and .70, compared to total raw score reliabilities of .94 and .86. As the number of students at a campus (the sample size) increases, so does the reliability of these scores.

If discrepancy score reliabilities are expected to be low, the difference between two such scores should be really low. To see if this were so, Klein et al. (2007) estimated value-added score reliability to be .63. Contrary to what might be expected, this is a strong indication of consistency given the complexities of the value-added score. Again, as sample size increases, so does the reliability of value-added scores.

This said, the CLA's value-added approach is a pragmatic solution to a difficult real-world problem; over time it will inevitably be revised as better methods become available. To see its limitations, consider the "ideal" way of estimating value added, in which the same cohort of students is followed from freshman to senior year—a longitudinal design. In this case, CLA's value-added approach, adjusting for that cohort's mean SAT score upon matriculation to the college, works well. But longitudinal studies are expensive and difficult to carry out with the churning of students in and out of a college. Moreover, it takes four years to get an estimate of value added. Consequently, most campuses opt for a cross-sectional design. This design collects SAT and CLA scores for freshmen in the fall and for the senior class in the spring of an academic year (e.g., fall 2006 and spring 2007). The design uses the freshman SAT-CLA scores as a proxy for what the seniors' scores would have been when the seniors were freshmen four years prior. But the "surviving" seniors are not the same as the entering class four years previously; not all students in the freshman cohort have become seniors. That means that both the freshman and senior discrepancy ("residual") scores need to be estimated to control for differences in SAT scores over time. And that leaves room for doubt as to whether the adjustment is proper. If the adjustment is not proper, interpretation of value-added scores in one year is tricky for a campus, and change over years is even trickier. Bottom line: Multiple indicators are needed to make informed decisions about areas in need of improvement.

Summary of Reliability Evidence.   Fairly extensive evidence suggests that CLA raw scores are adequately reliable, especially for reporting school-level performance. Moreover, both discrepancy scores and value-added scores are, perhaps, unexpectedly adequate, based on the magnitude of measurement error that they might introduce.

Validity

Validity refers to the degree to which a proposed interpretation of a measurement is warranted by conceptual and empirical evidence. In the case of the CLA, validity depends on the evidence that supports its claim to measure analytic reasoning, critical thinking, problem solving, and communication. There are variety of ways a validity argument can be built. One way is to argue that the tasks on the CLA are representative of real-world tasks drawn from a variety of life situations. Often, expert judges are used to evaluate this representativeness claim. Another way to establish validity is to show that scores on the CLA correlate with other measures as expected. For example, a positive correlation between the CLA and a measure of, say, critical thinking would provide such evidence. A third way is to show that the CLA predicts future performance of experts and novices, or life outcomes, perhaps through correlations with grade-point averages. And a fourth way is to establish that the kind of thinking expected—analytic reasoning, problem solving, for example—is actually demanded when students perform CLA tasks. This is typically done via a "think aloud" method, in which students verbalize their thoughts as they work through a task.

A measurement is never "validated." That is, validation is an ongoing process of building evidence—confirmatory and disconfirmatory—that leads to changes in the measurement, in the conceptual underpinnings, or in both. The CLA, being a new instrument, is in the beginning stages of validation, as we will see. Much progress has been made, but more remains to be done.

Content Representativeness.   The CLA claims to contain real-world, holistic tasks sampled from domains such as education, science, health, environment, art, and work. Of course, these are not the real-world tasks themselves but simulations of such tasks. The question, then, is to what extent students and faculty view the tasks in this way and believe that the capacity to perform the tasks is valuable—what a college education is supposed to prepare students for. To a small degree, data exist to address the question of representativeness, but only for the performance tasks, not the critical writing tasks.

Faculty Perceptions of Performance Tasks.   In a study designed to set performance levels on the CLA's performance tasks, Hardison and Valamovska (2008) collected faculty members' perceptions of the tasks. These data are important because the forty-one faculty members were selected to be widely representative of faculty across the country, regionally, by public or private college, by academic field, and by rank. Moreover, the faculty members became intimately familiar with the CLA performance tasks through extensive review of the tasks themselves and extensive reading and discussion of student responses to the tasks. More specifically, faculty responded to a questionnaire on a five-point Likert-type scale (1=strongly disagree . . . 5=strongly agree), with items tapping whether the following occurred:

- An important educational construct was measured.
- What is measured on the CLA is taught in college courses.
- Performance tasks measured what they were intended to measure (critical thinking, etc.).
- Performance on the test would predict important life outcomes.
- Training students on the tasks would help them get ahead in life.
- Known groups would perform better on the tasks (e.g., professors would be expected to perform better than dropouts on the CLA).

These faculty seemed to be in a position to judge issues of importance, overlap with courses taught in college, whether the tasks measured analytic reasoning (etc.), and perhaps differences between known groups. However, it is a stretch to believe that they could predict the future. Nevertheless, for completeness, those findings are reported along with the others. In general, the lowest mean might be expected for the scale tapping the overlap between courses taught and the CLA. College courses tend to focus more on knowledge in the subject being taught and less on broad reasoning abilities (Figure 2.1).

The results are shown in Figure 4.3. Consistent with expectation, the lowest mean rating was given to the overlap between CLA performance tasks and what is taught in college courses. With respect to whether the performance tasks measure an important educational outcome and whether they measure what they are supposed to measure, the faculty agreed or strongly agreed. As for pre-

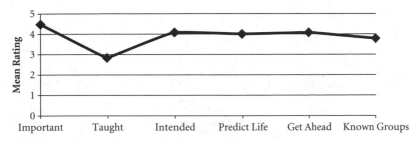

Figure 4.3 Faculty perceptions of the CLA's performance tasks.

SOURCE: R. Shavelson; www.cae.org/content/pdf/CLA.in.Context.pdf.

dicting the future, the faculty agreed that the CLA would do so, although that is a far conjecture. Finally, faculty agreed that the performance tasks would distinguish known groups, but that, too, is as much conjecture as experience.

The evidence, such that it is, suggests that faculty who have studied the performance tasks and read a substantial number of student papers varying in quality viewed the CLA performance tasks as reflecting important educational outcomes, measuring what they were intended to measure, and distinguishing "experts" from "novices." They also felt that these tasks were somewhat different from what was taught in college courses. And finally, they viewed the tasks as predictive of life outcomes and getting ahead if taught.

Student Perceptions of Performance Tasks.   The CLA regularly collects students' perceptions of its performance tasks (e.g., Klein et al., 2005). The most recent data available are for freshmen in fall of 2006 and seniors in spring of 2007. They were asked to evaluate the tasks on a set of eight items, six of which are pertinent to content representativeness. Unfortunately, the Likert-type scales associated with each item on the questionnaire differ from one another in number of scale points, and so a succinct summary of findings like that in Figure 4.3 is not possible. The questions are paraphrased and the mean (standard deviation) response provided for freshmen and seniors in Table 4.4.

Freshmen and seniors agree that the CLA performance tasks are "mostly different" from those encountered in their classes (Question 1). This is what might be expected if the CLA were measuring broad ability to perform holistic, real-world tasks. Just as the faculty did, students saw the differences between CLA and classroom tasks; this difference perhaps reflects broad reasoning ability and knowledge in the major. Moreover, they considered the tasks to be good at tapping their ability to analyze and communicate (Question 3).

Table 4.4. Students' Mean (Standard Deviation) Perceptions of CLA Performance Tasks

Question	Freshmen	Seniors
1. How similar are the CLA tasks to those you do in college (1 = Very Different . . . 4 = Very Similar)?	2.08 (.87)	1.96 (.87)
2. How interesting was the task compared to course assignments and exams (1 = Boring . . . 5 = Far More Interesting)?	2.98 (.99)	2.93 (1.01)
3. How good are the CLA tasks at measuring ability to analyze and present a coherent argument (1 = Very Poor . . . 5 = Very Good)?	3.59 (1.05)	3.61 (.97)
4. How difficult was the task compared to your college exams (1 = Much Easier . . . 5 = Much Harder)?	2.74 (.92)	2.47 (.92)
5. Do you agree that more professors should use tasks like this one in their courses (1 = Strongly Disagree . . . 5 = Strongly Agree)?	2.91 (1.08)	2.99 (1.09)
6. What is your *overall* evaluation of the quality of this task (1 = Terrible . . . 4 = Fair . . . 7 = Excellent)?	4.86 (1.10)	4.86 (1.11)

SOURCE: R. Shavelson.

Both freshmen and seniors viewed the performance tasks to be about as interesting as college tasks (Question 2) and at about the same level of difficulty as college tasks (Question 4). They were neutral about having more professors use these tasks (Question 5) but rated the overall quality of the tasks as "fair" to "good" (Question 6).

Perhaps the most important evidence for the validity of CLA task-score interpretation is the finding that students say the tasks are different from what they encounter (Question 1), *and* that the tasks tapped their ability to analyze and communicate (Question 3). This is just what the CLA says about its tasks. Students are neutral about having more such tasks in courses and view the tasks as about as interesting and challenging as those encountered in their courses.

Relationship of CLA Scores to Related Measures. Another way to examine the interpretative validity of CLA scores is to see whether they "behave" as might be expected. For example, since both the CLA and the SAT measure broad abilities, the latter measuring broader abilities than the former (see Figure 2.1), CLA scores and SAT scores should be positively correlated with one another. Also, since CLA tasks tap critical thinking (in part), scores on these tasks should be positively correlated with scores on other critical-thinking measures. Moreover, science majors would be expected to perform slightly higher on science-like CLA tasks than humanities or social science majors would, and vice versa. Even though all CLA tasks tap broad reasoning (etc.) abilities, some special domain knowledge might help, at least in comprehending the task presented (see Figure 2.1).

Males and females might be expected to perform similarly, but the majority-minority gap might be found on CLA tasks.

Correlation with SAT.   The correlation between SAT scores and CLA performance and writing scores should be positive and of moderate magnitude, as both tap into cognitive abilities, although the SAT score taps verbal and quantitative aptitudes and the CLA tasks tap broad domain abilities more closely tied to education (more "crystallized abilities" than the SAT). The correlations between the SAT and CLA for seniors in 2006 and 2007 ($N \sim 4,000$), for example, are as follows: performance task—.55 and .57, respectively; analytic writing—.57 and .50, respectively. The freshman correlations are of similar magnitude (Klein et al., 2007). So the CLA is "behaving" as expected.

The SAT-CLA correlation at the school level, however, is considerably higher, on the order of .88 for freshmen and seniors on CLA total score (available at the school level and not the individual level due to matrix sampling); .91 and .88, respectively, for the performance task; and .79 and .83, respectively, for the writing task (Klein et al., 2007). The higher reliabilities at the school level than at the individual level arise because school mean scores are more reliable than individual scores, and there are systematic differences between campuses on both the SAT and the CLA.

The high correlation at the school level does *not* mean that the SAT and CLA measure the same thing, as some believe (Klein et al., 2007). Rather the two measures share about 60 percent to 80 percent of their variance at this level, leaving room for college effects. Such effects are reflected, in part, by seniors at all SAT levels scoring higher than freshmen across campuses (Figure 3.2). Moreover, the CLA and SAT measure different things. As a thought experiment, imagine coaching students on the CLA and the SAT. The coaching would take very different forms, because the two assessments measure different things and require somewhat different thinking processes. Incidentally, there is about a .91 correlation between LSAT and bar exam scores at the school level. The rank ordering of school means on the LSAT corresponds almost perfectly with the differences in bar exam passing rates among law schools. Does this mean that the LSAT and the bar exam are measuring the same knowledge and skills? Hardly (see Klein, 2002b).

Correlation with Grade-Point Average.   It seems reasonable to expect a positive correlation between CLA scores and college grade-point averages. However, given the unreliability of GPA, the variability of GPA from one instructor to another or one major to another, and the fact that seniors' GPA is based on a diverse set of courses, the magnitude of the correlation should be fairly low—say, about .35 (Sackett, Borneman & Connelly, 2008). This is typically the range for SAT– freshman GPA correlations *within campuses*. And this is what is found with the CLA for seniors in 2007. The CLA-GPA correlation for performance tasks was .28, for Make an Argument .23, and for Critique an Argument .25. The direction and magnitude of these correlations did not change when carried out by students' major area of study. Note that these values are the average *within*-school correlations for the nonrandom sample of students who elected to participate in the CLA at their campuses.

Correlation with Critical-Thinking Measures.   If the CLA taps important aspects of critical thinking, CLA scores should correlate positively and moderately with other measures of critical thinking, such as the Watson-Glaser Critical Thinking Appraisal. The relationship among the CLA, MAPP, and CAAP scores, along with specific measures of critical thinking, are currently being studied; but results are not yet available.

Correlation Between Academic Domain and Task Type.   The CLA taps broad cognitive abilities developed in humanities, social science, and science domains. This leads to the conjecture that science and engineering majors might do better on performance tasks based on science and engineering scenarios, humanities majors better on humanities scenarios, and social science majors better on social science tasks. A counter conjecture would be that while these tasks vary, they all tap basically the same cognitive abilities. Moreover, students take courses in all three domains. Any differences, especially after adjusting for differences in SAT scores between majors, should be very small at most.

It turns out that differences do exist across the academic domains, both before and after adjusting for differences in SAT scores. In Figure 4.4 seniors' adjusted mean SAT-adjusted CLA scores in 2007 are presented for three types of performance tasks (science-engineering, social science, and humanities) and four academic-major groupings (science-engineering, social science, humanities, and "other," including business and service majors).

The mean scores for the academic groupings after SAT adjustment are science-engineering ($n = 855$), 1,178; social science ($n = 788$), 1,204; humanities ($n = 641$), 1,199; and other ($n = 2,036$), 1,168. These mean differences are statistically different: "Other" performs, on average, below the remaining groupings; science scores do not differ significantly from those of either the humanities or

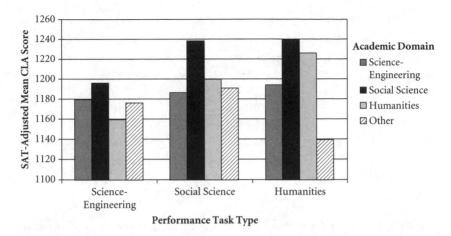

Figure 4.4 Relationship between academic domain and performance task type (SAT-adjusted scores: seniors 2007).
SOURCE: R. Shavelson.

the social sciences, although the social sciences scores are higher than the humanities scores.

The interaction of task type and academic domain bears directly on competing conjectures: Is there or isn't there a relationship between academic domain and task type? First, and perhaps surprisingly, students majoring in the social science domain scored, on average, higher than students in other domains across all three task types (Figure 4.4). However, the mean difference between social science and science-engineering students on the science-engineering task type is quite close (means of 1,197 and 1,189, respectively), as is the mean difference between social science and humanities students on the humanities tasks (1,239 and 1,226, respectively). Across the board, the "other" grouping fell considerably lower than the rest. There does, then, seem to be a small (about 1 percent of variance) relationship between academic domain and task type, but the high performance of the social science students across domains muddies the water a bit.

Correlation of Performance Task Scores with Gender and Minority Status.   It is important to ensure that measures of learning do not contain bias or have an adverse impact on various groups of students. Consequently, attention focuses, for example, on the performance of men and women and of majority and minority students. No statistically significant relationship was found between gender and mean unadjusted performance task scores. However, when an adjustment is made for SAT, women scored, on average, .30 standard deviations higher than men. Moreover, white students scored about .50 standard deviations higher than nonwhite students (a smaller difference than what is typically observed on other cognitive tests) before covariate adjustment. However, adjusting for SAT, this mean difference is not statistically significant ($p < .071$).

Cognitive Demands.   Finally, if CLA tasks tap students' reasoning, problem solving, and critical thinking skills, having students think aloud while performing these tasks should reveal the degree to which the tasks are having their intended impact on thinking (e.g., Taylor & Dionne, 2000). Unfortunately, such "cognitive validity" data have not yet been collected for the CLA.

Summary of Validity Evidence.   Validating test score interpretations is an ongoing process. This is especially true of the CLA, as it has only recently been developed. Much remains to be done. That said, the evidence that does exist supports the proposed interpretation of CLA scores. The tasks on the CLA, according to faculty and students, do vary from typical tasks found in college courses. Moreover, the CLA scores correlate with SAT scores, as would be expected. And CLA scores tend to be sensitive to students' academic domain and the type of task presented (science-engineering, social science, humanities), with social science students scoring, on average, higher than students in the other domains (adjusting for SAT). Finally, the white-minority gap disappears once CLA scores are adjusted for SAT; a gender gap appears (women scoring higher than men) once SAT is taken into account.

Reprise

The Collegiate Learning Assessment was developed as a measure of students' broad abilities—critical thinking, analytic reasoning, problem solving, and communicating. These abilities appear to be the kinds of college outcomes valued by educators, policy makers, and the public. The CLA took an approach that differs from the traditional approach of analyzing complex performance into component psychological components and measuring each with, typically, a multiple-choice test. Rather, the CLA adopted a criterion-sampling approach to measure complex performance by sampling holistic, real-world tasks drawn from life situations. The CLA assumes that the whole is greater than the sum of its psychological-component parts. The evidence from both faculty and student encounters with CLA tasks ("content representativeness") supports this claim so far.

The assessment was developed to send a signal to campuses as to how well their students are performing (Benjamin, 2008). This the CLA does by providing value-added scores and benchmarking a campus's performance with those of its peers (Klein et al., 2008). The parent organization of the CLA, the Council for Aid to Education, is on record as stating that the intent of the CLA is to provide feedback to campuses for the improvement of teaching and learning and *not* for high-stakes external comparisons (Benjamin, 2008). CLA's board recognized the diversity of college student bodies and missions and noted that one size does not fit all.

The CLA is a relatively new assessment (with a pedigree dating back to the 1930s), and so information about its reliability and validity is being gathered. At present, although there is fairly extensive and strong evidence of reliability, some validity studies have been done and reported here, some are in progress, and some remain to be begun. This said, validation is a process, not an end; hence, studies need to be done continually to improve the measurement and the construct definition.

One way of reprising the technical information about the CLA is to address its more vocal critics (Banta, 2008; Banta & Pike, 2007; Kuh, 2006; Pike, 2008; Shermis, 2008).[6] Banta (2008, p. 4) laments shortcomings of the CLA (and other measures of broad abilities, including the MAPP and CAAP), saying, "Dear colleagues, the emperor has no clothes." She, Pike (2008), and Shermis (2008) enumerate a number of limitations. Evidence from this chapter, and Klein et al. (2007) and Klein et al. (2008), will be brought to bear on each claim.

- *Tests like the CLA are measures of prior learning,* as evidenced "by the near perfect .9 correlation between CLA scores and SAT/ACT scores at the institution level" (Banta, 2008, p. 3). There is no doubt that tests of cognitive ability reflect prior learning or achievement at a given point in time (see Chapter 2). Indeed, prior learning has been found to be the best predictor of future learning. Just how much prior learning is tapped by the CLA is another story. The .9 correlation reflects the SAT-CLA correlation for total scores at the school level. This school-level correlation ranges from .6 to .8 when performance and writing task scores are examined separately. However, the best measure of prior learning is not the school-level correlations that aggregate over students and capture campus-level SAT-CLA relationships but the individual-level correlations between students' SAT scores and their CLA scores. This correlation was found to be in the .5 realm. Even adjusting for unreliability, these correlations are not perfect, suggesting that the CLA measures something other than the SAT, which Banta uses as an index of prior learning.

- *The high correlation between CLA and SAT scores means that there is little room in which to observe college impact on student learning.* That is, a correlation of .9 accounts for 80 percent of the total variation in CLA scores. (Recall the square of the correlation coefficient can be interpreted as the percent of variance shared by two measures.) Surely some of the remaining 20 percent, so the argument goes, is captured by demographic differences at campuses, test-taker maturation, motivation and anxiety, and measurement error. To be sure, some of that 20 percent is taken up by such factors. However, when CLA scores are predicted from SAT scores and student demographics, the proportion of variance shared in common stays roughly the same (Klein et al., 2007; Klein et al., 2008). Finally, measurement error cannot take up shared variance, as it is unpredictable, by definition.

- *A corollary of this reasoning (Pike, 2008) is that the variation among students is large within a campus, and the variation between campuses is small.* However, there is ample evidence of substantial variation among campuses' CLA scores (see Figure 3.2). And campuses with the same mean SAT score vary considerably in the level of their students' mean performance on the CLA.

- *There is inadequate evidence of the technical quality of CLA scores*—retest reliability is missing, construct and content validity studies are sparse to non-existent, and so on (Banta, 2008; Pike, 2008; Shermis, 2008). As described in this chapter, extensive reliability information has been reported for the CLA, and it appears to be adequate. True, retest reliability has not been reported, but what would that look like? Traditionally, to find retest reliability, the same test is given on two separate occasions about two weeks apart, assuming no intervening learning has occurred. Such information's value is far less than the cost of collecting such data with the CLA, for two reasons. The first is the high cost (financially, motivationally, logistically) of retesting within a short time period. The second is that, except in longitudinal applications of the CLA (which have been few),[7] retest reliability is much less relevant than internal consistency and inter-rater reliabilities that speak to the quality of scores at a particular point in time (freshman and senior years with the CLA). Moreover, as pointed out previously, there is evidence about the content representativeness of CLA tasks and of the CLA's construct validity in the form of correlations with other measures. This said, a great deal of work needs to be done in collecting additional evidence regarding correlational validity (e.g., correlation with other measures of critical thinking) and "cognitive" validity, making sure the CLA tasks evoke the kind of thinking they are intended to evoke (critical thinking, problem solving, etc.).

- *Value-added scores are unreliable and to be mistrusted.* "I also confess to a great deal of skepticism about the wisdom of attempting to measure value added," states Pike (2008, p. 9). Banta (2008, p. 4) tells readers that "the reliability of value-added measures is about .1, just slightly better than chance." To be sure, there is room for skepticism about value-added scores; from a measurement perspective they are prone to errors and misinterpretation. Also, there are different methods available for measuring value added, and each method might paint a somewhat different picture. However, the evidence summarized in this chapter shows that both discrepancy scores (the discrepancy between expected and observed scores for seniors across campuses, for example) and value-added scores (the difference between senior discrepancy scores and freshman discrepancy scores) were reasonably reliable, the former around .70–.75 and the latter around .63 (see Klein et al., 2007; Klein et al., 2008). The CLA uses discrepancy and value-added scores because simply comparing campuses' raw scores would be misleading due to the great variability in the ability of these campuses' entering freshmen. Discrepancy and value-added scores attempt to level the playing field and provide benchmarks for campuses by which to judge their performance.

- *No tasks are content free, so differential performance on tasks is to be expected, depending on a student's academic preparation.* As we saw, there is a slight relationship between academic domain and performance on CLA tasks. But this was very small. Moreover, since the CLA focuses on campus-level (or program-within-campus–level) performance with matrix sampling, by randomly assigning students to tasks, such differential academic preparation by task-type relation is balanced out.

- *A corollary of this reasoning is that there is no course on college campuses in which students would learn the broad abilities assessed by the CLA.* Shermis (2008, p. 10) asks whether CLA-measured competencies are "something that would likely be an outcome of a general education course? If so, which one? English? Math? Introductory psych?" These questions are revealing. In the CLA view, the goal is to transcend "course" fixes and speak of an integrated general or liberal education that builds over the college years toward these competencies. Shermis is right: No single course can do the trick, and that is just the message the CLA intends to send.

• *Students are not motivated to take the CLA, and, consequently, their observed performances are not reflective of their true performances.* Without doubt, motivation is an issue for all testing, not just the CLA. We know that motivation is high on college and graduate-school entrance examinations and on certification examinations. These are high-stakes tests for students' futures. Where the stakes are low for the test taker, as with the CLA, motivation is an issue. To address this issue (and to get an adequate sample) campuses vary in the incentives they do or do not provide students, and this might account for between-campus differences. Klein et al. (2007) have studied, correlationally, the relationship of various incentives and no incentives with campus CLA scores. They found no systematic relationship (Klein et al., 2007). Moreover, CAE believes that assessments of learning—the CLA and campus measures—need to become an integral part of college students' education. Once students see the benefit of having information about their ability to reason analytically, solve problems, and communicate clearly, that becomes a source of motivation (see the CLA's frequently asked technical questions 2007–2008, www.cae.org/content/pdf/CLA.Facts.n.Fantasies.pdf). As will be seen in Chapter 5, some campuses have achieved this, but it is rare at present.

• *There is no urgent need to compare institutions.* Homemade assessments are to be preferred because they are more likely to be closely linked to a campus's curriculum than a test designed to assess "a generic curriculum" (Shermis, 2008, p. 12). While there is clearly a role for campus assessment programs in the improvement of learning (see Chapter 5), there is also a need for benchmarking (Benjamin, 2008). Campus-grown assessments cannot tell administrators, faculty, students, and the public whether the campus is doing as well as it might do in fostering student learning. As Graff and Birkenstein (2008) point out,

It is simply not true, as the antistandardization argument has it, that colleges are so diverse that they share no common standards. Just because two people, for example, don't share an interest in baseball or cooking, it does not follow that they don't have other things in common—or that, just because several colleges have different types of faculties or serve different student populations, they can share no common pedagogical goals. A marketing instructor at a community college, a biblical studies instructor at a church-affiliated college, and a feminist literature instructor at an Ivy League research university would presumably differ radically in their disciplinary expertise, their intellectual outlooks, and the students they teach, but it would be surprising if there were not a great deal of common ground in what they regard as acceptable college-level work. At the end of the day, these instructors would probably agree—or should agree—that college-educated students, regardless of their background or major, should be critical thinkers, meaning that, at a minimum, they should be able to read a college-level text, offer a pertinent summary of its central claim, and make a relevant response, whether by agreeing with it, complicating its claims, or offering a critique. Furthermore, though these instructors might expect students at different institutions to carry out these skills with varying degrees of sophistication, they would still probably agree that any institution that persisted in graduating large numbers of students deficient in these basic critical-thinking skills should be asked to figure out how to do its job better.

The CLA, then, represents a different approach to the assessment of student learning than other such measures (e.g., CAAP, MAPP). Moreover, it measures students' critical thinking, analytic reasoning, problem solving, and communication competencies in a realistic, holistic manner. And it does so reliably and validly. Not surprisingly, I believe it is the best alternative for measuring undergraduates' learning of broad abilities.

5 Exemplary Campus Learning Assessment Programs

IMPROVEMENT OF TEACHING AND LEARNING in our colleges will proceed only so far with summative assessment of student learning, the focus of the previous chapter. Such assessment *signals* the need for improvement overall and perhaps in some specific areas. It also may provide formative information when used to guide instruction in class (Benjamin, Chun & Shavelson, 2007). At worse, however, these assessments punish colleges that are not meeting expectations without providing adequate information on what to improve and how to improve it.

For substantive, not symbolic, responses to accountability to payoff, campuses need in-depth, context-sensitive diagnostic information about student learning. Such information cannot be provided by external assessments alone. External assessment, then, needs to be supplemented with closely aligned internal assessments of students' learning *and* with an analysis of organizational structures and processes that afford or constrain students' learning.

In a somewhat overused phrase, colleges and universities need to become "learning organizations." Moreover, they need to recognize that "doing good" is not enough. Their goals should be such that the proverbial bar is raised higher and higher in response to their own prior performance and their peer institutions' performance. And to do so, they need both external assessments of learning that provide benchmarks for judging how well they are doing (Benjamin, 2008) and internal measures to diagnose where improvement is needed (Shavelson, 2008a,b). Finally, once diagnosed, campuses need to adopt a spirit of experimentation to judge which alternative solutions to diagnosed problems are effective. In a word, alignment of external assessment with internal assessment is essential for a campus to learn and grow productively.

Campuses, then, need to develop internal, formative assessments for generating context-sensitive diagnostic information for improvement. Is this possible beyond a symbolic response? Are there examples—existence proofs and models—to guide those institutions seeking to respond substantively to improving teaching and learning? If so, what do these campus assessment programs look like? How did they start? What keeps them going? Have they had the impact they intended? What challenges have they faced?

These questions are posed with the recognition that a great deal has been written about campus assessment of learning and that literature is readily accessible (e.g., Banta & Associates, 2002; Peterson, Vaughn & Perorazio, 2001). Here we look closely at six campus assessment programs that, within the past ten years, have been widely recognized by peers as "successful" and "exemplary" at one time or another (recently, the Council for Higher Education Accountability has given awards to exemplary programs; see Eaton, 2008). These are not "representative" in some statistical sense, they are not unanimously acclaimed, and they will not necessarily be at the top of their game by the time you read this chapter. Nevertheless, they were selected to give a sense of the variation in approaches campuses have taken to assessing student learning and to improving. The goal is to identify a range of campus assessment practices that might be adopted and adapted by other campuses seeking to assess learning and experiment with the improvement of teaching and learning.

This chapter begins by describing two benchmark campus learning assessment programs that reflect the variability in possible approaches. It then focuses on the findings from a case study of campuses recognized by the field as exemplary, examining their inception, philosophy, operation, and impact. It concludes by drawing conclusions for the design of campus learning assessment programs.

Benchmark Campus Learning Assessment Programs

Over the past twenty-five years, two campus assessment-of-learning programs have arguably stood out as exemplary, serving as benchmarks for other campuses. To be sure, they have evolved over time, but their distinctive features remain. Perhaps somewhat surprisingly, they are as different as they are similar in many important respects. While both programs sprang from visionary leaders, one focused on individual student development of holistic, problem-focused, real-world critical thinking and social responsibility abilities and skills. The other focused on campus-level improvement of underlying, general psychological abilities and skills. While both campuses—Alverno College and Truman

State University—view assessment of learning as part of their mission, they have varied as to how much they integrated that assessment into their teaching and learning processes. The goal here is to characterize the similarities and differences between the two assessment programs, along a set of dimensions that can then be applied to the campuses in the case study that follows.

Although Alverno and Truman have been identified over the past ten years, at one time or another, as exemplars by peers and experts in the learning assessment community, the potential for rhetoric about accomplishments even from these two campuses (let alone the campuses in the case study below) sometimes exceeds reality. And although both have been widely recognized, they have their critics, for different reasons.

Alverno College

Alverno College has a four-year, undergraduate liberal arts program for women and coeducational graduate programs. The college is dedicated to the student— her learning, personal and professional development and service to the community. Located in Milwaukee, the nineteenth-largest city in the United States, Alverno serves about 2,500 students and offers more than sixty undergraduate programs (majors, minors, and associate degrees) in four schools: School of Arts and Sciences, School of Business, School of Education, and School of Nursing.

Alverno believes that education means "being able to do what one knows" (Loacker & Mentkowski, 1993, p. 7). Since 1973, students graduate only if they have demonstrated an appropriate level of *performance* on eight *abilities:* (1) communication, (2) analysis, (3) problem solving, (4) valuing in decision making, (5) social interaction, (6) developing a global perspective, (7) effective citizenship, and (8) aesthetic engagement.

To assess the level of student performance, Alverno developed an extraordinary program of performance assessment. The program was initiated in response to concerns about the quality of its academic programs raised about thirty-five years ago, in accreditation. The then president, Sister Joel Read, challenged each department to identify important questions being raised in its discipline and then to decide on the critical concepts that should be taught and the most appropriate methods for teaching them. This exercise led to a key question that drove the curricular reform and the assessment process: "What kind of person were we [Alverno faculty] as educators seeking to develop?" (Loacker & Mentkowski, 1993, p. 6). This question triggered the definition of the outcomes, characteristics, and abilities that were expected from the students as a result of their education at the college.

The basic notion that emerged at Alverno was that assessment of these learning outcomes should incorporate *samples of the performances the college seeks to prepare students for*. Consequently, Alverno built a performance assessment system. The system assessed students' performance, in realistic tasks and contexts, on the specific abilities the college considered essential learning outcomes. Students were expected to demonstrate competence within a range of situations (assessment tasks) in which they might find themselves (Loacker & Mentkowski, 1993), such as giving a speech, writing a business plan, or designing a scientific investigation.

This program embraced a criterion-sampling philosophy based on Mc-Clelland's (1973) approach to the measurement of competence. For McClelland (1973, p. 7), learning assessment tasks should be samples of criterion situations: "If you want to test who will be a good policeman, go find out what a policeman does. Follow him around, make a list of his activities, and sample from that list in screening applicants."

Assessment at Alverno is considered an integrating, developmental experience. Its main purpose is to support students in developing their own strengths on each of the learning outcomes. The assessment process is integrated into curriculum and teaching to enhance students' developmental experiences. Supporting individual student development, then, is the core of the Alverno system, a system in which both faculty and administrators take responsibility for their roles in student development.

Moreover, the assessment program is built to measure *developmental trajectories,* a concept that Alverno has used from the program's inception, and one that has been put in the spotlight by the National Research Council (2001). Indeed, in the early 1970s, Alverno conceived the development of the eight abilities as successive and increasingly sophisticated as students moved through their studies; for example: "To meet general education requirements, the student will show analytical skills at the four basic levels: observing, making inferences, making relationships, and integrating concepts and frameworks. All these are integrated with the content of her general education courses" (Loacker & Mentkowski, 1993, p. 9).

All assessments are developed to provide an opportunity for students to demonstrate one of the eight abilities. Tasks are sampled, and a student's performance or "criterion behavior" is evaluated. The assessments' criteria for success are public. Students receive feedback on their performance and on how to improve it. They are encouraged, as well, to assess themselves and their own goals (Loacker & Mentkowski, 1993). The idea is that if students can be taught to perform on samples of criterion tasks, they have been taught to perform in real-world situations. "Cheating," in the sense of performing on various samples of criterion tasks, is not problematic. If students can perform well on the assessment, that means they are likely to perform well in a comparable real-world situation.

Upon entry to Alverno, for example, students are videotaped as they give a persuasive talk; each subsequent year they give another persuasive talk and are videotaped again. Over a four-year period, then, students' development on this criterion task is monitored and evaluated. Formative feedback from a review panel, including representatives from the Milwaukee business and government communities, provides for individual development in this criterion situation. At the same time, external participation at Alverno develops critical links with the community and public service.

Since the beginning, faculty has sought different strategies to ensure multiple perspectives and data sources on student learning. For example, since the start of the program faculty have kept written portfolios with copies of key performances as a cumulative record of each student's development. About seven years ago, a digital portfolio was created. The portfolios enable students to follow their learning progress throughout their years of study.

Although the assessment program focuses on student learning trajectories on the eight critical abilities, this information is also used to evaluate academic programs and the institution as a whole. In this way, Alverno evolves over time with feedback as to how well it is meeting its goals for student learning in a systematic, rather than an intermittent, way.

Alverno has run its assessment program organizationally first through an Office of Research and Evaluation (which later became the Assessment Center). Three years after the assessment program began, the college created the Office of Research and Evaluation and charged it with describing (1) developmental trajectories, (2) models of professional performance, (3) knowledge and skills students should develop, and (4) expectations of what graduates would need (Loacker & Mentkowski, 1993). The Assessment Center now is a department that works closely with students, faculty, staff, and the southeastern Wisconsin business community to provide services related to assessment at Alverno.

The assessment program, then, is a coherent system created by the faculty and embedded in a supportive culture. Coherence is achieved by articulating and integrating educational mission, values, assumptions, principles, theory, and practice. Moreover, "it relies on the re-conceptualization of the use of time, academic structures, and other resources to bring about increasingly effective learning for students" (Loacker & Mentkowski, 1993, p. 20).

Perhaps the signature characteristic of the assessment program is that assessment has been tightly integrated into the students' learning processes, the faculty's vision and enactment of their teaching and learning, and administrators' commitment to student development. This "assessment as learning" approach has earned Alverno worldwide recognition (Banta, 2002).

Truman State University

Truman State University, formerly Northeast Missouri State University, is located in Kirksville, Missouri. A four-year, liberal arts university with more than six thousand students, Truman offers forty-five undergraduate and six graduate areas of study in twelve academic divisions, such as science, language and literature, mathematics and computer science, education, and social science. The university seeks to advance knowledge; create an environment for freedom of thought and inquiry; and develop the personal, social, and intellectual growth of its students.

Truman State's widely recognized institutional culture of assessment was spurred in part by the State of Missouri's approach to higher-education accountability and in part by a visionary president. Missouri early created financial incentives to encourage its colleges and universities to assess and report on student learning. Administrators at Truman State took leadership among the state's campuses and spearheaded student-learning assessment, capitalizing both on that leadership and on the resources made available.

Learning assessment began in the 1972–73 academic year, when President Charles J. McClain invited graduating students to sit for comparative (senior) exams. Early in his administration McClain made clear that the traditional use of inputs for assessing the quality of the institution (e.g., resources, reputation; see Chapter 8) would be replaced by methods focusing on student learning outcomes and value-added models for measuring quality (Cartwright Young & Knight, 1993). He wanted to demonstrate that the university made a difference in students' knowledge, skills, and attitudes, and that graduates were nationally competitive in their chosen fields. The university referred to its assessment program as value-added, even though the data collected did not always fit a value-added model (Cartwright Young & Knight, 1993).

The assessment program typically has tested students in their first, third (at 75 credit hours), and senior years at the university with multiple methods. The assessments provide both indirect and direct outcome measures. In contrast to

Alverno's use of performance assessments, Truman focuses on surveys, questionnaires, and nationally standardized instruments that measure broad, underlying cognitive abilities (knowledge and broad domain reasoning; see Figure 2.1). The important advantage of using these types of assessments over locally developed assessments is that they provide an external reference for benchmarking student achievement against peer institutions (Magruder & Cartwright Young, 1996a).

Different sets of instruments are used, depending on the student's academic year. For example, freshmen are administered the Cooperative Institutional Research Project (CIRP) survey, which profiles the entering class on field of study, highest degree planned, college choice, ethnic background, and self-ratings of various abilities and skills. At the senior year, students take a majors' test prior to graduation. Recently, the Collegiate Learning Assessment (CLA) has been administered to a sample of freshmen and seniors, providing a value-added measure. Although seniors are tested in every discipline with externally normed tests (e.g., ETS's major field tests) their graduation does not depend on test performance.

Since 1985, seniors have taken capstone courses that seek to integrate subfields within a major. Many of the courses require that students demonstrate the knowledge and skills that faculty have determined as learning priorities within the major. Faculty in each major, then, determine the content of the capstone. This flexibility acknowledges the faculty responsibility for the curriculum. However, it also leads to considerably different capstone experiences across majors. For example, in one major students write a thesis, in another they present papers or projects at an organized forum outside class, and in still another they take a comprehensive exam (Cartwright Young & Knight, 1993).

One of the few assessments developed by the university is a student portfolio, a requirement created in 1988 in response to a petition from President McClain for an instrument that could demonstrate students' achievement and learning. Currently, all students are required to develop a portfolio of their best work, accompanied by a reflective essay, written in the senior year, on their growth in knowledge, skills, and attitudes in college (Kuh, Gonyea & Rodriguez, 2001; Magruder & Cartwright Young, 1996b). Students learn about the portfolio requirement as freshmen, hear more about it periodically during their course of study, and fully develop the portfolio as seniors.

A final type of assessment employs interviews. Since 1992 faculty-student teams have conducted interviews to gather information not collected in other surveys on issues such as teaching-learning strategies and learning experiences (Cartwright Young & Magruder, 1996).

Compared with the program at Alverno, Truman's assessment program focuses less on individual student improvement and more on aggregate measures of performance that reflect the campus's academic programs. Portfolios, the exception, are used for formative feedback in meetings between advisors and students. Portfolios have been identified as the characteristic that has put Truman's assessment program back on the map as an exemplar (Kuh, Gonyea & Rodriguez, 2001).

Critical to the success of the Truman assessment program was its incremental and low-key manner of implementation. Unlike the way things were done at Alverno, at Truman the president chose not to create a central assessment office. (An Advisory Committee for Assessment was created at the beginning of the 1990s.) The rationale was that such an office would reduce faculty interaction. What was critical for the success of the development and implementation of this assessment program was the extensive role modeling that President McClain and Vice President Darrell Krueger did in the use of assessment data at the assessment program's inception (Cartwright Young, 1996; Cartwright Young & Knight, 1993). They were particularly "adept at suggesting program innovations that increased faculty interaction, conveyed higher expectations for students' academic development, and heightened students' involvement in learning" (Cartwright Young & Knight, 1993, p. 29). Assessment became the university's mechanism for using a common vocabulary and an organizational focus (Cartwright Young & Knight, 1993).

Other keys in the success of the program have been the faculty's role in implementing the program and the type of assessment information provided to them. Faculty-administration conversations grounded in assessment data have been critical for developing assessment-based improvements at the university (Magruder & Cartwright Young, 1996b). Also, faculty have been directly involved in developing specifications for assessing students. The process of determining what learning objectives to assess has benefited faculty, curriculum, and courses develop (Magruder & Cartwright Young, 1996b). Faculty receive, annually, information on their students', along with university averages and norms when available. However, they do not receive comparative departmental data (Cartwright Young & Knight, 1993).

Exemplary Learning Assessment Programs

That Alverno and Truman State are so very different but also so highly regarded demonstrates that, not surprisingly, there is no consensus as to the "best" way to assess learning in higher education. But it also raises questions as to what it is about these programs and perhaps others that has made them archetypes in the field.

While Alverno and Truman State are, arguably, benchmarks in the learning assessment community, other institutions have become well known as exemplary, too. In order to learn from these institutions, answers were sought to questions such as how their assessment programs originated; what assessment of learning means on the campus, including its underlying philosophy; how the assessment program was organized and used; and how it impacted teaching and learning.

Because there is often a gap between rhetoric and reality in the world of higher-education assessment and accountability (e.g., Newman, 2003), an in-depth case study approach (Yin, 2003) seemed appropriate to develop an understanding of campus assessment programs. Much of the current assessment literature is descriptive and champions innovation and effort more than it analyzes program design and use. The case study reported here collected data from a broad variety of individuals and documents to characterize or profile four campuses' assessment programs. *Assessment program* was defined quite broadly—as a college's or university's effort to systematically measure undergraduate student learning indirectly (by proxies such as graduation rates, student surveys) or directly (via instruments such as the CLA, MAPP, CAAP, GRE, or certification examinations; see Chapters 3 and 8).

Here we provide an overview of the questions that drove the study and describe the campuses that participated. Site selection and methods used for data collection and analysis are described in the appendix at the end of this chapter.

Research Questions

The study sought to understand the origins, philosophy, operation, and impact of exemplary campus assessment-of-learning programs. To this end, it addressed four questions: (1) How did these programs come into being—e.g., were they institutionally initiated, externally mandated, or both? (2) What philosophy underlies the program's assessment of students' learning—e.g., performance competence or cognitive ability? (3) How does the assessment program operate—e.g., what structures and policies shape the program? (4) What is the impact of the program, intentionally and unintentionally, on administrators, faculty, and students and on the improvement of teaching and learning? In sum, four dimensions of campus assessment programs were addressed: *development, philosophy, operation,* and *impact.*

Case Study Sites

Four campuses participated in the study. Site selection took into account a number of institutional and program characteristics, as well as recommendations from researchers and policy analysts who pointed to the colleges and universities as having a particularly innovative or effective assessment program. Case studies were conducted during the 2003–4 academic year at these institutions. In order to protect their anonymity pseudonyms are used for the campuses. Each is described briefly here:

- *Learning Outcomes University* (LOU) is an urban state university committed to outcomes-based education. With an enrollment of about thirty thousand students, the campus offers more than 180 academic programs, from associate degrees to doctoral and professional degrees. This university has been considered a service-learning campus, linking university programs with the community. The campus is noted for graduating a high percentage of professionals (e.g., dentists, nurses, physicians, and social workers) in this state. Its learning assessment program encompasses both general education and the majors, with emphasis on the former.
- *Student-Centered Learning University* (SCLU) is a small, somewhat rural state university. It is committed to outcomes-based education, both in general education and in academic majors. The campus offers about fifty academic programs, including graduate degrees. Most of the university's roughly 3,700 students come from segments of society that have been traditionally underserved by the educational system. Its learning assessment program encompasses both general education and the majors, with emphasis on the latter.
- *Assessment-Centered University* (ACU) is a medium-size public university located in a rural setting. The campus of about seventeen thousand students is also committed to outcome-based education. This university offers about seventy academic programs, including bachelor's and graduate degrees. More than 60 percent of the students come from within the state, and most are white. The university's learning assessment program encompasses both general education and the majors, with emphasis on the former.
- *Flexible University* (FU) is a large public university located in a suburban area of a large city. It offers about seventy academic programs, including associate, bachelor, graduate, and professional degrees, to about thirty

thousand students. More than 91 percent of the students come from within the state. The learning assessment program encompasses both general education and the majors, with emphasis on the former.

Findings: Comparing and Contrasting Campuses

Here the four campuses' learning assessment programs are compared and contrasted on four dimensions: development, philosophy, operation, and impact. Within each dimension specific, concrete evidence portrays a campus.

Development—Impetus

Accreditation served as the common impetus for assessing learning on all four campuses (Table 5.1). Given the popular perception that accreditation has "no teeth" and has not been an effective accountability mechanism, especially for those who seek cross-campus comparative information, this finding might be somewhat surprising. However, in support of the skeptic, the research team found that seeking accreditation might be a necessary, but is certainly not a sufficient, condition for stimulating campus learning assessment. The desire for accreditation *combined* with a campus vision, especially a vision espoused by the president or chancellor—or *combined* with state policy incentives—led all four campuses to assess student learning. With respect to vision, the president at ACU believed in data-based evidence on the value the campus adds to student learning and the key role that assessment played: "It's perhaps a little cliché to say, but it really is true—we were interested in better understanding what value we add before someone told us that we had to do that. . . . So I think it's important that the learning assessment really take the lead in our efforts, because that is, after all, our primary reason for being" (ACU president).

The effect of the accreditation application was especially strong on campuses with professional schools. Specialized accreditation, combined with a certification examination, created a culture of assessment within the particular school. A LOU department chair reported, "A lot of it's driven by accreditation, but I think it's also driven by the faculty's dedication to quality of teacher education. . . . Because the [State] Professional Standards Board mandated that we were going to have a unit assessment plan and have it in place and operating by this past year."

Moreover, state incentives played directly into the ACU president's vision. The executive director of the assessment office at ACU recalled, "We had a legislative mandate from the state . . . that mandated assessment at all of the

Table 5.1. Cross-Campus Comparison on Dimensions of Development, Philosophy, Operation, and Impact

Assessment Program Topic	Learning Outcomes University	Student-Centered Learning University	Assessment-Centered University	Flexible University
Development—Impetus				
• State higher-education policy / $	✓	✓	✓	
• Accreditation	✓+	✓	✓	✓+
• University leader	✓	✓+	✓	
Philosophy				
• Processes vs. outcomes	O	O	O	O
• Trait vs. criterion sample	T	C	T	T
• Focus				
- student centered	✓	✓	✓	✓
- feedback to programs		✓	✓	
- feedback to students		✓+		
Operation				
• Chancellor/provost support	✓	✓	✓	
- faculty hiring policy		✓	✓	
- promotion and tenure		✓	✓	
- link to improvement		✓	✓	
• Assessment director				
- stature	✓	✓	✓	
- coherent vision		✓	✓	
- work with faculty		✓	✓	
• Assessment vs. planning office	A+P	A	A	A
• Oversight committees	✓			✓
• Program-based committees	✓–	✓	✓	✓
• Size vs. relationship with faculty	Large–	Small+	Large+	Small+
• Top-down or bottom-up or both	Top–	Both+	Both+	Bottom–
• Feedback to program in place		✓	✓	✓–
• Technical (psychometric) capacity	✓–		✓	

(continued)

Table 5.1. (*continued*)

Assessment Program Topic	Learning Outcomes University	Student-Centered Learning University	Assessment-Centered University	Flexible University
Stages of maturity				
- age (years)	>10	5–10	>10	<5
- outcomes developed	✓	✓	✓	✓–
- assessment system developed		✓	✓	
- feedback systems in place		✓	✓	
• Instrumentation				
- in-house assessment office	✓		✓	
- in-house program committee	✓	✓	✓	✓
- standardized commercial	✓		✓	
Impact—Consequences				
• Faculty burden	✓	✓–	✓	✓+
• Faculty improvement around student, learning, and assessment	✓–	✓	✓	✓

SOURCE: R. Shavelson.

NOTE: ✓ indicates presence modified by less or more (– or +). O=outcomes, T=traits, C=criterion sample, A=assessment, P=planning office.

institutions of higher ed. . . . And [the university] took it seriously. The dust never settled, and [the president] began to see that assessment is a political policy tool. He was a skilled politician, and we provided him with information that was useful, and they [the state higher education board] continued to invest in this center."

Learning Assessment Philosophy

Whether implicit or explicit, and in these case studies it was primarily implicit, each campus had a distinctive philosophy about learning assessment. In common, all campuses focused on *student outcomes,* in contrast, say, to having particular *processes* in place to serve student learning. Yet beyond espousing outcomes, campuses varied dramatically—for example, as to whether they focused on individual students (SCLU) or on programs (the other three campuses) and as to the types of student outcomes targeted.

As part of a campus vision, LOU (not surprisingly) moved to make outcomes a campus-wide focus:

> I think there's a lot of work under way right now by [the chief assessment officer] with regard to [learning outcomes] and the ways in which we assess them. We're looking at [them] again; this is not a novel approach, but a beginning, intermediate, and senior or graduating level of competence in these [learning goals], so that you don't look at them as there's simply one way of assessing student mastery or student competence. (LOU chancellor)

Following its accreditation review, Flexible University also began to focus on student outcomes, in particular on outcomes related to speaking and writing: "Yes, it was sort of bubbling up then, and the provost at that time and all the deans have said that the colleges' departments would be responsible for writing and speaking in those disciplines, and to hold their feet to the fire, provost said, and they must do this, they must have outcomes-based assessment" (FU faculty member).

Another dimension of assessment philosophy is whether the assessment taps student cognitive abilities (e.g., as at Truman State University) or competence on criterion samples of real-world (problem- or project-based) tasks (e.g., as at Alverno College). For example, although each of the campuses espoused students' ability to think critically, they took different approaches in assessing critical thinking in general education. For some campuses (e.g., ACU), critical thinking was a trait students possessed more or less of, and it was measured efficiently and reliably by a campus-made multiple-choice test that drew largely on logical reasoning and syllogisms: "The third area, an area in which I'd say we have the most trouble over the entire program, is critical thinking. We have tried probably every standardized critical thinking test in the country; we don't like any of them. We designed our own" (ACU dean).

In contrast, at SCLU critical thinking was assessed holistically by assessing performance on criterion tasks, such as finding the sources of pollution in a stream outside the local town:

> The Humanities and Social Sciences dean had . . . [come] from our visual and public arts [assessment], and the student . . . did a mural with a local high school in [Town]. And that mural involved his putting together various aspects of himself as a student and as a person contributing to society. He had to go and convince the school district to let him use a huge brick wall on the school

grounds and to get the art classes to participate, and then he was the art instructor himself, teaching the students how to do art, which was going to then trans-
late to their working on the mural. Then he supervised, organized the mural and
then made a movie about the experience and then designed a display board with
the art that the students did. . . . And it was really about how art was a means by
which people can both develop self-esteem, develop their own confidence in
their ability to contribute to a community and collaborative project, and also to
come together on values that express community. It was a community-building
exercise.

Finally, although all campuses focused on student outcomes, only two, SCLU
and ACU, sufficiently implemented assessments of these outcomes to provide
feedback to students and programs across most of the campus (see Table 5.1). The
other two campuses, at the time, were primarily at the outcome-definition stage
or the initial-assessment-of-outcomes stage, so that feedback was not widely
available.

Both SCLU and ACU used student-outcome assessments for program improvement. SCLU stood out among the four cases in feeding back performance
information to students. For example, "entering students are briefed in a first-
year freshman seminar about individual learning plans, and feedback is provided
on their progress. An advising office and peer advisors support each student's
learning" (SCLU faculty member). Moreover, feedback to students is designed
into their assessments, capstone projects, and portfolios; students have access to
the same information that all others do, since data are public.

Assessment Program Operation

On each campus, the assessment program operated, to a greater or lesser extent,
out of a campus-wide assessment office. The office at each campus was headed
by a visionary assessment director whose view of learning assessment permeated the program. Indeed, perhaps what distinguished these campus programs
in the learning assessment community was the visibility of the director and his
or her accomplishments.

The assessment offices had responsibility for facilitating and promoting
student-learning assessment goals. Organizationally, these assessment offices reported through the provost's office or a related vice chancellor. Only at LOU was
the assessment office also the Planning and Improvement Office. Depending on
the campus's academic program offerings, assessment office professionals might

also hold faculty appointments in relevant departments, such as education or psychology, and students majoring in those departments might have assistant-ships in the assessment office.

The LOU assessment office had a staff of more than a dozen professionals, in addition to the director. In contrast, SCLU, a much smaller institution, relied on one professional and an assistant; FU, a large campus, relied on a part-time assessment associate. ACU's assessment office fell in between but closer to the size of LOU's.

Campus Leadership Support

The learning assessment programs on three of the four campuses were champi-oned by leadership. The presidents and provosts not only supported the campus's assessment program, they also saw it as part of their own vision for what the cam-pus should be. At SCLU, for example, the assessment program's impetus came from the top of the organization, the president and the provost, both of whom were committed to outcomes-based education. In the president's words,

> I was able to convince the founding faculty . . . that talking about learning out-comes would in fact be friendly to first-generation or historically underserved populations, because one of the great reported, sort of frictions for them in or-ganized education is the subjectivity of the faculty member . . . [and students] not having any public standards. . . . I argued that if we were serious about keeping ourselves honest, we should decide what we meant by general education exit standards, and for graduating baccalaureate and master's degrees, and then we should begin to organize the learning experiences that we offered or the as-sessment experiences that we offered.

On the two campuses with the strongest assessment-of-learning cultures, in the research team's judgment, campus leaders had linked their vision and sup-port for the assessment program with strong incentives for the faculty. Both SCLU and ACU had created policies that spoke directly to the value of assess-ment. In hiring new faculty, the commitment to student learning and assessment was a major goal:

> We . . . try to be very careful when we're hiring, and we try to be very clear about what it is we're looking for. So, for example, the person who writes to the Physics Department and basically says that they need $350,000 start-up funding and they're going to be bringing six graduate students and post-docs, the application

doesn't go very far. We're looking for a scholar teacher who is interested in undergraduate education and interested in involving undergraduate students in
their research and scholarly work. So we're hiring a certain kind of faculty member, and we're doing that very intentionally, because I think we're interested in
the learning outcomes for undergraduate students and providing solid research
experiences. (ACU dean)

In a similar vein, SCLU and ACU had promotion and tenure policies that
signaled the importance of student outcomes and learning assessment. In the
words of the SCLU president,

If a person wants to stay home and do research, they've got to do it on their own
time, basically. If you want us to be excited about and supportive of your research, then you have to show how it would become the basis for the pedagogy
that you are employing. . . . It's a matter of making your research and the doing
of your research available to undergraduates and graduate students and integrating it with the pedagogy. And then people who do that get a lot of (a) support, (b) thanks, (c) move faster through the ranks—and I mean, we reinforce
it, which means we don't reinforce other things.

SCLU's and ACU's positions on hiring and promotion and tenure contrasted with LOU's focus on research. There the impact of the assessment program on the faculty was viewed with some skepticism. Pressures at this research
university led a dean to report that the reality was that disciplinary research was
privileged in hiring and in tenure and promotion over scholarship in teaching
and learning: "Faculty are hired on the basis of that, they are tenured on the
basis of that, and they are promoted on the basis of that."

Finally, SCLU and ACU focus, as *learning organizations,* on improvement,
from the president through the deans to the faculty. Learning assessment, for
example, is integral to SCLU's commitment to developing students' competencies with assessment information feeding back to improve teaching and learning. This focus, in the words of the president, "is absolutely intentional. And [it
has] . . . implications for our organization and becoming a learning organization, a notion of a culture of evidence. We ask students to be attentive to evidence, and we ourselves are then attentive to evidence. It is all linked. You can't
do one without the other is our view."

ACU focuses on programs, especially on improving its general education program. General education courses must pass review periodically and demonstrate

student improvement. According to the dean, "Where we do, theoretically at least, hold their feet to the fire is the requirement that they demonstrate performance on assessment for reapproval—we have a five-year reapproval cycle. . . . This is our own general education curriculum reapproval."

Assessment Office Role in Organizing Campus Assessment

One pattern was similar on all campuses: Assessment offices played a more critical role in assessing learning in general education than in the majors, where departments took primary responsibility. Moreover, the better articulated the general education curricula were, the stronger an influence the assessment office had on assessments in this area. Although all sites articulated goals or outcomes for a liberal education, campuses that tied goals closely to the curriculum (i.e., SCLU and ACU) had better-developed assessments in those areas.

At LOU, the assessment office took responsibility for organizing a campus-wide assessment committee composed of two persons from each of its schools. The two representatives constituted a small subcommittee within a school and worked as a link between the campus committee and the school. The subcommittee typically coordinated learning assessment within the school, but not always; sometimes other faculty members performed that function. One faculty member defined the campus committee as "a committee and a forum for people to present their assessment methods for the edification of the rest of the university. . . . [It] recognizes excellence in the assessment efforts of their colleagues and provides advice on how to improve those efforts." Similar types of committees were found at FU.

At ACU, and to a lesser extent SCLU, the main instrument for implementing the assessment program was program-based committees. At SCLU, a clear committee structure could be found when the campus started its assessment program. The chancellor along with the founding faculty hammered out a vision of outcomes-based education and the kinds of outcomes sought for students. As it set about building assessments, this faculty committee recognized that it did not possess the competence to do that and concluded that it needed an assessment director to provide technical expertise and vision for the program. Once hired, the director worked closely with faculty, less in a formally organized committee structure than in loose groups of faculty with common interests (e.g., general education), to build assessments and create an assessment program.

ACU organized the assessment office and assessment committees around its undergraduate learning goals. The goals were packaged into five "bundles" (categories; e.g., critical thinking and communication in the humanities, arts, natural sciences, and social sciences). Each of the bundles had a steering committee composed of faculty who taught the courses involved in that bundle. The leader for each bundle coordinated activities with all departments that taught in that bundle.

In sum, assessment offices differed in the ways student-learning assessment was conceptualized, developed, and implemented on their campuses. Some offices formed oversight committees; others used program- or department-based committees. Assessment office policies varied from primarily top-down (e.g., LOU) to primarily bottom-up (e.g., SLCU).

Perhaps the most telling aspect of assessment center organization was the relationship with faculty across programs. We found important differences in the roles these offices played vis-à-vis faculty involvement—that is, the extent to which faculty lead, develop, oversee, administer, analyze, and use assessment. It was clear at each site that the faculty who helped select and deliver assessments found the program to be more meaningful than bystanders. Whereas one assessment program office was a clear leader and innovator in areas such as instrument selection and development, others played a more facilitating role and kept faculty members in central control. As will be seen, this relationship made a significant difference not only to the faculty's ownership of the assessment program but also to its level of implementation success. The pervasiveness of assessment in the campus culture was directly related to the leverage held by assessment staff in the facilitator role.

Assessment Office Approach to Assessment Policy and Practice

LOU's central assessment office took a somewhat top-down approach, at least for certain policies, which proved difficult to implement at the school level. This situation created among faculty a sense of misdirection and a perception that the assessment office did not have a clear vision for the program:

> And for each program in your department, your schools, [the program had to] write intermediate and introductory performance criteria. And I've calculated for our school, we did a good job, writing just four intermediate and four intro for each degree. We have associate degrees, we have bachelor's degrees, we have a graduate degree. Some departments have four degrees. I counted 52,920 statements of behavior [performance criteria], and I said, "We can't do this!" So, that, the e-mail came back: "Okay, stop everybody and let's let the [learning goals] committee do this first." So, that's the kind of thing I'm talking about. (LOU faculty member)

I don't think they have a strong vision, being involved from the get-go in the entire assessment. This situation creates some misdirection. (LOU faculty member)

At the other three campuses, the assessment office played a consultancy role. An important difference among the three was that at SCLU the assessment director had a general assessment strategy that was implemented and adapted by individual programs. At the other two universities, the assessment strategy was more open and flexible. However, across all three campuses faculty ownership of the assessment program was, in the research team's estimation, higher than at LOU.

At SCLU the assessment office director, having worked closely with the campus community to develop and implement workable policies that were well received by the faculty, was recognized by all informants as the cornerstone and resource for assessment. Assessment policies were modified and adapted based on program and faculty needs. The assessment director became the key player in developing a "culture of evidence" across the entire campus. Feedback mechanisms to improve teaching and learning were well established and valued. In the words of one faculty member, the assessment office director "actually is the person that made this happen. Before she got here, we really just were wandering in the wilderness."

At ACU the assessment office had at least one liaison on each bundle committee. (Some of the liaisons held academic positions, as well, and consequently knew firsthand about teaching and assessment.) The assessment office, in collaboration with faculty within each bundle committee, selected and/or designed, administered, and analyzed assessments, particularly in general education. The office, then, played a consultative role throughout the campus, helping academic departments design instruments and analyze data. As the ACU assessment director said, "We consider ourselves to be the full-time consultants. . . . We see our task as helping institutions and programs to develop reasonable goals and objectives, help them to initiate and design and craft methods that provide information that will be useful and meaningful to them."

At FU each school had faculty leaders who coordinated assessment efforts. Consistent with flexible policy, the assessment office's role was to educate faculty within programs on assessment issues by conducting workshops and serving as a consultant and facilitator to help faculty define objectives, select assessment methods, and interpret and use results.

Technical Quality Assurance

The assessment offices' capacity for evaluating the technical adequacy of campus assessment instruments varied. Only at ACU did we find an assessment office strongly oriented to measurement. This, then, was the only assessment office that stressed the importance of certain technical issues, especially reliability. Rigorous statistical analyses of assessment results were conducted at the assessment office, although interpretation of the data was always done by the faculty: "I mean, that's my proudest moment, you know, to have faculty take that data and interpret it. That's an interpretive report. We do not interpret the results for faculty; we provide them with results, the interpretation is theirs" (ACU assessment director who also holds a faculty position).

LOU focused to a lesser degree than ACU on the technical quality of its instruments. At SCLU quality control and quality assurance were not a priority; over time both the quality of the assessments themselves (their reliability, validity) and the inferences drawn from them about individual students and educational credits would need to be addressed. At the time of the visit the will was there, but the capacity was not. A similar situation was found at FU, where instruments were in a development phase; gauging their technical qualities was neither a priority nor a capacity.

Finally, assessment program maturity across the four campuses was unrelated to the number of years the program had been in operation. With more than ten years in place, LOU's assessment program did not have a system fully developed that provided systematic feedback throughout the institution. ACU, at a similar age, had an assessment system in place that fed back assessment findings to programs at the bundle level, but not at the student level. SCLU's assessment program was at a similar stage of maturity as ACU's but with many fewer years of life. At SCLU we found evidence that assessment information affected students, although a formal feedback system was not in place. FU, the site of the youngest program, had a new assessment office that was dealing with defining student outcomes and developing assessments. At the time of our visit, this campus was completing a first assessment cycle in some schools, focusing on a single student-learning outcome.

Nature of Assessment Instruments

At each campus, we sought to understand what constituted the battery of examinations, portfolios, presentations, or other tools used to assess learning. The purpose was not to conduct a psychometric study of the relative merits of different instruments but to focus on the intentions behind their selection and use. A particular assessment format, for example, might be chosen for department-level curricular planning, whereas another might be chosen for internal or external accountability reporting.

LOU's primary learning assessment instrument was a self-report student survey—the National Survey of Student Engagement (NSSE)—chosen in response to accreditation demands. Specifically, general education was assessed by student self-reported learning gains as compared with peer NSSE institutions. Although the current survey strategy seemed to successfully appease the external mandate from the institution's accreditor, the information was not used otherwise. Strategies for direct assessment of student learning were being developed and implemented in some schools and departments, especially when professional accreditation was involved. Faculty reported wide variance in the extent to which their departments participated in a comprehensive assessment strategy. At the time of the visit, the campus was in the early stages of developing a student portfolio assessment aimed at directly measuring the campus's agreed-upon undergraduate learning outcomes. Portfolios were viewed as the best tool for connecting what students were expected to learn with what was actually taught and with what students actually learned, because, as one assessment official opined, you "can see it, taste it, feel it, in domain-specific ways."

At SCLU assessments were developed to provide formative and summative feedback to students and formative feedback to programs. The assessment strategy had two components. First, well-articulated general education and major program outcomes were embedded in and assessed in course work. Second, a campus-wide capstone experience was used as a performance assessment to demonstrate mastery of outcomes: Students designed, carried out, and reported on applied research or other projects in their major field. These projects had to deal with social and environmental contexts in which the university was embedded.

At ACU the assessment office took a deliberate step away from external assessments and focused on developing its own measures and helping departments develop their own. Most of the assessment instruments, then, were designed in house, but some standardized instruments also were used. This was unique to ACU and happened because of the technical competence of the staff.

The ACU assessment office developed a range of assessments from direct learning measures, including content- and skills-based tests such as multiple-choice tests, performance assessments, and capstones, to indirect measures such as development, motivation, attitude, and disposition questionnaires. Diverse types of instruments were used across the different bundles and majors. The assessment office preferred assessments that allowed the campus to speak to the value that the curriculum adds to students' learning. For example, some instruments took a "value-added" approach by assessing students longitudinally in their freshman and junior years. Students also took a battery of developmental instruments that explored areas such as identity and values. These instruments were primarily multiple-choice, with some constructed response. Afterward, the office conducted rigorous statistical analyses to evaluate the technical quality of the assessments.

At FU the research team had difficulty getting a sense of the instruments used, although clearly they were mostly developed in house. Instruments were based on the outcomes, and outcomes were program based. At least two schools were using student portfolios. One department chair used the NSSE, but she was not sure whether NSSE was appropriate, based on student demographics at the campus.

Impact

In examining the impacts of the four campuses' assessment programs, two of Gormley and Weimer's (1999) criteria for evaluating organizational report cards are used. The first criterion, reasonableness, asks whether the assessment program's burden is reasonable or strains the institution's human, fiscal, or time capacity. The second criterion, functionality, asks about intended and unintended consequences, both positive and negative.

A consistent finding across the four campuses was that the assessment programs imposed, at different levels, a sense of faculty burden without reduction of other responsibilities. That is, most of the faculty experienced a tension between what they were asked to do by their assessment office and their teaching, research, and administrative duties. This sentiment was higher at some campuses (LOU, FU) than at others (SCLU, ACU). Examples of comments follow:

> There's also the perception that we spend too much time assessing assessment, and the faculty is very frustrated. . . . They're willing to do service, but when you're asking them to do service on service, they get kind of tired of it. . . . And in addition to that, there are always new things coming out of the dean's office and things coming out of [the assessment] office, and it really complicates the

job of middle management and chairs. But when you're trying to protect faculty members . . . I think it's very counterproductive. (LOU faculty member)

Over the last four to five years, times have not been flush here at State, and I would imagine some other institutions, as well. That's important because with things like assessment and lots of other initiatives, it's difficult . . . to motivate faculty who have been subjected for one year after another of no raises and no extra resources—if anything, cutbacks. . . . So there is a little bit of built-in resistance to any kind of additional work that we're asking. And I believe that was one of the reasons that it was a little bit more difficult this last fall to get all the departments to go through all the work, which they did; it just took a little bit longer than we had hoped. (FU assistant dean)

Even at the smallest campus, SCLU, which was confronting a growth spurt, the assessment burden was evident. At the time of our visit, faculty and the assessment officer were making plans to have small groups of students, rather than each individual student, do a capstone, for example.

Many faculty who were directly involved in assessment programs, however, found the experience to be constructive. The assessment program allowed them to learn about assessment and how to improve their teaching; in some cases it had opened communication channels that had not existed before. For example, at LOU, faculty who participated on the campus-wide assessment committee felt they had gained a valuable opportunity to learn more about assessment and about what other schools were doing to assess their students' learning. But even for those who were part of that committee, there were disconnects. For example, being committee members did not help them understand the feedback mechanisms that the central assessment office had implemented: "I did go [to the campus-wide assessment committee] kicking and screaming into it and found it to be way more interesting than I expected. . . . Although I still have the same categories of negative reactions to the idea of assessment, I actually have seen that in ideal circumstances, you can learn from it and make changes that will make things better" (LOU department chair).

Similar experiences were heard at the other campuses, including FU, where administrative and financial supports were so limited:

From a faculty point of view, not from an administrative point of view—after having that discussion on what do we actually want this to look like, I changed the way I taught. I added elements in my course that I didn't have before, and I changed the way I approached even the material. So that discussion, for me . . . as a faculty member, changed the way I delivered the course. So I'm sort of sold. (FU associate dean)

This is not to say that all assessment committee faculty went along with the assessment willingly. One faculty member at ACU who had become heavily involved in assessment reported, "We do it because we have to do it"—for their accreditor—and "with anguish and gnashing of teeth."

Reprise

Assessment of learning for external accountability provides an important but limited tool for improving organizational performance. It *signals* areas in which strengths and weaknesses have been observed; however, these signals are diagnostically weak. Such external learning assessments need to be supplemented with internal assessments that focus on the college's curriculum and its teaching and learning, and that are aligned with external measures. Since campus assessment of learning plays such a critical role in organizational learning, and in improving teaching and learning, it seemed reasonable to look at exemplary campus learning assessment programs to see what could be learned.

How Did These Programs Come into Being?

The conduct of national and regional accreditation played a catalytic and symbiotic role in creating an emphasis on learning assessment at the four case-study campuses. This was especially true of professional schools facing certification examinations. Certainly, the desire for accreditation played a role, as well, at Alverno. Accreditation led to fundamental changes in that campus's curriculum and learning assessment and led it to become internationally recognized.

Institutional leadership—presidents and provosts and assessment directors— also played a critical role in spurring learning assessment on each of the campuses. The visioning of assessment by such leaders also played an important role at Alverno and Truman, albeit in different ways.

Finally, state policies that encouraged learning assessment with (e.g., monetary) incentives contributed to the assessment programs on two campuses in states that had them. (But not on all campuses in those two states jumped on the assessment bandwagon; see Naughton, 2004). Such was also the case at Truman, where strong incentives were available.

All three policy instruments—the accreditation process, state policies, and institutional leadership—taken together proved to have synergistic effects on learning assessment. They provided necessary but not sufficient conditions to stimulate assessment programs at these campuses.

What Philosophy Underlies Assessment of Learning?

All four campuses shared a common, overarching philosophy: outcomes-based education. This is in contrast to a philosophy of content (e.g., "great books") or one of process (e.g., the Socratic teaching method). Each campus wanted to be clear as to what knowledge, skills, frames of mind, attitudes, and the like the campus sought to engender in its graduates.

Student-Centered Learning University parted company from the other campuses, however, with its emphasis on criterion-sampling assessment (cf. Alverno) in contrast to cognitive ability or trait assessment (cf. Truman). That is, SCLU developed learning assessments that sampled criterion performances (e.g., stream monitoring in a local town); whereas the others might assess general knowledge or broad reasoning abilities. To be sure, the distinction was not always so clear-cut, as all four campuses varied in their approaches to learning assessment. We speak of the preponderance of assessment methods.

Finally, the campus philosophies differed as to the use of assessment information—program focused (cf. Truman) or student focused (cf. Alverno). Once again, the distinction was not so neat, but the relative emphases were clear. Only two campuses could be used to test whether differences in program- and student-centered philosophies could be seen firsthand on campus (in spite of all four campuses' recognition in the assessment community). We found that the philosophies could be recognized, quite clearly. SCLU focused on student feedback, as well as program improvement; and Assessment-Centered University, vice versa.

How Does the Assessment Program Operate?

All campuses had both charismatic assessment directors and a central assessment office. The directors were well known in the learning assessment community, and their stature helped put the campuses' assessment programs on the map. Typically, a campus-wide assessment office was responsible for promoting the program. (Incidentally, the size of the office was not necessarily associated with its effectiveness, but size was associated with the number of functions carried out.) On three of the four campuses, the assessment function was separated organizationally from the planning and improvement function (the exception being Learning Outcomes University). And three of the four campus assessment offices and directors had very strong support (in vision and material) from the president or provost (Flexible University was the exception).

The campuses varied in approach to assessment implementation. Two of the campuses (LOU and, to a lesser extent, FU) took a top-down approach. The office and director led the development of campus outcomes and encouraged assessment of those outcomes. The other two campuses, those with operational assessment programs, took what might be called a "pandemonium approach." Assessment implementation was simultaneously top-down and bottom-up. The assessment office pressed for program implementation while supporting department and faculty assessment efforts and, when called upon, guided their outcome definition and assessment development efforts.

At three of the four campuses, various committee structures were created to accomplish the work of defining outcomes and building assessment. At SCLU, beyond the faculty committee that initiated outcomes-based education and assessment, it was often difficult to discern a committee structure. To be sure, work groups could be identified, characteristic of the strong bottom-up approach on this campus, but they were far less formal.

Both SCLU and ACU, the two campuses with operational assessment programs, had campus-wide policies that supported learning assessment. With respect to faculty hiring, priority was given to teaching and assessment over research accomplishment; a commitment to the campus's philosophy was critical. With respect to promotion and tenure, the scholarship of teaching, in contrast to research, was given priority. Finally, both campuses had policies that brought the findings of the assessment programs to the attention of the president and on down to the department faculty and students. It said loud and clear that assessment was valued, important, and used in decision making.

Instrumentation and attention to technical quality varied across campuses. All four campuses embraced homemade in contrast to off-the shelf assessments. This varied, however, especially when a department or school used certification examinations. Instruments ranged from indirect measures of learning, such as student surveys (e.g., NSSE), to portfolios, performance assessments, capstone projects, and multiple-choice and constructed-response tests. Only at ACU was there a concern about and capacity to deal with the technical quality, especially the reliability, of the instruments used. The lack of overt technical evaluation (if not concern) might be expected when assessments are used formatively to improve programs and when students' performances are aggregated. Nevertheless, more attention to the quality of the assessments, especially to whether the assessments are measuring what they are intended to measure, seems warranted.

What Was the Program's Impact?

Our evaluation of each campus's learning assessment program focused on reasonableness (whether it created a burden) and functionality (the intended and unintended impacts). Across the campuses, assessment of student learning was described as an add-on to current duties. At three of the four campuses, it was clearly a burden, especially at a time of diminishing resources and increasing student enrollments. At two of the campuses, the absence of a link to faculty incentives made the burden even more vivid. Even at SCLU, the smallest campus, whose entire history was one of assessing learning, faculty reported that maintaining a commitment to assessment with fiscal restraint and, especially, growing enrollments was creating a strain. It was only a matter of time before the detailed assessment and feedback processes would have to give way to the reality of time and cost constraints. Alternatives would have to be sought. Although it is understandable why assessment is an add-on, given the constraints, except under the most unusual circumstances of commitment and moral support (e.g., Alverno), assessment programs will ebb and wane unless this matter is addressed by higher-education institutions.

The good news is that there was general agreement that the assessment programs, whether in operation or still developing, focused faculty attention on teaching and student learning. The exercise of building assessments, reviewing student work, and trying to figure out how to improve programs had a positive, "professional development" effect.

Some Tentative Conclusions

Preliminarily, several very tentative conclusions can be set forth to characterize a model campus assessment program:

- The program most likely would be spurred by accreditation criteria, a state policy with incentives, leadership, or some combination of those factors. Accreditation criteria and policy could be catalysts, but even more important are campus visionary leaders in the persons of the president (or provost) and the assessment director. Leadership support is essential.
- All four campuses philosophically supported the idea of outcomes-based learning assessment, but they varied in focus from program improvement to student improvement. Both program and students should be the focus of a learning assessment program; program focus seems to come naturally, but student feedback does not. Moreover, the campuses varied in the extent to

which "criterion" performances or cognitive abilities were the focus of assessment. This philosophical stance on criterion performance or ability translated into campus practice with an impact on curriculum and teaching.

- Faculty need to be engaged in and committed to the program. A top-down approach is unlikely to succeed. The assessment office director plays an important role in setting the tone and engaging and supporting faculty, as do the campus academic administrators (presidents, provosts, deans, department chairs). In the end, responsibility needs to be placed in the hands of the faculty, with support and expertise from administrators and the assessment office.

- The program must articulate agreed-upon learning outcomes (general and major specific) that are measurable by campus-constructed or externally identified assessment instruments. The key here is that such assessments should be useful in diagnosing strengths and weaknesses and providing the information needed to conjecture possible courses of action for improvement and for the campus to test them out empirically.

- Campus leaders must champion learning assessment and support faculty to be heavily involved in designing, scoring, analyzing, reporting, and using assessment data. Perhaps the most persuasive metric of success for an assessment program is the extent to which faculty are genuinely involved.

- Assessment data must be relevant for improving faculty (program) teaching and student learning. Individual-level data are pertinent to student feedback, and aggregated data are pertinent to program improvement and tracking campus-wide progress.

- The campus needs to put in place policies for hiring faculty, rewarding faculty for scholarly work on teaching, and using assessment findings to improve programs and inform students of their progress. Such policies should also recognize the time and effort commitment needed for a learning assessment program to succeed and adjust faculty responsibilities accordingly.

- To make learning assessment manageable over time, a balance needs to be struck between faculty involvement in assessment development and the use of off-the-shelf assessments that are now becoming available and seem to fit with what campuses want to see in their assessment programs (e.g., Collegiate Learning Assessment, National Survey of Student Engagement). The balance is necessary because current practice, which places a heavy load on the faculty, creates morale problems and threatens the program. Making the assessment program manageable is also necessary because in so doing faculty then focus on teaching and student learning.

A program with these characteristics would be useful to faculty, students, and campus leaders *and* would be capable of demonstrating accountability for meeting the college's mission of teaching and learning.

Appendix

This appendix presents the details of case-study site selection and then describes the data collection and analysis methods.

Site Selection

Case studies were conducted during the 2003–4 academic year at four institutions with purportedly exemplary assessment-of-learning programs. Site selection took into account a number of institutional and program characteristics, as well as recommendations from researchers and policy analysts who pointed to the colleges and universities as having a particularly innovative or effective assessment program. More specifically, model learning assessment programs were identified through conversations with experts in the field, through a review of literature, and through the research team's knowledge of assessment in higher education. The study focused on four-year public institutions because they educate most college students and in order to observe a variety of assessment strategies in general education and in liberal arts, science, and professional majors.

From approximately a dozen possible sites that were originally identified, four emerged that demonstrated different conceptual frameworks for assessment, dissimilar institutional contexts, and diverse state contexts. The sites were deliberately chosen to follow the spectrum of public, four-year higher education, as they included research universities and colleges focused on undergraduate teaching; drawn from urban, rural, and suburban areas that varied in assessment program longevity; and situated in three different accrediting commission regions.

In order to ensure candor from a variety of constituencies at each of the sites, we agreed not to reveal the identities of these campuses. There are trade-offs to this choice, such as an inability of researchers at these sites and elsewhere to build on this work. For anonymity, the sites were named for their signature approach to assessment-of-learning programs: (1) *Learning Outcomes University*, an urban state university with about 30,000 students; (2) *Student-Centered Learning*

University, a small, somewhat rural, state university with roughly 3,700 students; (3) *Assessment-Centered University*, a medium-size public university located in a rural setting, with about 17,000 students; and (4) *Flexible University*, a large public university located in a suburban area of a large city, with about 30,000 students.

Methods

Site Contacts.   In order to arrange site visits, we contacted campuses' assessment offices and explained the study to the director with the goal of establishing initial interest. If such interest was expressed, then, typically, the president's or chancellor's office was contacted to formally request permission for a site visit. All four initially selected sites agreed to participate. University administrators were then contacted for interviews, and the assessment office helped to identify faculty and students to interview.

Interviews. Two or three researchers visited each site and spent two or three days for interviews and document collection. Before each site visit, the university and the assessment program were reviewed, using documentary evidence from Web sites, publications, and reports. Familiarity with the assessment program allowed the interviewers to pose questions directly related to the program and to better understand informants' responses. At each site eight to twelve individual interviews were conducted, with presidents, provosts, deans, department chairs, faculty on assessment committees, other faculty, campus assessment professionals, and students. Several group interviews were conducted with faculty and students ("focus groups"). (For details, see Shavelson & Ruiz-Primo, 2006.) Interviews characteristically followed a three-step sequence, adapted to the role of the particular informant: (1) introduction to the study, informant consent to participate, and collection of informant background information; (2) questions about the assessment program (goals, philosophy, initiation, relation to accreditation and accountability, intended audience); and (3) questions about the intended and unintended impacts of the program (reliability and validity of assessments, learning outcomes measured, information relevance to and use by "consumers," unintended consequences).

All individual and group interviews were tape recorded and transcribed. These transcripts were then integrated with associated field notes and documentary evidence from Web sites, publications, reports, and other sources. This created a rich data set for analysis. The transcripts were coded to reflect the four dimensions of assessment programs that guided our work: *development, philosophy, operation,* and *impact.* For example, *program development* had four main facets: *motivation*—what or who was the impetus of the program; *goals*—the explicit goals for the assessment program; *focus*—whether the program focused on general education, majors, or both; and *initiation*—how the program started. A similar process was followed for each assessment program dimension.

Analyses.   In analyzing the informants' responses to questions about assessment program development, philosophy, and operation, we focused on information that provided some indication about the principles of good practice for assessing student learning proposed by the American Association of Higher Education in 1992. For example, to get information about principle 1—The assessment of student learning begins with educational values—we asked about the institution's vision or philosophy of learning and about what was chosen by the institution to be assessed and how it was assessed.

The evaluation of assessment program impact followed Gormley and Weimer's (1999) criteria for organizational report cards: (1) *validity*—Do the assessments accurately measure important aspects of undergraduate learning? (2) *comprehensiveness*—Do the assessments cover the important outcomes of the undergraduate program? (3) *comprehensibility*—Are the reports based on assessments understandable to administrators, faculty, and students? (4) *relevance*—Is the information provided relevant to improving teaching and learning? (5) *reasonableness*—Is the burden of the assessment reasonable, or does it strain the institution's fiscal and time capacity? (6) *functionality*—What intended and unintended consequences, both good and bad, emerge? and (7) *feedback*—Is there a capacity to feed back information at all levels of the institution?

6 The Centrality of Information in the Demand for Accountability

OVER THE LAST TWENTY-FIVE YEARS policy makers, educators, and the public have increasingly debated about what information and how much of it higher-education institutions should provide about their "quality." Policy makers are held responsible by the electorate for ensuring quality education. Consumers want comparative information on quality as they choose among campuses. And campus administrators and faculty seek information for improvement.

Just as we saw with the assessment of learning, the debate surrounding higher-education accountability has a much longer history than the current debate recognizes, also dating back to the turn of the 20th century. In this chapter that history is traced briefly, in an attempt to understand how we arrived here today and what the fundamental enduring issues are. A case is then made for the centrality of information in the accountability debate, information that is useful for "consumers," government officials, and educators. What proves useful to one stakeholder is not necessarily useful to another, and there is an inherent conflict of cultures when it comes to how the information is used.

Brief History of Higher-Education Accountability Demands

Accountability concerns in the United States date back more than one hundred years, to when colleges began popping up in the late 1800s. At issue then were questions of what counted as a college or university and how admissions procedures might be made consistent across them. To address these questions, self-regulating groups of colleges and universities created regional, nongovernmental accrediting agencies early in the 20th century,[1] which continued through World

War II. These agencies were established to benchmark minimum standards for higher-education quality.

Current-day accountability emerged as higher-education enrollments surged at the end of World War II and service men and women, so-called GIs (after their general issue uniforms), flocked to colleges with dollars in hand from the GI Bill. Higher education responded to this swell in demand by rapidly growing colleges, including some of dubious enough merit to raise concern about how federal dollars were being spent. Were GIs and the government getting the education the government was, in large part, paying for (e.g., Fishkin, 1978)?

To address this question, the federal government, through the Veterans' Readjustment Assistance Act of 1952, turned to accreditation agencies to serve as a reliable authority on education quality. These agencies had been around for over forty-five years, initially to address concerns about college admissions policies and transfer of credits among institutions, and later on to verify an institution's existence and a minimal quality of curriculum, faculty, facilities, and the like (e.g., Bloland, 2001; Alstete, 2004).

The government's goal with the Veterans' Readjustment Act was to weed out incompetent from minimally competent colleges and universities, and its tool was a set of preexisting regional accrediting agencies. The intent at that time, as today, was to assure the public that federal dollars were being spent at institutions that meet acceptable levels of quality (e.g., Thelin, 2004).

However, it was not until 1968 that the federal government, through its Office of Education, linked itself directly to accreditation and indirectly to ensuring college quality. Now the U.S. secretary of education reviews accrediting agencies every five years and publishes a list of those approved. In this way, the government warrants, and regulates (Fishkin, 1978; Bloland, 2001), the reliability of an agency in evaluating the quality of education provided by a college or university and its educational programs.

Accreditation is widely used by higher education to account for its performance and to weed out institutions that do not meet minimum standards. The federal government continues to use accreditation as its major higher-education accountability mechanism, although its displeasure with this mechanism has been made clear by the Spellings Commission. States, as well, have adopted a variety of accountability mechanisms ranging from widely variable report cards to published comparative measures of student learning. And a nonprofit organization, the National Center for Public Policy and Higher Education, entered the picture at the turn of this century to hold states accountable for the quality of their higher-education systems. Most recently, higher-education professional associations have entered the fray. The approach to accountability taken by each of these mechanisms—accreditation, states' demand for accountability, an independent agency publishing a state report card, and professional organization self-regulation—are briefly described in what follows.

Accreditation

Today accreditation agencies, private educational associations of regional or national scope, function to assure the public that the education provided by higher-education institutions meets minimally acceptable levels of quality. They do this by developing quality criteria and conducting peer evaluations to assess whether their criteria have been met. The accreditation process involves five characteristic steps: (1) standard setting by an accrediting agency; (2) campus-developed program description (goals, objectives, faculty, governance, facilities, curriculum, and self-evaluation); (3) on-site peer review by an accrediting team that examines and comments on items in the program description and provides a written report of findings; (4) institutional and faculty responses to a preliminary peer-review report; and (5) a decision by the accrediting agency to grant, reaffirm, or deny accreditation based on available information (Lubinescu, Ratcliff, & Gaffney, 2001). Institutions and programs that request an agency's evaluation and that meet that agency's criteria are accredited by that agency. What the public learns is whether the campus was or was not accredited. Further information goes only to the campus.

For much of their history, accrediting agencies focused primarily on inputs and processes such as student and faculty quality, curricular quality, student-faculty ratios, finances, and capital resources, including libraries and classrooms (e.g., Wergin, 2004). This carried the accountability weight for higher education well into the 1970s. However, in the late 1970s, concerns were raised about the lack of *outcome* information—in particular, information about student learning outcomes—in accreditation. Accreditation, according to Bowen in 1979, "may be entering a new era. As higher education has expanded and proliferated, the need and the demand of society for consumer protection and accountability have become more urgent. In meeting new societal needs and demands, the procedures of accreditation must become more concerned with outcomes and less preoccupied with resource inputs" (p. 19).

Bowen's comments were prophetic. Today, student learning outcomes have become the top priority of the nation's major college accrediting agencies. This is in response to the 1998 reauthorization of the Higher Education Act, which made student academic achievement the top standard for accreditation. Although it does not satisfy the demand for higher-education accountability today (e.g., U. S. Department of Education, 2006), in synergy with state accountability requirements accreditation has moved campuses—from small liberal arts colleges to research universities—toward increased self-monitoring of student-learning (and other) indicators and external reporting (e.g., Naughton, 2004; see Chapters 5 and 8).

Pressure to Account for Student Learning: Beyond Accreditation

Toward the end of the 1970s and into the early 1980s, pressure to account for student learning had risen palpably. This pressure grew out of both the academy's discontent with the college curriculum (e.g., Grant & Riesman, 1978; Massy & Zemsky, 1994) and the public's concern about the quality of student learning spurred by rising costs, increased time to degree, and questionable readiness of graduates for employment. Campuses began to get pressured to assess student learning[2] and to respond to external accountability[3]—assessment and accountability beyond accreditation (e.g., Dill, 1997; Ewell, 1991, 1997; National Governors Association, 1991). That is, the public, and state-level policy makers and staff wanted a more *open exchange of information* between the academy and the public than that provided by accreditation agencies. The public and policy makers did not consider an agency's posting of an institution's accreditation status adequate. They wanted information that differentiated among institutions on various quality criteria.

By the mid 1980s, states began to take up, in earnest, the assessment of student learning and program impact for college accountability. State involvement was spurred on by a number of national commission reports on precollege education (e.g., *A Nation at Risk*, National Commission on Excellence in Education, 1983) and higher education (e.g., *Time for Results*, National Governors Association, 1991 *Transforming the State Role in Undergraduate Education: Time for a Different View*, Education Commission of the States, 1986). The reports asked for evidence of what was being produced by the states' colleges and universities. The public and policy makers wanted evidence of student learning. That is, they wanted to know about "skills, abilities, and cognitive learning" (National Governors Association, 1991, p. 156; the Tennessee value-added experience—Banta, 1986). In addition to cognitive learning they wanted students to be able to think critically and communicate clearly (Ewell, 1997, 2001). Alverno College served as an exemplar (National Governors Association, 1991 see Chapter 5). As then Missouri governor

John Ashcroft put it (National Governors Association, 1991, p. 154), "The public has the right to know what it is getting for its expenditure of tax resources; the public has the right to know and understand the quality of undergraduate education that young people receive from publicly funded colleges and universities."

The Push for State-Level Higher-Education Accountability

The push for accountability increased into the 1990s (e.g., Ewell, 1997) in large part spurred by two sources of frustration. One source of frustration was accreditation, because accrediting agencies did not provide comparative information on quality across campuses. To some degree, the source of this frustration—accreditation without comparative information—is understandable. But accrediting agencies are caught between a rock and a hard place—or in a tug-of-war. On the one hand, their membership—colleges and universities—focus on the private, internal use of accreditation information, ostensibly for institutional improvement. On the other hand, policy makers and the public want comparable externally published information on cross-institution student learning and program effectiveness (e.g., Wergin, 2004). From many policy makers' perspectives, accrediting agencies had simply provided insufficient information to satisfy the public's and policy makers' demands. They wanted information to judge among accredited institutions and to enable students and parents to make decisions about which institution to apply to and, if admitted, enter.

The second source of frustration lay in the diversity of ways campuses measured student learning. With good intent some states had crafted policies creating incentives for individual campuses to assess and report on student learning. The result was a decentralized, incoherent picture of institutional quality. Once again, comparisons among institutions were next to impossible to make. Yet the public expected politicians and staff to account for rising costs and concerns for quality.

Changing View of Higher Education and Push for Increased Accountability. With the onset of the 1990s, in the context of a mild recession, demands for increased "productivity" (Dill, 1997), and an increasingly conservative political environment, policy makers and the public were coming to view higher education as a business. In this view, colleges produce a private good with benefits accruing primarily to individuals. This view replaced the predominant view up to that time—that colleges were a public good. That is, they were viewed as social institutions reflecting the public's investment in a collective social asset (e.g., Ewell,

1997; Gumport, 2000). From this emerging business perspective, higher education was increasingly seen in Gumport's (2000, p. 71) words:

> as a sector of the economy; as with firms or businesses, the root metaphor is a
> corporate model of production—to produce and sell goods and services, train
> some of the workforce, advance economic development, and perform research.
> Harsh economic challenges and competitive market pressures warrant better
> management, which includes swift programmatic adjustment, maximum flexi-
> bility, and improved efficiency in the direction of greater accountability and
> thus customer satisfaction.

Efficiency and the market, then, not necessarily quality, became the focus
(Burke & Minassians, 2002a). Students came to be viewed as consumers (e.g.,
Zemsky & Massy, 1990); accounting for results, not just expenditures, spilled
over from business and government (Burke & Minassians, 2002a); information
asymmetries between campuses on the one hand and overseers on the other
hand were anathema to the developing view; mutual trust between higher-
education institutions and state policy makers was winnowing (e.g., Naughton,
2004). Business served as part of the guiding vision (e.g., Gumport, 2000). K-12
standards-based reform served as the other part of the vision, with its shift away
from regulation to increased flexibility at the price of greater accountability.

By the mid 1990s, then, accountability and learning assessment programs had
evolved from more to less institutionally autonomous—that is, from campus defined to state defined. The central context of assessment shifted from quality to
compliance—from assessment for improvement to accountability for standards
(Dill, 1997; Nettles, Cole & Sharp, 1997). States began focusing on "report cards"
(Dill, 1997; Gormley & Weimar, 1999) to assure the public of institutional quality.

External Accountability in Full Swing.   By the late 1990s into the new millennium, state-level external accountability had moved into full swing (e.g., Alexander, 2000; McLendon, Hearn & Deaton, 2006). Performance reporting and
indicators of institutional quality, featuring direct and indirect measures of student
learning, became commonplace (Chapter 2). States had assumed responsibility, at
least enough to satisfy the public, for their institutions of higher education.

While state accountability programs varied, three types could be distinguished: performance funding, performance budgeting, and performance reporting (Burke & Minassians, 2003). A performance-funding program tied
institutional performance to direct appropriation incentives. Tennessee was the

first state to adopt this approach, in 1979, and by 2003, twenty-five states had tried such a policy. Performance budgeting was less concrete and related indirectly to budgetary decisions based on campus performance. Illinois was first to adopt this policy, in 1984, and by 2003, thirty-five states had established such a policy. Finally, performance reporting publishes indicators of campus and system performance, as Tennessee had begun; by 2003, forty-two states had some form of this policy (McLendon, Hearn & Deaton, 2006). All three accountability-for-results approaches share common purposes: "demonstrating external accountability, improving institutional performance, and responding to state needs" (Burke & Minassians, 2002b, p. 11).

The emerging predominate type of accountability program at the turn of the millennium was "performance reporting" (Burke & Minassians, 2002b); elected lawmakers were the prime movers behind it. Both performance budgeting and performance funding, especially the latter, proved costly and unstable in changing economic times (for details, see Burke & Minassians, 2002b). With performance reporting, public higher-education institutions are required to track a set of indicators and report these indicators to legislators, state boards, and the public (Burke & Minassians, 2002b). Before the 1990s, only Tennessee, South Carolina, and Oklahoma had legislated reporting mandates. By 1996, twenty-three states had such laws (Burke & Associates, 2002b). This growing legislative interest "sought to increase the quality, productivity, and efficiency of public colleges and universities" (Burke & Associates, 2002b, p. 9) by calling for centrally defined assessment methods that could be reported publicly and compared across institutions and states. Additional mandates from other sources, especially state higher-education boards, brought the total number of states with performance reporting requirements to forty-four by 2002 (Burke & Minassians, 2002b), and now "virtually all states monitor performance indicators as part of budget review" (National Commission on Accountability in Higher Education, 2005, p. 31).

Most recently, the Spellings Commission (U.S. Department of Education, 2006) reinforced the view that policy makers and the public needed a more transparent accounting of the performance of the nation's colleges and universities. The commission concluded that despite the achievement of American higher education, "U.S. higher education needs to improve in dramatic ways," ". . . the unfulfilled promise that remains," and "past attainments have led our nation to unwarranted complacency about its future" (p. ix). The commission went on to say that more accountability and transparency were needed: "To meet the challenges of the 21st century, higher education must change from a system primarily based on reputation to one based on performance. We urge the creation of a robust culture of accountability and transparency throughout higher education" (p. 21). And in that culture, indirect (e.g., the National Survey of Student Engagement) and, especially, direct assessments of student learning and the value added by the college experience (e.g., the Collegiate Learning Assessment) are needed and should be published in a consumer-friendly database that permits policy makers, parents, and students to compare institutions.

State Report Cards

The federal government, states, and campuses, however, were not the only actors in higher-education accountability. In 2000 (and subsequently in 2002, 2004, 2006, and 2008), the National Center for Public Policy and Higher Education (NCPPHE), established in 1998 as "an independent, nonprofit, nonpartisan organization" (National Center for Public Policy and Higher Education, 2000, p. 4) published a state-by-state report card on higher education—*Measuring Up 2000*. According to James B. Hunt Jr., NCPPHE board chair and former North Carolina governor, "The first state report card on higher education . . . was created to assist the nation and each state in assessing and addressing the [economic and labor force] challenges that lie before us" (p. 9). *Measuring Up* compares the performance of each state in six key areas of education and training through the baccalaureate degree: (1) *preparation* of students for education and training beyond high school (i.e., the quality of the state's K-12 system); (2) *participation* or access of the state's students to enrollment in education and training beyond high school; (3) *affordability* or the cost of postsecondary education to students and their families; (4) *completion*, or the timeliness of degree completion; (5) *benefits* of a highly educated population to the state; and (6) *learning*—"What do we know about student learning as a result of education and training beyond high school?" (National Center for Public Policy and Higher Education, 2000, p. 23).

In the first three report cards, the National Center was able to publish data and grade states on five of the six indicators. The only indicator for which insufficient information was available was student learning, the indicator that had been called for since the late 1970s. Data on student learning simply was not available across the states.

To demonstrate how states might provide information on student learning, NCPPHE enlisted five states—Illinois, Kentucky, Nevada, Oklahoma, and South Carolina—in a project designed according to the center's vision of learning assessment (Miller, 2006). For four-year colleges, NCPPHE's learning indicator included (1) data from the National Adult Literacy Survey, which could be used to index the literacy level of the state's population; (2) scores from admissions and licensure examinations; and (3) a direct measure of "general intellectual skills" (Miller, 2006, p. 2), using the Collegiate Learning Assessment (see Chapters 3 and 4 for description). The center used these data to present state-by-state comparative "learning profiles that . . . gave an idea of each state's strengths and challenges . . . with regard to collegiate learning" (p. 2). By 2006, the center was able to report learning indicators for nine states. However, in 2008 the center gave each and every state in the nation, once again, an incomplete on this indicator.

Colleges and Universities Get into the Accountability Act

Although they were reluctant partners with "clients" and "government" in accountability, colleges and universities have grabbed the proverbial bull by the horns and jumped into the accountability act. Most notably, the Association of American Colleges and Universities (AAC&U, 2005) issued a set of goals for higher education in three domains: knowledge of human culture and the natural world, intellectual and practical skills, and individual and social responsibility. The AAC&U also sponsored assessment efforts to enable campuses to provide evidence of progress toward these goals (e.g., see www.aacu.org/Rising_Challenge/index.cfm).

Perhaps the most radical step that associations of colleges and universities have taken is the Voluntary System of Accountability (VSA; see www.voluntarysystem .org/index.cfm). The VSA, developed through a partnership between the American Association of State Colleges and Universities and the National Association of State Universities and Land-Grant Colleges, is a voluntary accountability reporting program for four-year public colleges and universities. It is designed to demonstrate accountability and stewardship to the public; provide measures of educational outcomes to identify effective educational practices; and assemble information for the public that is accessible, understandable, and comparable. The VSA's "College Portrait" reports a set of indicators in the following areas: consumer information, student experiences and perceptions, and student learning outcomes.

Centrality of Information in Accountability

The debate over the past quarter century among policy makers, educators, and the public is, in essence, a debate about information—what and how much information about quality should be provided, and how that information should be used. The debate has peaked today. After all, for many years campuses enjoyed a high degree of autonomy in accountability matters and generally rejected external intrusion. Until recently, policy makers and politicians went along with the presumption of autonomy. As we have seen from the chapters on the history of learning assessment and campus assessment programs, as well as the brief history of accountability, all this has changed. Students and their parents want *comparative information* in order to choose among colleges, and government and business entities seek such benchmark information as they invest in training and research from colleges and universities. Elected officials, likewise, want to benchmark the quality of higher education, as they are held accountable for doing so by their constituencies. If consumers do not get the information they want about a college, in a timely manner and at an affordable price, politicians and bureaucrats may well have to take a hike. And campuses will come under increased criticism and external pressure.

Campuses, however, have self-regulatory processes, based on professional judgment, that are a centerpiece of academe. Not surprisingly, campuses closely guard their autonomy, arguing that the extensive internal information they regularly and periodically collect through accreditation leads to organizational improvement. As we saw in the brief history of accountability, the AAC&U's work on college outcomes is consistent with this view—it seeks to put assessment information in the hands of colleges and universities, not in external indicator systems, for program improvement. In seeking to make external and explicit comparisons among campuses, the VSA runs counter to this culture.

Colleges and universities have been deeply concerned about the potential negative impact of institutional comparisons. Many higher educators argue, for example, that the diversity of their missions precludes the potentially distorting effect of a one-size-fits-all accountability approach. Moreover, they are concerned that comparative information, once made public, is open to political "spin." Indeed, political accounts may very well lead to considerable mischief, and to the detriment of the institutions the information is intended to improve (e.g., March & Olsen, 1995; Shavelson & Huang, 2003; Shavelson, 2007a; see Chapter 7).

What has evolved over time is a clash of three cultures—the political, the consumer, and the academic. The political culture involves politicians and bureaucrats responsible for assuring their constituencies that the higher-education institutions under their aegis are producing high-quality education. The consumer culture includes students and their parents, as well as governments and businesses, purchasing education, research, or both from higher-education institutions. This culture seeks comparative information about campus quality in order to make informed decisions as to where to invest time and money. In-creasingly, both these cultures view higher education instrumentally—as a mechanism for labor force supply (jobs) and economic competitiveness. The academic culture includes administrators and faculty responsible for producing education and research. This is a professional, self-regulating culture focused on the use of information for improvement. Higher education's goal for this culture transcends training and the economy and focuses on the development of liber-ally educated citizens, believing students should possess the capacity to learn throughout their lives, not only as contributors to the economy but also as in-formed citizens and purposeful individuals.[4]

The clash of cultures is over *information*—Who provides and interprets what kinds of information? How much of it is provided? And with what conse-quences? To reiterate, members of the political culture want comparative infor-mation to judge quality, to reassure the public, and to hold higher education accountable to its goals with possible sanctions. Members of the consumer cul-ture seek comparative information to judge quality relative to its goals, as well, but for the purpose of deciding where to purchase education or research. In contrast, members of the academic culture seek information to improve their processes and outcomes toward academe's goals.

The two kinds of accountability information sought—for comparative judgments and for educational improvement—are not necessarily aligned. The intensity with which these contrasting positions are held—comparison versus improvement, with varying goals—is reflected in the Spelling Commission's re-port and by a university assessment administrator (see Table 6.1).

The clash is also over the use of that information, with low and high stakes for colleges. Making certain kinds of information available may have negative or at least uncontrollable consequences. From a college's perspective, making com-parative information widely available, especially when its interpretation be-comes politicized and its consequences come with high stakes (e.g., reputation, funding), may have a negative impact on higher education. However, from both political and consumer perspectives, such information should have a positive impact on institutional behavior (organizational improvement) through com-petition. In contrast, making available the kinds of information needed to im-prove teaching and learning processes within an institution may enable campuses to improve the education they deliver, but the information is more detailed than desired by and less interpretable to the political and consumer cultures.

Table 6.1. Competing "Cultural" Views of Accountability

Spellings Commission	Assessment Administrator
"The collection of data from public institutions allowing meaningful interstate comparison of student learning should be encouraged and implemented in all states. By using assessments of adult literacy, licensure, graduate and professional school exams, and specially administered tests of general intellectual skills, state policymakers can make valid interstate comparisons of student learning and identify shortcomings as well as best practices" (U.S. Department of Education, 2006, p. 24).	"So those of us in the assessment community are asking each other, 'Can assessment for accountability and assessment for improvement coexist? Can the current accountability focus actually strengthen assessment for improvement? Or will an accountability tidal wave roll across the fields, crushing the fragile green sprouts of assessment for improvement that have begun to appear?' " (Banta, 2007, p. 9).

The cultural clash can be viewed in a complementary way—as forces likely to shape institutional behavior. Clark (1983) noted three such forces that if orchestrated well in public policy might enhance performance: professional authority, governmental authority, and the market. Burke and Associates (2005) called these three forces the vertices of the "Accountability Triangle."

The culture of academic institutions led them to establish professional authority or self-regulation in the form of accreditation as an accountability mechanism focusing on improvement. Accreditation agencies were created for, funded by, and served the campuses. To be sure, the federal government "accredits" accrediting agencies, but the agencies, having met federal standards, serve their higher-education sponsors. Information, collected for internal campus use, is provided by a campus-initiated peer review of curriculum and research, and from acceptance and accreditation by professional organizations, as well as from voluntary accreditation through regional agencies.

In contrast, government and consumer cultures seek to influence behavior by external means. Governmental authority includes regulating institutional behavior or increasing campus autonomy. Increased autonomy, of course, comes with a price—that of campuses providing comparative, public information about performance (i.e., accountability). As we have seen, policy makers have increasingly moved away from regulating colleges to permitting them greater autonomy in return for greater accountability.

Finally, "the market" stands somewhere in between campus autonomy and government oversight. Market forces operate through competition, reflecting the fact that unlike precollege education in the United States, college education is voluntary. From this perspective, accountability comes through campuses competing for students, research dollars, high-quality faculty, and capital resources. The market, however, depends on high-quality information about higher-education performance to operate reasonably well. That is, market forces rely on comparative information about institutional performance, which is hard to come by.

So now here is where the cultures clash. Government oversight and market forces seek institutional performance information, especially of a comparative nature, in order to judge institutional quality and to choose among institutions for allocation of scarce resources. However, campuses are wary of providing such information externally for a variety of reasons, arguing, for example, that their missions are diverse—one size doesn't fit all—and that politicians and others might potentially misuse such information leading to unintended, negative consequences. Rather, they seek information for improvement of processes and outcomes.

Summative and Formative Functions of Information for Accountability

The distinction between accountability information for external audiences and accountability information for campuses themselves is a distinction between the "summative" and "formative" functions of accountability. The summative use of accountability provides summary judgments of the quality of the education-processes in place (e.g., academic press, access to advisors, faculty-student ratios) and of the quality of the outcome (e.g., value added to students' learning) to interested, external parties. The summative function addresses the question: To what extent are colleges and universities carrying out the charter they were entrusted with? The intent, then, of the summative function is to hold campuses accountable to external authority and assure the public that quality education is being provided in the state.

The formative function of accountability information is to signal to campuses the strengths and weaknesses in their education processes and outcomes, and to lead to conjectures as to possible courses of action for improvement. The formative function addresses the question: How can colleges monitor and continually improve their processes and outcomes? The intent of the formative function, then, is educational improvement.

Summative Function of Accountability.   Two forms of summative accountability can be identified (cf. Gormley & Weimer, 1999)—top-down and bottom-up. They are not mutually exclusive and are often mixed in accounta-

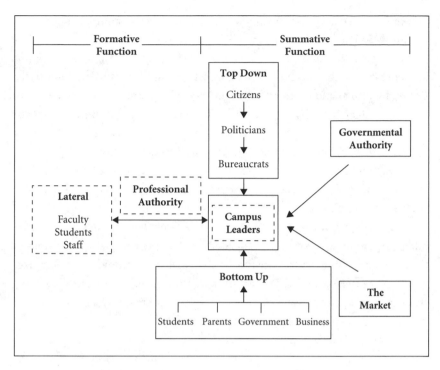

Figure 6.1 Accountable to whom?

SOURCE: R. Shavelson.

bility rhetoric and practice. Top-down accountability refers to campus oversight by public officials, such as members of a state congress or state board of higher education. Such oversight is part of the authority delegated to them by the state's citizens (Figure 6.1). This is what Clark (1983) meant by governmental authority. Top-down accountability operates when the public, through its elected officials, expects campuses to be held accountable for the quality and cost of higher education and bureaucrats to be accountable for seeing that this happens.

Bottom-up accountably operates like an economic market—Clark's market force. It operates, for example, when students (and their parents) choose a college to attend, when they express satisfaction (or dissatisfaction) with campus policies and experiences, and when they contribute to campus fund-raising efforts. The market also operates when governments or businesses contract with campuses to provide training or to conduct research.

Formative Function of Accountability.   In contrast to the summative function, the formative function of accountability serves to provide information to improve the processes and outcomes of the organization. Clark (1983) spoke of this influence on the behavior of academic institutions as professional authority. Formative information is typically useful internally in an organization, where it serves a regulatory purpose (e.g., are faculty teaching their minimum load?) or an improvement purpose (are the results of student learning assessments in general education used to improve the program and student outcomes?). The formative function ultimately focuses on teaching, learning, and research processes and outcomes and the level of support provided for them in pursuit of the campus's education mission.

This formative form of accountability is self-regulating, "lateral" accountability (see Figure 6.1). Administrators and faculty play complementary roles in the academy. Administrators are responsible for the operation of the organization and to external bodies. The faculty is responsible for curriculum, teaching, student learning, and assessment. Such lateral accountability is built into accreditation processes but has its tensions.

For this shared governance to operate effectively, a campus must freely exchange information at all levels of the organization. This seemingly reasonable presumption presents a challenge within academe. The separation of responsibilities between academics and administrators—the separation of deans and higher-level administrators from department chairs and faculty, in particular—has cultural conflict built in. As Jim March and colleagues (Cohen, March & Olson, 1972) noted, this decentralization compact leads to "organized anarchies."[5] Where, traditionally, academic decision making rested within the department, the push for greater accountability both within academe and from outside has required college administrators and even state higher-education systems to get more deeply involved in these traditional academic functions because of both external pressures and the practical need for data centralization.

For lateral accountability to work, then, it must address internal cultural conflicts and have structures and processes in place that put this information into action. There needs to be a concerted effort by all levels of administration and faculty to support the use of this information and the changes that ensue. And there needs to be a mechanism that evaluates how effectively this is being done. In the absence of such effort, campus responses to accountability demands may simply be symbolic at best.

It turns out that information useful for summary judgments is often not detailed enough to inform decisions for improving teaching and learning (e.g., Nettles & Cole, 2001; see Chapter 5). Moreover, once summary information is in the public eye, who gets to put what spin on the information may have unintended consequences for education quality when campuses respond symbolically rather than substantively to external pressures (typically sanctions). This said, information about education processes may not get at the bottom line for external parties (consumers, government officials), which is whether students are acquiring the knowledge, skills, and habits of mind that are needed to support the economy and are expected of a college education.

Access to Information

Whether accountability is lateral, top-down, or bottom-up, *information is central*. In order to judge whether campuses are acting responsibly, the public, parents, students, businesses, and policy makers need to know whether actions that campuses have undertaken to improve processes and outcomes are reasonable within the bounds of known technologies. In order to improve teaching and learning in the academy, and to allocate resources appropriately, campus administrators, faculty, and students need to know the current level of performance, the gap between current and desired levels, and how to bridge the gap.

And there's the rub. Within an organization, information for improving teaching and learning (e.g., improving general education) may not exist, organizational mechanisms may not be in place to make this information available to relevant parties, incentives may work against faculty spending time on teaching, or the technology needed to transform information into appropriate action may not be known.

Similarly, external to the organization, information currently available on campus quality (e.g., for accreditation) has been inadequate—inadequate for parents and their children to make informed choices among colleges, for government and business to make informed choices among potential service providers, and for bureaucrats and policy makers to assure the public of the quality of education or to make informed decisions about budgets.

Information asymmetries, then, abound. Policy makers and the public do not have all the information they would like, especially comparative information about quality, to evaluate campuses. Moreover, higher-education institutions and accrediting agencies have more information than they provide to external audiences. The call for increased accountability over the past twenty-five years, and especially the call to measure the value campuses add to student learning (U.S. Department of Education, 2006), reflects the frustration with information asymmetries. Higher-education overseers and consumers are no longer willing to stand for the current situation.

The remainder of this text, in large part, is intended to offer analyses and visions as to how these information imbalances might be addressed. The intent is to do so in a manner that assesses student learning in meaningful ways and provides accountability information in ways that improve education yet also inform the public and government officials.

Reprise

For well over the past hundred years, concern for higher-education quality has led to a demand for accountability, initially created by consortia of colleges and universities themselves as members of regional accrediting agencies, which served at their members' pleasure. The focus of these accrediting agencies was then and is today on serving higher-education institutions and assisting with improvement. Through tumultuous times, these agencies have moved from a focus on resources (inputs and processes) to embrace student learning and other outcomes, but they have held steady to their commitment to internal (formative) use of such information by member institutions, publicly reporting only accreditation status. These agencies have buffered the demand for external reporting throughout the accountability movement chronicled here, recognizing the centrality of student learning, but arguing that due to the diversity of campuses and missions, a common measure of student learning on which comparisons could be made does not make sense. Rather, these agencies have pushed for institutions to define learning goals, make them public, and provide evidence that reveals how well they are meeting these goals (Wergin, 2004). Accreditation alone, then, will not entirely meet public and governmental demands for the summative function of accountability—external information of a comparative nature. Put another way, accreditation will not, in itself, correct the information asymmetry between education consumers and providers.

States are now attempting, to a greater or lesser extent, to fill this comparative information gap for clients and government officials, above and beyond the usual popular reputational rankings of institutions published by a variety of organizations (the summative function of accountability). Some form of performance planning, budgeting, or reporting of comparative indicators has taken hold, using mostly "indirect" measures of student learning (e.g., graduation rates) with the long-term vision of moving to comparative, "direct" measures of student learning (e.g., achievement, ability). *Measuring Up*'s state-by-state higher-education report card, call for measures of learning (Miller, 2006), and use of the Collegiate Learning Assessment (Chapters 3 and 4) foreshadow near-term developments as examples of a college learning measurement system.

Three cultures—the political culture, the consumer culture, and the academic culture—seek somewhat different kinds of information to judge educational quality on the one hand and to improve quality on the other. Differences in information sought reflect, in part, differences in visions for higher education—instrumental development of the economy or means for a liberally educated citizenry. The political and consumer cultures are closely aligned in their quest for *comparative* information—of how colleges and universities stack up against one another on some summary measure of "quality," with emphasis on economic competitiveness. In contrast, the academic culture seeks information that can be used to improve its educational processes and outcomes, with emphasis on liberally educated citizens. We can distinguish, then, the summative function of accountability information (information used for comparative summary judgments) from the formative function (information for educational improvement). These different types of information do not necessarily have to be misaligned, but typically in accountability they are.

The cultures also clash as to how the information should be used—that is, the consequences that should follow from the information. The political culture seeks comparative information to hold higher education accountable for (typically) its outcomes and resorts to sanctions if campuses fall short of standards. The consumer culture seeks to use comparative information to decide where to spend scarce resources on education, training, or research. The consequence is that stiff competition among campuses would significantly affect organizational behavior, potentially both positively and negatively. Finally, the academy seeks to use information aligned with its mission and core processes for monitoring, reporting, and improving.

The cultural conflict has led to distrust among the academy, politicians, and consumers. Politicians and consumers are skeptical that colleges are actually using formative information for improvement, and accreditation only signals to them that the college has met minimal standards. The academy does not trust politicians and their political agendas and does not believe that "league table" comparisons among institutions capture their diversity of students, missions, and resources adequately for wise consumer choice.

Any proposal for improving accountability intended ultimately to improve higher education must deal with the forces at play in the accountability triangle. That is, any proposal must deal with two dimensions of conflict (and distrust): the kinds of information collected for accountability purposes—summative versus formative information—and the use of that information with low versus high stakes. This is easily said. As we will see, these fundamental tensions have not yet been adequately addressed in the debate over higher-education accountability.

7 Accountability: A Delicate Instrument

THE NOTION THAT INSTITUTIONS IN A DEMOCRACY should be held accountable and the indignity that arises when stakeholders perceive that they have been uninformed underlie the debate about what and how much information higher education should provide to garner continuing public trust and support. That stakeholder support depends on campuses being able to account for their actions and their "products" seems indisputable. What is disputable, however, is just how to "do accountability." Disagreement abounds.

This chapter takes up the conception of accountability. It briefly sketches accountability's history in higher education and then delves into underlying facets of the notion. Variation among facets gives rise to variability and disagreement in definition, and the disagreements have important implications for how to hold higher education accountable. The chapter concludes by enumerating a set of factors that make doing accountability difficult. The goal is to make clear that "doing" accountability is complicated and that knee-jerk, "tough" responses to the question of how to hold higher education accountable are wrongheaded. Accountability is a delicate instrument. Wielded incompetently or inappropriately, it can have devastatingly negative consequences rather than the intended positive ones. Making transparent the complications surrounding accountability serves to enumerate a set of constraints and affordances that need to be considered in the last chapter on design recommendations for holding U.S. higher education accountable.

Notion of Accountability

The idea of accountability is fundamental within a democratic society. Individuals representing themselves and officials representing institutions such as colleges and universities are expected to act rationally and honestly in accord with relevant facts and the best practices available (March & Olsen, 1995). They are also expected to deliver the "product" or "outcome"—such as student learning—that they say they will deliver at some acceptable level of quality and cost.

This notion of accountability includes *responsibility for* actions and outcomes.[1] That is, given public trust, campus officials are expected to take responsibility for their actions, for the products of their actions, or both. *Responsibility for* processes and outcomes carries with it, significantly, the expectation that individuals and officials must be prepared to account for—explain, justify—their actions and the products of those actions when called upon to do so. The expectation, then, is that campus leaders are responsible for their campus's performance. When asked to, they are obliged to justify their approach to educating students and the results that are produced (e.g., student learning).

The accounts that actors give by way of explanation or justification are assessed, according to March and Olsen (1995), by the following kind of logic: The campus official's behavior is matched with society's codes of proper or legal behavior and is evaluated—Did the official act reasonably and in a manner consistent with, say, best practices? Moreover, the products, results, or outcomes of the official's actions are evaluated as to their social or political attractiveness—For example, did students learn to think critically and express themselves clearly? Outcomes are then attributed through some ostensive rational process to the motivations and actions of the official and evaluated accordingly.

The idea of accountability also includes *responsibility to* not only oneself but also external authority. Internal responsibility—responsibility to oneself per se or in the role of an official—refers to moral standards such as honesty, duty, and honor. External responsibility refers to campus leaders being accountable to an external official or body (e.g., a state board of higher education) through formal institutional arrangements of observation (accountability methods or "mechanisms") and sanction (accountability consequences). Ultimately, campus officials are accountable to the citizens, typically through their elected or appointed officials (see Figure 6.1).

Finally, underlying the notion of accountability is the *belief that rationality and order can be imposed* on social and political life through planning, intervention, monitoring, and sanctioning. Beliefs such as these make reasonable the expectation of accountability. Put another way, accountability creates the presumption of capability and causality, and a presumption of choice, thus a freedom to act intentionally (March & Olsen, 1995).

To a great degree, and not surprisingly, the *Oxford English Dictionary* captures much of this notion of accountability in a couple of somewhat cryptic phrases: "The quality of being accountable; liability to give account of, and answer for, discharge of duties or conduct; responsibility, amenableness."

Some Implications for Higher-Education Accountability

This notion of accountability makes clear that it is reasonable to expect public and private higher-education institutions to be held accountable to the public. "Trust me" is an inadequate response to the demand for accountability. The presumption of accountability holds for American higher education, even if it is considered the best in the world, or if its complexities defy simple accounting, or if the diversity of its missions does not comport with a one-size-fits-all approach. Accountability is fundamental to a democracy, and the public has a right to hold colleges and universities to account. The notion of accountability, however, is silent as to *how* to hold higher education accountable so as to achieve accountability goals such as informing citizens and public officials *and* improving educational quality.

The notion of accountability also makes clear that, ultimately, college and university presidents are responsible to the public for their institution's performance. Moreover, these officials are obliged to justify the processes used to carry out their missions and the results produced. The educational processes should be consistent with best practices and should lead to the outcomes set by the campus or external authority. How much weight is placed on processes and how much on outcomes, however, is unclear. Once again, how to do accountability and hold higher education accountable *is* at issue.

Accountability also implies that processes and outcomes can be observed and measured, and that there should be some consequences ("sanctions") attached to poor performance. Again, the question of what observations and measures to take is not addressed by this notion of accountability (let alone with what measurement reliability, validity, and utility). And so the measurement question is hotly debated.

Likewise, the notion of accountability implies that public officials are expected to respond to the consequences of actions taken and outcomes achieved by campuses. Typically, responses to consequences are expressed as sanctions or punishments to get campuses to comport with some set of expectations. Such a response to consequences is an important part of K-12 accountability in the form of high-stakes testing (as in the federal No Child Left Behind Act, NCLB). However, what these sanctions (or incentives) should be remains an issue, as does their actual—intended and unintended—consequences on the behavior of campuses. Indeed, the notion of sanctions rather than incentives is a major point of contention between the academy and public officials.

Finally, campus leaders are responsible to three sets of actors (see Figure 6.1): internally to (1) faculty, students, and staff; and externally to (2) citizens and their elected officials; and (3) clients—parents, students, business, and government. As we saw in Chapter 6, accountability information that is useful to one set of actors (e.g., faculty and department chairs) may differ from what is useful for another set of actors (e.g., elected officials). The notion of accountability does not tell us how to satisfy multiple audiences. Experience shows that misalignment of information for educational improvement (formative function of accountability) and for justifying performance to external audiences (summative function) can work against improving performance.

Complications Surrounding Accountability

While the notion of accountability seems somewhat straightforward, as just pointed out, its practice is not. Moreover, decisions about practice (e.g., what to hold campus leaders accountable for) need to consider a number of complications that arise. Five such complications are enumerated here.

Accountable for Actions or Outcomes?

One complication arises from what March and Olsen (1995) call the interweaving of two logics of human action. One logic is that of *consequences*, the idea that actors should be held accountable for the consequences of their actions—Were the outcomes of the level of quality expected? The second logic is that of *processes*, the idea that actors should be held accountable for the appropriateness of their actions—Was their behavior consistent with what political and cultural norms would call for? The problem is that, by coming down on either side—outcomes or processes—good actions (processes) may result in negative consequences; improper behavior may lead to positive consequences. In practice, actors may be held accountable for both right acts and right consequences. At issue, then, is the balance between interpretations based on actions and interpretations based on outcomes (see "Interpretations as Accounts" below).

This complication has direct implications for higher-education accountability. To what extent should an accountability system hold actors accountable for consequences—in this case, the amount or level of learning their institutions produce in their students, the so-called value added by the institution? In K-12 education accountability under NCLB, consequences predominate—a single test of student achievement in reading and a single test of student achievement in mathematics are the sole output indicators on which sanctions are based. Performance reporting and its variants draw heavily on this logic of outcomes (see Chapters 6 and 8).

To what extent should an accountability system hold actors accountable for appropriate behavior—are the processes engaged in likely to improve student learning? Historically, accreditation has been largely or entirely based on accountability for actions or processes—that is, appropriate behavior. However, in the past ten years or so, accountability for student outcomes has assumed highest priority.

To what extent can the two—output and process—be combined in accountability? "Academic audits" found in Scandinavia, Great Britain, New Zealand, and Hong Kong, for example, might be one such middle ground. Audits focus on the existence of institutional processes that provide feedback from assessments—say, of student learning (e.g., Dill et al., 1996)—to campus actors in positions of authority to respond to this information (see Chapter 9).

Attribution of Causality with Uncertainty and Multiple Outcomes

A second complication surrounding accountability involves the attribution of responsibility to actors. Political accountability is filled with ambiguities, ambivalences, and contradictions (March & Olsen, 1995). Assigning responsibility and blame is complicated by multiple actors—who is responsible and who should be blamed? Assigning responsibility and blame is also complicated by causal complexity. Who or what caused an event, and how can causal responsibility be attributed? How can extraneous factors and counter interpretations be ruled out in the complexities of social and political life? Finally, assigning responsibility and blame involves outcomes—what outcome or outcomes do we seek and by what criteria or standard of performance do we seek them? Agreement on outcomes and corresponding performance standards is hard to come by and often contested, especially in social and educational institutions.

Outcomes, Outputs, and Standards.   While all three sources of uncertainty for accountability—multiple actors, causal attribution, and standards of performance—apply to higher education, the challenge of deciding upon and measuring outcomes for higher education stands out. Americans hold diverse goals for their colleges and universities, ranging from "specific expertise and knowledge in a chosen career" to "improved problem solving and thinking ability" to citizenship to a sense of maturity (Immerwahr, 2000).

Two challenges present themselves. The first challenge is to create trustworthy measures of these outcomes. In creating these measures, it is important to recognize that they are "output measures" and as such do not measure perfectly the valued outcomes colleges seek to instill in their students; hence, something has been lost already (e.g., Gormley & Weimar, 1999). Moreover, while these outcomes are all valued, some are easier to measure and hold more political currency than others, especially knowledge outcomes. Yet to measure some outcomes and not others creates imbalance. The act of measuring and reporting some indicators and not others transforms output measures into outcomes themselves—that is, the limited output measures become *the* valued outcomes; the originally valued outcomes are lost (e.g., Shavelson, 2007a,b; Shavelson & Huang, 2003).

These points can be seen in the standard organizational input-process-output-outcome production model (Gormley & Weimar, 1999; Romzek, 2000; see Figure 7.1). Inputs in higher education often include the materials and resources available to institutions, such as student and faculty quality, facilities, and finances. Processes transform inputs into outputs and may include such indicators as faculty-student ratio and class size. Outputs are measurable products that might include graduation rates, time to graduation, scores on licensure or certification examinations, or employer satisfaction with graduates. And outcomes are the valued goals that institutions seek to attain, such as those surveyed by Immerwahr (2000).

When outputs are closely matched with outcomes, they provide a strong means for monitoring performance. The consequences of such monitoring are those largely intended. For example, in many businesses, the output measure (e.g., sales, revenue, or stock price) is a close proxy to valued outcomes. The output measures can be used to advantage for business decisions and actions.

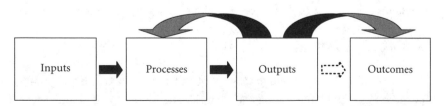

Figure 7.1 Standard organizational production model.
SOURCE: R. Shavelson original.

In education, however, outcomes are many and debated. The outcome indicator, such as a multiple-choice achievement test score, is an *output measure* that is a distal *proxy* for the desired *outcomes*. When high-stakes sanctions such as budgetary consequences are placed on the output measure, as NCLB has done in K-12 education, for example, the indicator becomes an end in itself. Well-intentioned accountability, then, may very well distort the system it was intended to improve (cf. Gormley & Weimar, 1999).[2] Moreover, when outputs do not provide informative feedback to an organization, they have limited value in the absence of collateral (e.g., campus-specific) information (see Chapter 5). Rather, they serve a signaling function (Shavelson, 2008a) that something may be amiss but go no further toward improvement.

The model in Figure 7.1 also points out a fundamental conflict inherent in (education) accountability systems. That conflict is between the summative function and the formative function of accountability (e.g., Lingenfelter, 2003; see Chapter 6). The summative function permits the public and responsible officials to reach a summary, comparative judgment about the performance of, say, higher-education institutions against some standard of performance or in comparison with one another (outputs). However, this information is too sparse to enlighten campuses on what and how to improve education (processes). Accountability information for improvement falls in the province of the formative function—to gather and feed back information on how to improve education processes, and to monitor improvement. One implication of this analysis with the organizational production model is that a system of measures, rather than a few distal output measures of "learning," such as graduation rates, may be necessary if the intent of accountability is to go beyond sanctioning poor performance and lead to improved institutional performance.

Balancing Diversity of Outcomes.   Another challenge is how to hold institutions accountable for achieving the diversity of outcomes, as espoused, for example, in their mission statements. It is well known that an institution cannot optimize on multiple, potentially multidimensional outcomes such as cognitive achievement, civic engagement, and self-understanding at once. Institutions must "satisfice" (a blend of satisfy and suffice) and balance (or weigh) outcomes against one another (March, 1994). Institutions of higher education have been doing this throughout their history—hence, the diversity of institutions. In the absence of consensus about how to weigh outcomes, comparisons among institutions become suspect, and institutions are motivated to argue for those outcomes they value or look the best on (cf. Gormley & Weimar, 1999).

These challenges—measuring valued outcomes and satisficing on multiple outcomes—must be addressed in considering options for higher-education accountability. To this end, in the next two chapters we will look at how various U.S. states and other countries handle this balancing act for hints of what options might be most viable in the future.

Sanctions and Desired Behavior.   Accountability carries with it the notion of sanctions for undesirable actions or consequences. A third complication arises, then, from the application of sanctions in accountability. The idea is that if an actor is found culpable, sanctions should be applied. The intent of sanctions is to get actors to behave properly, even to improve their performance. Sanctions may, indeed, work this way. If the sanctions are strong enough, most officials will behave as desired, at least symbolically—but that behavior will persist only so long as the sanctions are hanging overhead. Once sanctions are lifted, individual and institutional behavior may spring back to what it was before the sanctions were imposed (Baldwin & Baldwin, 1998; Sidman, 1989).

Sanctions are problematic for another reason, as well. They can lead to self-fulfilling prophecies. For example, K-12 schools failing to meet NCLB standards are penalized and ultimately can be disbanded. The remedies in NCLB are rather draconian and range from externally imposed technical assistance to replacing staff or curriculum, all the way to reopening the school as an autonomous public charter school or state takeover school. Schools attempting to improve to get out from under the sanctions have to do so with less flexibility and fewer resources, as their resources have been diverted to respond to sanctions. While we would like to reward appropriate behavior and positive outcomes and punish the reverse, sanctions may in themselves build in more failure, the very failure they are intended to correct.

The challenge for designing higher-education accountability is to figure out what mix of rewards and sanctions lead at least to substantive institutional compliance and, more desirably, to improvement. The State of Missouri, for example, has had experience with the use of incentives instead of sanctions in its assessment-of-student-learning program (e.g., Naughton, 2004). Institutions building assessment programs were given added fiscal incentives to do so; institutions struggling were given fiscal resources to move a plan for improvement forward. Perhaps lessons learned from Missouri will inform the nature and use of sanctions (and rewards) in higher education.

Interpretations as Accounts

The fourth complication arises from interpretations of accountability information, or what March and Olsen (1995) call *accounts* of events. Accounts are stories in which plot, characters, and setting are created to convey information in an accurate yet persuasive way (e.g., Shulman, 2007). They provide "explanations" that make events meaningful and actionable within an accountability framework. That is, accountability systems provide "observations" of an institution in the form of indicators. Indicators, however, are simply statistics or combinations of statistics; they need to be interpreted, or, in today's vernacular, they need a "spin" to fit within prevailing political and social ideologies or myths. By *accounts*, March and Olsen (1995) mean explanations, interpretations, or stories that bring order to the obscurities of the causes of an event. They make actions in the event imaginable and consequences interpretable. They mold assessments of history and the roles of individuals in it. Outcomes must fit a recognizable story line and thus are bound by conventions of explanations. "Accounts define political reality, and the reality they define can attribute events to a variety of causes, including acts of fate, incomprehensible external forces, malevolent enemies, or beneficent gods" (March & Olsen, 1995, p. 149).

An excerpt from Ohanian's (2005) article in *The School Administrator* illustrates this point clearly, both in content and manner:

> Nowhere is the smoke of deception thicker and trickier than in the lingo the corporate-politico-media squad uses when talking about public schools. At first glance, their talk seems plain and to the point: "failing schools," "caring about education" and "education as war." In contrast, education progressives befuddle the public with "authentic means of assessment," "decision-making processes" and "triangulated learning." But the simplicity is deceptive. The expression "failing public schools" has a lot in common with "war on terror." After the media parrot these phrases often enough, we find ourselves at war and in the morass of radical public school deformation. Familiarity breeds acceptance.

Accountability data, be they quantitative indicators or qualitative reviews, are open to interpretation along social and political lines; *they do not speak for themselves*. Given the ambiguities surrounding actors, causes, and outcomes, this leaves plenty of room for mischief (Shavelson & Huang, 2003). This is a major reason the academy is concerned about who holds it accountable, for what, and with what consequence.

To meet the implied contract between policy makers and campus leaders, accountability must deal with this issue of "cultural conflict" (see Chapter 6). Ostensibly, both policy makers and educators agree, in the abstract, on the importance of student learning and institutional improvement. They disagree, however, on the means for bringing this about, and here lies the cultural conflict.

In government culture, the summative function of accountability prevails. Officials are ultimately held responsible for higher-education performance by the citizens of the state. Consequently, they take their perceived responsibility and power and collect and report "objective" indicators of campus quality. These officials have come to distrust lateral approaches (see Figure 6.1), wherein campuses conduct and report their own performance assessments, for, as we have seen, intercampus comparisons are impossible to make and, consequently, quality difficult to compare.

In contrast, the campus culture embraces the formative function of accountability with a faculty-driven lateral approach. The professed intent is to improve curriculum, teaching, and learning. The academy distrusts top-down and bottom-up, decontextualized summative approaches to accountability that challenge or proscribe these traditional areas of faculty decision making. Accountability systems need to address this distrust and create a new compact for improvement, recognizing that tension is inherent (e.g., Mansbridge, 1998; Bailey, 1974):

> Today, as we perceive this elemental paradox in the tensions between the academy and the state [e.g., academe's need for dependence upon and autonomy from the state], it is useful to keep in mind its generic quality. For at heart we are dealing, I submit, with a dilemma we cannot rationally wish to resolve. The public interest would not, in my estimation, be served if the academy were to enjoy an untroubled immunity. Nor could the public interest be served by the academy's being subjected to an intimate surveillance. Whatever our current discomforts because of a sense that the state is crowding us a bit, the underlying tension is benign. (Bailey, 1974, p. 5).

Wielding a Two-Edged Sword

The fifth and final complication arises from individual and institutional responses to accountability. As March and Olsen (1995) pointed out, accountability is a two-edged sword. It sharpens social control and makes actors more responsive to social pressure and standards of appropriate behavior. Yet it also can lead to procrastination and indecision, reduced risk taking, persistence in a course of action that is failing in order to avoid disclosure, nonparticipation in data collection, cherry picking (taking the best examples for data), manipulating numbers, blaming the messenger, and the like (e.g., March & Olsen, 1996; Gormley & Weimar, 1999, especially pp. 7–17 and 36–37).

Reprise

Individual and institutional accountability is a fundamental presumption of a democratic society. All agree that individuals qua individuals, or as officials representing institutions, should act rationally, reasonably, and honestly and produce expected outcomes. They are held responsible for their actions and the outcomes produced, and they are held accountable by an external authority—ultimately, the citizens of the polity. When actions or outcomes fail to meet legal and societal expectations, sanctions are applied, with the intent of both punishing and correcting behavior.

At first blush such accountability seems reasonable; however, in practice, a great deal of misinterpretation, misguided sanctions, and just plain mischief can be done in the name of accountability. Accountability, then, is both a powerful policy tool and a very delicate instrument. It is a powerful policy tool because of its potential to significantly affect individual and institutional behavior. It is a delicate instrument because if it is not fine-tuned, it may give rise to unintended consequences—even to the very behavior it was designed to correct.

In order to fine-tune higher-education accountability, we have identified six related factors to consider. First, consideration needs to be given to the relative emphasis on accounting for the reasonableness of education processes and for the level of education outcomes within current technological know-how. As pointed out, well-implemented processes may not lead to expected outcomes, and expected outcomes might arise from intolerable processes. An accountability system needs to reach a balance on accounting for actions and for outcomes.

Second, consideration needs to be given to what processes and outcomes get measured and what do not, recognizing that what gets measured may be quite distal from the process or outcome it is intended to measure. Moreover, what gets measured is often what is easy and inexpensive to measure, narrowing the range of processes and outcomes measured and increasing the distance between what is measured and what is desired. From this it should be clear that simple, single measures of process or outcome are inadequate; multiple indicators are needed in an accountability system.

Third, based on these measurements, sanctions (and, less frequently, incentives) are applied with the intention of changing and improving performance. However, sanctions are very powerful policy instruments. The behavioral evidence is that they are only effective in a very narrow way and do not last beyond their intense application. Moreover, sanctions often have unintended consequences, so that they need to be monitored and fine-tuned over time. Crafting and monitoring sanctions, and exploring positive incentives, are essential in the design and conduct of an accountability system.

Fourth, information produced by an accountability system needs to serve multiple audiences: educators, governments, and consumers (see Chapter 6). Yet the information sought by educators is typically formative in nature and intended to improve education processes; whereas the information sought by the other two groups is typically summative and meant to be used to compare quite different higher-education institutions. To the extent possible, the two information functions—formative and summative—need to be linked in an accountability system, recognizing that there is a potentially productive tension between the two, as Bailey (1974) pointed out.

Fifth, education process and output indicators are multiple, multiply caused, and do not speak for themselves. They require interpretation to make them culturally and socially meaningful. Herein lays potential accountability mischief, as competing political views vie to spin the interpretation of the indicators. There need to be checks and balances in an accountability system to minimize the chance that a single, simple, well-spun interpretation will predominate over other potentially viable explanations.

And finally, sixth, accountability is a double-edged sword. On the one hand, it can move institutions to comply with societal and political expectations, and on the other hand it can reduce flexibility and innovation. An accountability system should be constructed to balance the two.

The intuitive appeal of accountability and the widespread acceptance of its position in a democracy, then, need to be tempered with its potential for unintended consequences. Perhaps mechanisms need to be in place to hold accountable those who would hold higher education accountable—a co-accountability scheme (e.g., March & Olsen, 1995). In the end, this awareness of the delicacy of a powerful policy instrument should lead us to be very much concerned with the design and implementation of accountability mechanisms in higher education, a concern that motivated this text and is the focus of its last chapter, after we have seen how others within and outside the United States have attempted to assess learning and hold higher education accountable.

8   State Higher-Education Accountability and Learning Assessment

INCREASING PRESSURE TO HOLD CAMPUSES accountable have reinforced a higher-education accountability and assessment "movement" over the past two decades (e.g., Ewell, 2002) and led states in a frenzy to mandate various student learning assessments (Shavelson & Huang, 2003). The question is not one of whether to hold higher education accountable but one of what campuses should be held accountable for and how they should be held accountable. Moreover, the question is not one of whether to assess learning but rather one of what learning should be assessed and in what ways. To understand this movement, it is necessary to see what states are doing to hold higher education accountable. While the federal Higher Education Act holds great sway regarding student access and financial support, and in saber rattling for accountability through, for example, the U.S. secretary of education's bully pulpit and the threat of economic sanctions, states are responsible for educating the majority of students in the United States and so are the major actors in assuring the public, clients, and policy makers that these students are receiving a quality education.

In this chapter states' approaches to accountability are briefly characterized, and then attention turns to what states are using as assessments and indicators of learning. Specifically, we examine various approaches states have taken to monitor higher-education performance and characterize the nature and variation in states' performance reports. We then dig down to characterize states' assessment of learning, ultimately focusing on direct measures and the nature of indicators reported.

By collecting and reporting information on some indicators and not others, states de facto stipulate what "counts" in higher-education accountability.

Especially in adopting specific learning assessment strategies as part of accountability programs, state legislatures and higher-education boards define, de facto, what is meant as learning. Such definitions can trump the best of schemes for assessing student learning. That is, states willingly and explicitly define, by the very indicators they report, not only learning output measures but also implicitly what outcomes are valued in higher education (Shavelson & Huang, 2003; see Figure 7.1). States exert their influence, for example, when campus budgets depend upon performance on these indicators. States have raised the stakes high enough in this case to change campus behavior, at least symbolically if not substantively. When this happens, output measures can replace the valued outcomes for which they originally served as proxies. At best, state accountability programs can provide only limited information for improving teaching and learning on campuses. At worst, when output measures replace valued outcomes, the opportunity for mischief grows, as does the possibility of unintended consequences, such as distorting teaching-learning processes. The goal of this chapter, then, is to understand what states are doing now to hold higher education accountable as a basis for asking whether this is the best or only way to deal with higher-education accountability or might there be alternative approaches that would coordinate external demands for accountability and internal demands for information to improve teaching and learning.

State Accountability Programs

Although state accountability programs vary considerably, Chapter 6 distinguished three types: performance funding, performance budgeting, and performance reporting. Performance funding programs tie performance to direct appropriation incentives. Performance budgeting, less concrete, relates indirectly to budgetary decisions based to some varying degree on performance information. Both have proven costly and unstable in changing economic times (Burke & Minassians, 2002b) as the states' shares of the cost of public higher education have dwindled over the past twenty-five years, dropping from 6.7 percent of state revenues in 1977 to 4.5 percent in 2000 (*New York Times*, October 16, 2005, p. 12).

State Performance Reporting and Report Cards

The emerging predominate type of accountability program is *performance reporting*. Performance reporting programs require public higher-education institutions to track a set of indicators and report them regularly to legislators, state boards, and the public (Burke & Minassians, 2002). Elected lawmakers are the prime movers behind performance reporting. Before the 1990s only Tennessee,

South Carolina, and Oklahoma had legislated reporting mandates; by 1996 twenty-three states had such laws (Burke & Associates, 2002). This burgeoning legislative interest "sought to increase the quality, productivity, and efficiency of public colleges and universities" (Burke & Associates, 2002, p. 9) and did so by calling for centrally defined assessment methods that could be *reported publicly and compared across institutions and states*. Additional mandates from other sources, especially state higher-education board policies, brought the total number of states with performance reporting requirements to forty-four in 2002 and forty-six in 2003, the last time a survey was conducted (Burke & Minassians, 2002b, 2003). Today, virtually all states have some form of performance reporting requirement. Institutional or statewide progress toward some defined standards or objectives, then, is often accounted for and communicated in some form of performance report.

Gormley and Weimer (1999) distinguish seven variations in performance reporting programs: (1) organizational report cards, (2) Government Performance and Results Act (GPRA) requirements, (3) benchmarking, (4) balanced score cards, (5) program evaluation, (6) social indicators, and (7) disclosure requirements. These programs vary, for example, as to whether the performance assessment is carried out in one of the following ways:

- internally as mandated by GPRA or externally as by report cards (e.g., *U.S. News* rankings) and social indicators
- on a single institution (GPRA, balanced score cards/self-assessments) or multiple institutions (report cards, benchmarking)
- with data collected and reported regularly (report cards, social indicators, GPRA) or only occasionally (program evaluation)

Gormley and Weimer (1999) argued that, among the alternative reporting schemes, for accountability an "organizational report card" for government overseers and public consumers is likely to be most effective. An organizational report card is "a regular effort by an organization to collect data on two or more *other* organizations, transform the data into information relevant to assessing performance, and transmit the information to some audience external to the organizations themselves" (Gormley & Weimer, 1999, p. 3; italics in original). Many such report cards transmit this information in a simplified form of rankings (e.g., those of *U.S. News*), ratings, or grades (e.g., via the National Center for Public Policy and Higher Education's *Measuring Up*).

Measuring Up 2006 (National Center for Public Policy and Higher Education, 2006) provides a concrete example of a higher-education report card (see

Chapter 6). The report card evaluates states with a letter grade on how well they are doing in providing higher education to their citizens. The report card has been issued broadly to the states and public biennially by an independent organization, the National Center for Public Policy and Higher Education, since 2000. It distills a large amount of data into six indicators and corresponding grades: (1) high school academic preparation, (2) postsecondary education participation, (3) college completion, (4) student and family affordability, (5) "educational capital" benefits, and (6) student learning (see Figure 8.1).

State report cards are rare, however; only NCPPHE produces what Gormley and Weimer (1999) would call a report card. Rather, most states do a version of what Gormley and Weimer would call *benchmarking*. With benchmarking, campus indicators are compared with those of other institutions within or outside the state, or against some national norm (e.g., mean GRE score). Note that an independent third-party organization is not required; often state higher-education boards cobble together the comparative indicators. But state boards are not independent actors in this accountability play and are in a position to create a narrative account of the data to serve partisan interests (see Chapters 6 and 7).

The logic of report cards goes as follows: By delineating performance expectations and having an independent organization collect, analyze, and regularly publish readily interpretable results (e.g., rankings), states would be in a position to shape the behavior of higher-education institutions and ultimately improve their performance (see Borden & Banta, 1994; Burke & Serban, 1998; Gormley & Weimer, 1999). A similar logic follows for benchmarking. What is not well understood is *how* exactly these reports—leveraged by public opinion, public demand in a competitive market, and funding consequences—would spur changes in institutional behavior (or, specifically, teaching and learning). In part, this lack of knowledge reflects the recent, rapid spread of higher-education performance–reporting programs.

Among the most important performance indicators (report cards and benchmarks) are those that purport to reflect student learning. The inclusion of these indicators in state higher-education reports has increased over time. Avoiding political, philosophical, and psychometric difficulties associated with measuring college-level learning, most performance reporting systems do not include direct measures of cognitive learning outcomes (Ewell, 1993). Indirect measures of learning, predominantly graduation and retention rates and surveys, have been and continue to be the most widespread way for states to judge

	PREPARATION	PARTICIPATION	AFFORDABILITY	COMPLETION	BENEFITS	LEARNING
Alabama	D–	C	F	B–	B	I
Alaska	B–	C+	F	F	B–	I
Arizona	D	B+	F	B	B+	I
Arkansas	D+	C	F	C	C	I
California	C	A	C–	B	A	I
Colorado	B+	A–	F	B	A–	I
Connecticut	A–	A–	F	B+	A	I
Delaware	C	B	F	A–	B–	I
Florida	C	C	F	A	B	I
Georgia	C+	D+	F	A	B–	I
Hawaii	C–	C	D	B–	A–	I
Idaho	C	D+	D	C+	C–	I
Illinois	B	A	F	B+	A	+
Indiana	C	C+	F	B+	C	I
Iowa	B+	A–	F	A	C	I
Kansas	B–	A	F	B+	B+	I
Kentucky	C–	B–	F	C+	C+	+
Louisiana	F	C–	F	C–	D+	I
Maine	B	B–	F	B	B–	I
Maryland	A–	A	F	B	A	+
Massachusetts	A	A	F	A	A	+
Michigan	C–	A–	F	B	A–	I
Minnesota	B	A	D	A	B+	I
Mississippi	D–	D	F	B	C	I
Missouri	C	B	F	B+	A	+
Montana	B+	C–	F	B–	C+	I
Nebraska	B	A	F	B+	B	I
Nevada	C–	C	F	F	C–	+
New Hampshire	B+	C+	F	A	A	I
New Jersey	A	A–	D	B	A	I
New Mexico	F	A	F	D	C	I
New York	A–	B–	F	A–	B+	+
North Carolina	B+	B–	F	B+	B	I
North Dakota	B–	A	F	B	C+	I
Ohio	B–	B–	F	B	B+	I
Oklahoma	D+	C+	F	C	B–	+
Oregon	C–	C+	F	B–	A	I
Pennsylvania	B	B	F	A	A–	I
Rhode Island	C+	A	F	A	B	I
South Carolina	C+	D+	F	B+	C	+
South Dakota	B	A	F	B+	C+	I
Tennessee	C–	C–	F	B	C+	I
Texas	B–	C+	F	C+	B–	I
Utah	A	B	C–	B	A–	I
Vermont	B–	C	F	A	A–	I
Virginia	A–	B	F	B+	A	I
Washington	B	C–	D–	A	A–	I
West Virginia	C–	C–	F	C+	D+	I
Wisconsin	B+	A–	F	A	B–	I
Wyoming	C–	B+	F	A	C–	I

Figure 8.1 State-by-state report card of the National Center for Public Policy and Higher Education.

SOURCE: National Center for Public Policy and Higher Education, 2006, p. 18.

learning gains. Direct assessments, such as certification examinations or the GRE, which show actual achievement levels or learning gains with comparable data, have been encouraged nationally since the U.S. Department of Education and the nation's governors adopted the National Education Goals in 1990. By the late 1990s, state capitals had stepped up their calls for statewide testing of undergraduates, with surprisingly little organized resistance coming from campuses (Ewell, 1998b).

The National Center for Public Policy and Higher Education provides an example of a report card containing direct measures of learning (Miller, 2006). For four-year colleges and universities, the NCPPHE envisioned a system (Figure 8.2) that would, as noted in Chapter 6, collect the following: (1) state data in parallel with the National Assessment of Adult Literacy Survey (NAALS) to index the literacy level of the state's population; (2) scores from admissions and licensure examinations; and (3) a direct measure of "general intellectual skills" (Miller, 2006, p. 2), using the Collegiate Learning Assessment (see Chapters 3 and 4 for a description).

While this is a step in the right direction, there are, as with all indicators of learning, several limitations. First, the state literacy level as indexed by the NAALS is influenced not only by the state's higher-education institutions but also by the in and out migration of adults in the state; attribution of findings to a state's colleges and universities is problematic. Second, the use of admissions and licensure examinations is limited by those undergraduates who self-select to sit for these examinations; they do not represent the entire undergraduate senior class. Once again, attribution to the campus's performance is problematic.

NCPPHE implemented its vision in a pilot study with the participation of five states: Illinois, Kentucky, Nevada, Oklahoma, and South Carolina. The center provided a profile of performance for each state (see examples in Figure 8.3). The profile compared state performance to national benchmarks.

Moreover, the center used the learning data to compare performance state by state in "learning profiles that . . . gave an idea of each state's strengths and challenges . . . with regard to collegiate learning" (Miller, 2006, p. 2). For example, it compared the five states' white and nonwhite students' performance on the CLA (see Figure 8.4).

Such profiles help signal to policy makers, educators, and the public areas where improvement is needed. However, these profiles have limitations. For example, they are so general as to be of limited value to particular campuses for

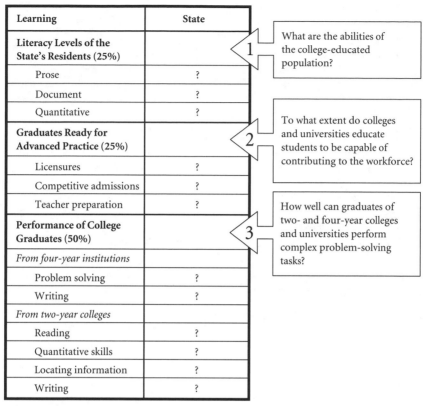

Learning	State
Literacy Levels of the State's Residents (25%)	
Prose	?
Document	?
Quantitative	?
Graduates Ready for Advanced Practice (25%)	
Licensures	?
Competitive admissions	?
Teacher preparation	?
Performance of College Graduates (50%)	
From four-year institutions	
Problem solving	?
Writing	?
From two-year colleges	
Reading	?
Quantitative skills	?
Locating information	?
Writing	?

1 What are the abilities of the college-educated population?

2 To what extent do colleges and universities educate students to be capable of contributing to the workforce?

3 How well can graduates of two- and four-year colleges and universities perform complex problem-solving tasks?

NOTE: Measures included under the first two clusters are available nationally and can be calculated for all 50 states. Measures included in the third will require special data-collection efforts similar to those undertaken by the five demonstration project states in 2004.

Figure 8.2 National Center for Public Policy and Higher Education's "Learning Model."

SOURCE: National Center for Public Policy and Higher Education, 2006, p. 23.

improvement purposes (see Chapter 5). Moreover, these profiles, in comparing states, ignore the enormous diversity of campuses and missions within states so as to make interpretation of differences among states problematic. This ambiguity blunts the signaling function.

Characteristics of State Performance Reports

Given the current wave of state efforts to hold public colleges and universities accountable for student learning, it is important to understand what data states require for benchmark reporting, especially as learning indicators. To this end,

KENTUCKY

Kentucky's recent substantial investments in both K–12 and postsecondary education have been a good public-policy response to its low literacy levels.

Its investments in community and technical colleges have paid off both in the form of higher-than-average proportions of graduates taking and passing licensing exams and in the high-level performance of those students on the WorkKeys exams, especially in the writing section.

But the state is less competitive when it comes to the proportion of its graduates taking and performing competitively on graduate-admission exams.

OKLAHOMA

Oklahoma's recent activity in improving the quality of its higher-education system is a response to the substantial challenges it faces in its K–12 system and in its low levels of college graduation. The disappointing literacy levels of its residents reflect those challenges.

Oklahoma's higher-education orientation toward workforce preparation is seen in the high number of students who take and do well on licensure exams, as compared to students' below-average performance on graduate admissions tests.

Written communication skills constitute a particular challenge for the state in both its two- and four-year colleges.

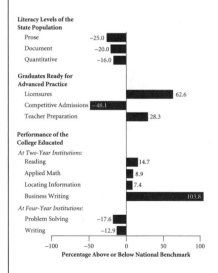

Figure 1.
Kentucky Learning Measures

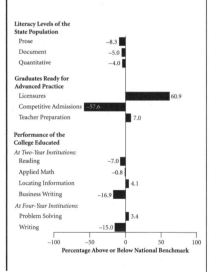

Figure 2.
Oklahoma Learning Measures

NOTE: Learning profiles for Illinois, Nevada, and South Carolina are available at: http://www.highereducation.org/reports/mu_learning/index.shtml.

Source for Figures and Tables: Margaret A. Miller and Peter T. Ewell, *Measuring Up on College-Level Learning* (San Jose, CA: The National Center for Public Policy and Higher Education, 2005).

Figure 8.3 State profiles of performance on learning assessment measures.
SOURCE: Miller, 2006, p. 3.

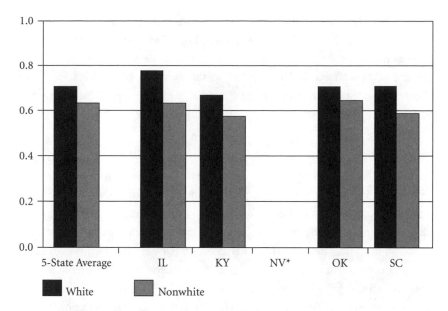

* Data for Nevada were unavailable due to insufficient numbers of test takers and logistical problems with test administration.

NOTE: To allow comparisons, the test results have been standarized by converting them to a scale from 0 to 1, with 1 being the highest score possible on the test.

Figure 8.4 State-by-state performance by white and nonwhite students on the Collegiate Learning Assessment.
SOURCE: Miller, 2006, p. 4.

in 2003, Blake Naughton, Anita Suen, and I (2003) began characterizing the input, process, output, and outcome indicators found in state performance reports.[1] We then focused on learning indicators, seeking to characterize what indicators were reported and how they fit with some reasonable framework for college outcomes—a framework that would define the nature of learning and achievement expected of students earning a degree. Admittedly, we were shooting at a moving target; state performance reports were and are in flux.

The goal was threefold: (1) to characterize the indicators of college performance that states included in their reports, (2) to characterize de facto definitions of student achievement and learning being promulgated in state accountability systems by surveying state learning output indicators, and (3) to map these learning indicators onto the broad conception of learning outcomes described in Chapter 2 (Figure 2.1). To this end we searched the State Higher

Education Executive Officers' (SHEEO) Web site and identified indicators that states reported in their performance reports. These indicators were then categorized as inputs, processes, outputs, or outcomes (for details, see Appendix A at the end of this chapter). The resulting database included information from twenty-six state performance reports (for a list, see Appendix B), including 748 performance indicators.[2]

Indicators Used in State Higher-Education Performance Reports

The top five "indicator keywords" (including indicators with tied frequencies) are reported by indicator type—input, process, output, and outcome—in Table 8.1. Since states used different labels or keywords to denote their indicators, and since some indicator keywords can be found under different indicator types, some explanation as to how to read Table 8.1 is in order. For example, twenty-two states used student admissions or enrollments as *input* indicators in their reports. "Admission/Enrollment" (key words) indicators included such things as the student body's academic qualifications (e.g., SAT, ACT scores) and demographic breakdown (e.g., first-time freshmen's racial identity, county of residence). Some indicator key words, including "Faculty," occurred under multiple types. Faculty *inputs* include indicators of faculty full-time status; whereas average faculty teaching load is a faculty *process* indicator. Research, too, occurred under more than one type, research dollars as an *input* and research publications as an *output*. Other key words in Table 8.1 worth defining include "K-12," used to designate those indicators relating to elementary and secondary education, like the *input* indicator of high school preparation or the *output* indicator of college graduates employed in a state's school districts. "Satisfaction" was used to denote any indicator derived from an opinion survey. Student progress or retention was coded as an *output* indicator because student retention into the sophomore year, for example, is an output of success in the freshman year.

These findings jibe with those reported by Burke and Minassians (2002b, p. 34), who analyzed indicators reported by the twenty-nine states that had issued at least one performance report by 2001. The most frequently used indicators in order of magnitude were as follows:

- graduation or retention (24 of 29 states)—our top *output* indicator
- enrollment or race (21)—our most frequent *input* indicator combined with our third-most frequent
- sponsored research (20)—our sixth-most frequent *output* indicator

Table 8.1. Most Frequent Indicators in State Higher-Education Performance Reports by Type

Input	# States	Process	# States	Output	# States	Outcome	# States
Admission or enrollment	22	Instruction	17	Graduation	24	Satisfaction	2
Finance	21	Finance	13	Progress/retention	23	Service	2
Demographics	18	Faculty	12	Learning	17	Learning	1
Faculty	17	Technology	10	Employment	12		
K-12	17	Collaboration	7	Satisfaction	12		
Research	17			Research	9		
Financial aid	11			K-12	9		
Total indicators: 306		*Total indicators: 130*		*Total indicators: 300*		*Total indicators: 6*	

SOURCE: R. Shavelson.

NOTE: With an additional 6 indicators coded as "combination/other," the total is 748.

- student transfers (19)—our second-most frequent output indicator (progress or retention)
- tuition and fees (18)—our second-most frequent input indicator

As Burke and Minassians (2002b) pointed out, indicators provide a direct expression of what states hold to be important in higher education. Burke and Minassians classified their indicators as to whether they reflected external, summative accountability concerns or internal, formative accountability concerns (our terms; see Chapter 6). They concluded that external summative concerns dominated performance reporting, and we, (Naughton, Shavelson & Suen, 2003) along with Nettles, Cole, and Sharp (1997), reached the same conclusion.

Moreover, Burke and Minassians (2002b) examined the distribution of indicators by type (input, process, and output). The number of indicators found in their classification jibed with that in ours: *input*—Burke and Minassians 37 percent vs. our 41 percent of all indicators; *process*—20 percent vs. 18 percent; *output + outcome* (due to some differences in classification)—41 percent vs. 41 percent. Note, as Burke and Minassians did, the emphasis on input and output indicators.

Our findings reinforced Burke and Minassians's conclusion that the summative or external focus of state performance reports were emphasized to a far greater extent than the formative function of institutional improvement. Moreover, the emphasis is also on output measures such as graduation rates, not direct measures of learning at all (see National Center for Public Policy and Higher

Education, 2006, and below). Nevertheless, it seems that state accountability systems—for good reason, including, especially, cost—need to track such output indicators as graduation rates, time to graduation, and the like. After all, taxpayers and parents (but perhaps not all students) are concerned about cost and timely graduation.

In order to improve performance, however, campuses need information on how effective their processes are in adding value to student learning over and above their inputs (e.g., Kuh et al., 2005). The focus of the state on external or summative indicators clashes with the concerns and cultures of campuses and their focus on improving their processes (Chapter 6).

Learning Indicators in State Performance Reports

With indicators in performance reports broadly characterized, consider now learning indicators specifically. How did they evolve and what do they look like?

Evolution of Learning Indicators

In 1997, the National Center for Postsecondary Improvement (NCPI) reported results from a comprehensive study of state and accreditation agency accountability policies; the report focused on the assessment of teaching and learning (Nettles, Cole & Sharp, 1997). Nettles and colleagues traced the antecedents to state accountability programs from 1987 to 1995 by reviewing both influential national association reports and four studies of state and accreditation agency assessment policies. From this series of studies two key trends emerged. First, assessment programs evolved from more institutionally autonomous to less— from campus-defined to state-defined. Second, the central theme of assessment shifted from quality to compliance—from assessment for improvement (formative function of accountability) to assessment for accountability (summative function).

The NCPI study constructed a common policy analysis framework for looking at states' and regional accrediting commissions' assessment policies, and used this framework to analyze assessment mandates. They found eight states that used common assessment instruments in their public institutions (Nettles, Cole & Sharpe, 1997). Two (Missouri and Kentucky) used a common instrument for teacher education programs, and six did so for general education. Of those six, Florida, Georgia, North Carolina, South Carolina, and Texas developed their own instruments, and Tennessee used commercially developed tests (ACT's College Outcomes Measurement Project or the College Basic Academic Subjects

Table 8.2. Early State Learning Assessment Programs

State	Learning Assessments
Arkansas	Collegiate Assessment of Academic Proficiency
Florida	College Level Academic Skills Testing
Georgia	Regents Testing Program
South Dakota	Collegiate Assessment of Academic Proficiency
Tennessee	College Outcomes Measurement Project (also the California Critical Thinking and Skills Test and ETS's Academic Profile)
Texas	Texas Academic Skills Program

SOURCE: R. Shavelson; Ewell and Ries, 2000.

Examination; see Chapter 3). In addition, twenty-two states required at least some common assessment indicators but did not mandate the specific instruments; twelve used institutionally defined indicators.

Ewell and Ries (2000) reported on how states tracked student-learning outcomes in their accountability programs. Of the twenty-two states then attempting to measure student learning directly, only six collected data that could be used to compare an institution against benchmark institutions or to aggregate data across institutions for within-state comparisons (Table 8.2). Two additional states pushed for reporting comparable data. Missouri required campuses to use nationally normed assessments in general education and the major (including licensure examinations); the state report aggregated the results into the percentage of students scoring at certain levels. Oklahoma's program was similar to its eastern neighbor's, although national instruments were not required. Other states reported that they were in various stages of exploring, developing, or piloting similar programs.

In addition to describing and classifying assessments, previous work has sought to align learning assessments into a conceptual framework. The National Postsecondary Education Cooperative (NPEC) situated available national tests (and not other types of assessments) into a framework of critical thinking, problem solving, and writing (Erwin, 2000). NPEC based this framework on the 1990 National Goals for Education's Goal 6, fifth objective: "The proportion of college graduates who demonstrate an advanced ability to think critically, communicate effectively, and solve problems will increase substantially" (www.ed.gov/pubs/EPTW/eptwgoal.html). NPEC recognized, however, that there were other cognitive outcomes of college to be measured.

Callan and Finney (2002), building on *Measuring Up's* 2000 and 2002 findings that all states earned a grade of "incomplete" in the category of assessment of learning outcomes, called for nationally comparable measures of undergraduates' learning. They tied legislators' and governors' accountability needs to a framework of a state's "educational capital." For them, educational capital was "the knowledge and skills of the population available for the workforce, for citizenship, and for community life" (p. 27). The knowledge and skills included critical thinking, problem solving, and communication. Callan and Finney argued that an "outside perspective" like educational capital (summative function of accountability) should take priority in assessment over an insider perspective, derived from institutions themselves (formative function), that was based on some local conception of learning and cognition. Moreover, they noted that no comparable measures existed then (but see NCPI's subsequent reports and Chapter 3): "More direct measures [of learning] are necessary to know what the public investment in higher education achieves over and above such investment in public schools. Direct measures of learning would also inform state policymakers about the educational capital available for state economic and social development" (Callan & Finney, 2002, p. 27).[3]

Reporting on findings of the 2001 National Forum on College-Level Learning, Callan and Finney (2002) recommended a long-term approach to measuring undergraduates' learning, one that resembled elementary and secondary education's National Assessment of Educational Progress (NAEP) but for higher education. For the short term, the forum encouraged states to collect and report assessment data currently available—including graduate entrance test scores, state and national licensure examination scores, workplace readiness assessments, the National Survey of Student Engagement (NSSE), the Collegiate Results Survey (CRS), ACT WorkKeys, and the National Assessment of Adult Literacy Survey (NAALS). The National Forum, then, proposed an assessment perspective that generalized the learning objectives of higher education into a utilitarian language of educational capital—a concept that enjoyed strong political currency. Somewhat in desperation, a mélange of direct and indirect measures of student learning had been recommended (Shavelson & Huang, 2003).

Following the advice of Callan and Finney (2002), the NCPPHE launched a pilot study to measure student learning in five states: Illinois, Kentucky, Nevada, Oklahoma, and South Carolina. They reported their findings in an addendum to *Measuring Up 2004* (National Center for Public Policy and Higher Education, 2004; see also Miller, 2006; National Center for Public Policy and Higher Education, 2006). Consistent with Gormley and Weimer's notion of a report card with complex data distilled into a readily interpretable, single indicator, their overall learning indicator was a weighted combination of three "themes." The first theme, "Abilities of the State's College-Educated Population," was measured with data from the 1992 NAALS (weighted 25 percent). The second theme, "Institutional Contributions to Educational Capital," was measured with a combination of the number of college graduates passing national licensure examinations, taking graduate admissions tests (e.g., GRE), and passing state teacher licensure examinations (weighted 25 percent). And the third theme, "Performance of College Graduates," was measured, in four-year colleges, by the Collegiate Learning Assessment (Klein et al., 2003, 2005; see Chapters 3 and 4) as a direct measure of learning (weighted 50 percent). The 2006 version of *Measuring Up* implemented these recommendations, as we saw earlier in this chapter. However, by 2008 states had regressed and "we are no further along than we were in 2000 when *Measuring Up* first awarded every state an 'Incomplete' in Learning" (National Center for Public Policy and Higher Education, 2008, p. 24).

For balance, and in contrast, at about the same time that Callan and Finney, NCPPHE, and the National Forum proposed cross-institutional direct and indirect indicators of student learning, Gray (2002) argued against a one-size-fits-all approach. Rather, he advocated a situated view of assessment that accounted for the complexity of institutions and the diversity of their missions. Effective evaluation and assessment, according to Gray, should be based on a tightly coupled relationship between the goals of learning and evidence—a complex relationship requiring the subjectivist reliance on the professional judgment of educators. This approach would require framing "a high degree of content correspondence between goals for student learning and assessment measures . . . for political as well as measurement reasons" (p. 138). Recognizing that preparation for jobs is one critical goal of an undergraduate education, Colby et al. (2003) and others (e.g., Shavelson, 2007a) urged that other learning goals, like making complex moral decisions, developing responsible citizens, and fostering independent inquiry, that are specific to institutions and majors ought not be forgotten in assessing learning outcomes (e.g., Colby et al., 2003; Shavelson, 2007a). This view has currency and is echoed by many educators and higher-education associations today.

Characteristics of Learning Indicators in State Performance Reports
What, then, are states using as output indicators for undergraduate learning? More specifically, what "indirect" (e.g., graduation rates, retention) and "direct" (e.g., cumulative examinations in the major, GRE) learning indicators have been

reported and what instruments have been used to measure them (e.g., GRE)? In our study, states were found to commonly use, for example, "freshman retention rates" (an indirect measure) and "student pass rates on professional licensure examinations" (a direct but not necessarily representative measure) to index learning. Focusing further, once we identified them, we placed states' direct measures of learning within the cognitive outcomes framework depicted in Figure 2.1.

An analysis of the twenty-six states' higher-education performance reports found 218 performance indicators related directly or indirectly to student learning.[4] By far, most of these were indirect measures of student learning—179 spread over twenty-five states. The two most common indirect measures were what may be called "behavioral" indicators, such as graduation rates or degrees awarded, because they reflected students' observable behavior in contrast to their surveyed opinions.[5] Some of the most frequently reported indirect indicators of learning included graduation rates or numbers (twenty-five of twenty-nine states), retention/student progress (seventeen), employment of graduates (twelve), and student/alumni self-reports of learning from surveys or interviews (nine). The majority of indirect indicators, then, were related either to program completion or to postgraduate success in further education or the workforce (including, in some cases, salaries).

At the time of our study only one state, Kentucky, reported a nationally normed survey of learning *processes* (National Survey of Student Engagement) as a statewide indirect indicator of learning. And only two states (Connecticut and Wisconsin) had measures of *personal*, *social*, or *civic* outcomes, as well as of cognitive outcomes of learning, hence the focus here on cognitive outcomes.

Of particular concern were direct measures of learning because the so-called indirect measures of learning are not measures of either achievement or learning (see Chapter 2). The only direct measures of learning reported by the states at the time of our study were scores based on standardized tests; no other direct measures, such as portfolios or performance assessments, were used statewide. Moreover, none of the scores reported were representative of a campus's undergraduate student population.

Once state performance indicators derived from direct assessments were identified, they could then be mapped onto the cognitive outcomes framework in Figure 2.1. Thirty-nine indicators (from seventeen states) directly assessed learning and are shown in Table 8.3.

Over the past few years, the scene has changed but slightly. NCPPHE reported the results of its pilot study with direct measures of community college

Table 8.3. Direct Measures of Learning Found in State Report Cards

Cognitive Outcome	Assessment Instrument	Number of States Using Instrument	States Reporting Direct Learning Indicators
General ability/ intelligence		0	
Crystallized/fluid intelligence		0	
General reasoning	GRE, GMAT, LSAT, MCAT	4	CO, MO, UT, WI
	Other	3	CT, ND, WA
Broad disciplinary abilities	ACT-COMP	1	TN
	ACT-CAAP	3	ND, SD, UT (pilot)
	Unspecified/various	2	MO, ND
Domain-specific knowledge	Major field examination	2	ND, MO
	Licensure examination	14	CO, CT, FL, MO, ND, NM, OH, SC, TN, TX, UT, WV, WI, WY
	Specific teacher examination	4	MO, NM, SC, TN
	Unspecified	2	HI, MO

SOURCE: R. Shavelson.

NOTE: States are counted in more than one category when applicable. Table does not show multiple indicators from one state under one category (e.g., reporting separate results across sectors, reporting both number taking exam and number passing).

and four-year college and university learning (e.g., Miller, 2006). Perhaps the state that has done the most with learning indicators as of this writing is Texas.

Texas' plan called Closing the Gaps by 2015, adopted in October 2000 by the Texas Higher Education Coordinating Board, seeks to close educational gaps within Texas and between Texas and other states. The state strives to close gaps in *student participation* indexed, for example, by enrollments of students by ethnic background; *student success* as indexed, for example, by degrees awarded by ethnic background; *excellence* in targeted academic areas reflected in rankings; and *research* indexed by federal funding (Texas Higher Education Coordinating Board, 2005–2006; see also 2006–2007).[6] Information on a variety of indicators in each category is reported overall and for each academic (and health-related) campus comparatively.

Student outcomes constitute one facet of the student success goal. Using multiple measures, "The U. T. [University of Texas] System . . . [put together] new and existing tools to create a new model to address the issue of student outcomes" (University of Texas System Board of Regents, 2005–2006, p. 45). The University of Texas (UT) System assesses student outcomes from four different perspectives: (1) pass rates on licensure examinations; (2) student satisfaction with their educational experiences (e.g., according to the National Survey of Student Engagement); (3) rates of postgraduate employment or further professional or graduate study; and, important for our focus, (4) "student learning outcomes: test results on assessments of student problem solving, critical thinking, and analytic writing" (CLA; University of Texas System, 2005–2006, p. 45; see Chapters 3 and 4). Moreover, the system notes the following:

> One or more of these measures are used in the State of Texas accountability system, by individual institutions, in other states' systems, or in national studies. However, it is still somewhat unusual for a public university system to present and analyze data in one place on this group of multiple measures. This is important because each measure alone can only address particular aspects of the student experience; all are needed to provide a fuller accounting of the value added by an educational experience in a U. T. System institution. (University of Texas System, 2005–2006, p. 85)

The Collegiate Learning Assessment is used system-wide "to understand how well students do on critical thinking, problem solving, and writing tasks, not on specific course-related knowledge. Nationwide, a total of 124 institutions participated in the 2004–5 assessment. The 2004–5 test results will help establish a baseline from which future progress can be measured" (University of Texas System, 2005–2006, p. 52).

The UT System reported, for example, value-added performance for seniors at six of its academic institutions (Figure 8.5). The report interpreted these findings overall to indicate that UT seniors "scored at expected or higher levels, compared with the national sample, on the CLA performance task—problem solving, analytical reasoning, and critical thinking" (2005–2006, p. 56) and then interpreted findings for each campus.

As noted above, Texas' approach is highlighted for several reasons. First, it indexes the higher-education system's performance broadly in four areas: student participation, student success, excellence, and research. Moreover, it provides multiple indicators for each of its four goal areas. It provides comparative data nationally, with benchmark peers vis-à-vis its various campuses. Finally, the UT System has taken seriously the call to measure student learning outcomes directly and has done so with what is considered to be one of the best possible measures available today for doing so, the Collegiate Learning Assessment.

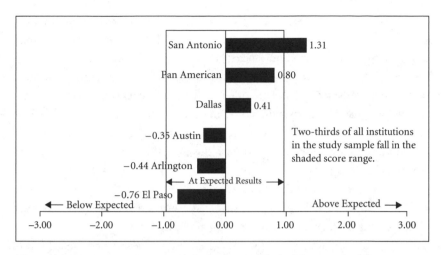

Figure 8.5 Value-added performance on Collegiate Learning Assessment.
Source: University of Texas System Board of Regents, 2005–2006, p. 56, figure I-25.

However, Texas' performance report comes closer to a benchmark report than a report card. First, report cards, like the ones we all received in grade school, typically provide a summary judgment, often in the form of a grade (or rank or rating). Texas' report does not do this, and so stakeholders are left with a considerable amount of data to wade through to reach some conclusion. Second, the 2005–2006 report (University of Texas System, 2005–2006) was the first comprehensive report of performance for the Closing the Gaps initiative (see University of Texas System, 2006–2007). For this endeavor to be a report card or benchmark, performance needs to be reported regularly over time, which the system currently intends to do. Third, the system is the organization responsible for collecting, analyzing, and reporting performance information; a report card is produced by an outside, independent organization. What is not known at present is the extent to which Texas' benchmarking will stimulate improvement, as Gormley and Weimer (1999) claim report cards are able to do and have done in other sectors (e.g., HMOs). This said, as the University of Texas System claims, what has been accomplished here sets a model for other states focusing on the summative function of accountability using direct learning measures.

Implications Drawn from State Performance Reports on Learning

This analysis of state higher-education accountability programs revealed conceptual gaps in the way student learning was conceived and measured. Indirect measures of learning such as graduation rates, which are extensively employed, may provide policy makers with a broad metric of student success, but they are not measures of student achievement or learning. They can produce little direct insight into what students have learned and can do, or into the strengths or weaknesses of particular programs for teaching and learning. Although student or employer satisfaction rates provide insights into the learning experience on college campuses, such instruments do not index achievement or learning and are not precise enough to tell campus administrators or faculty how to improve the education they provide. Importantly, however, they may pinpoint some institutional processes as candidates for study and improvement.

The few states attempting to measure learning directly are predominantly exploring ways to measure domain-specific knowledge and broad disciplinary abilities. This finding is encouraging, realizing that these outcome areas are or should be directly affected by the college classroom experience (Shavelson & Huang, 2003). The connections between student scores on these assessments and teaching and learning policy responses are plausible and perhaps outline the intended impact of accountability. They are commonly employed as tests of student achievement in the major and of abilities in general education—the basic structure of many undergraduate programs.

Nevertheless, several states attempted to measure general reasoning as a learning outcome, with four expressly using graduate admission examinations. Further, although data were not collected on campus-specific measures, performance reports suggest that even more campuses chose these graduate admission instruments as (possibly erroneous) proxies for disciplinary knowledge when an instrument had not been specified by the state. The connections between scores on these tests and the success of a curriculum are difficult to draw. Moreover, student self-selection and motivation in taking these tests lead us to conclude that results may not be representative of the college's student body. Such measures, then, might allow campus leaders to dismiss accountability for student levels of performance on the GRE, a measure that is not designed to reflect a particular college's course work.

The most common method of directly measuring student learning, licensure examination pass rates, was used in fourteen states. The measure, however, is applicable to only a small, nonrepresentative minority of undergraduate students—those in fields such as nursing, teaching, or engineering—and not undergraduates in general. This said, the rationale behind holding programs in these fields accountable to the success of their graduates on such examinations seems reasonable, as they serve as gateways to professional occupational entry.

The state role, however, is often complementary if not secondary to the quite meaningful accountability imposed by professional accreditation associations, as seen in Chapter 6.

Nationally, the two areas of cognitive outcomes most directly related to the college experience, domain-specific knowledge and broad domain abilities, are under assessed. At the time of this research, only two states had specified that assessment occur in the major field of study (domain-specific outcomes), and only a handful had specified a common instrument for general education (as viewed under broad disciplinary knowledge outcomes).[7] Moreover, states do not typically use both a major field and general education instrument— doing so would at least imply a rudimentary framework for learning outcomes. Only Missouri attempted to measure outcomes in the major and general education statewide, with a program that allowed campuses and departments to choose from nationally normed tests and then aggregated scores to institutional and statewide levels of performance (e.g., percentages of graduates scoring above the 50th percentile on major field examinations in all four-year institutions).

But overall, the evidence suggests that state learning assessment strategies are ad hoc. Beyond the limited application of licensure examinations, they do not reflect a full understanding of how people learn, develop knowledge, and perform, and therefore it is difficult to justify their power as an accountability instrument. In most states, it is doubtful that the assessment numbers reported in these performance indicators, indirectly or only narrowly connected to campus educational practices, will be able to help a president, dean, or instructor improve teaching and learning, unless the focus is on preparing students to pass the test—a case where the output measure becomes not the proxy it was intended to be but the highly valued outcome itself.

Reprise

Virtually all states now report indicators of higher-education performance. And over half report them regularly (e.g., annually), comparing campus performances with each other, with those of a norm group, or both. Finally, states are beginning to link their indicators to clearly stated outcomes, as we saw that Texas has done. Most states use these indicators to monitor performance (performance reporting). A few use this information in budgetary decisions, but the links between data and allocations are not clear (performance budgeting). A few states have based some very small percentage of their budget allocations on performance (performance funding). The last two uses of this information have been unstable and highly dependent on economic conditions.

States' Performance Reports of Learning

Among the many indicators reported in states' performance reports, student learning dominates the discussion today. In its biennial state-by-state report card, the National Center on Public Policy and Higher Education gave states a grade of incomplete in 2000 and 2002 on its Student Learning category. States did not have sufficient information on which to form an indicator. By 2004, the landscape had not changed greatly, but NCPPHE had conducted a five-state pilot study to demonstrate how other states might collect information bearing on student cognitive learning. In its 2006 report, all but nine states received an incomplete (Figure 8.1), but the nine had regressed by 2008, when all states received an incomplete.

Today, the movement to assess learning directly has proceeded, if by fits and starts. This acceleration is seen concretely in Miller's five-state study of literacy and problem solving (Miller, 2006); the Texas Board of Regents' Accountability and Performance report measuring communication and problem solving; and the report of U.S. Secretary of Education Spelling's Commission on the Future of Higher Education, which recommended standardized tests of cognitive learning such as those provided by the CLA and MAPP (U.S. Department of Education, 2006).

Progress in measuring and reporting student learning notwithstanding, a great deal of work remains to be done. Learning in the disciplines remains largely unreported. The exception is where external accrediting agencies require accreditation or certification of academic programs (e.g., clinical psychology, engineering, nursing, and teaching). The challenges are great here because of the breadth and depth of disciplines and subdisciplines and the disagreements within them. Nevertheless, Shavelson (2007a,b) noted the possibility for learned societies (e.g., American Historical Association) working in consort with, say, the Collegiate Learning Assessment, to create measures that tap knowledge and reasoning within a discipline (see Figure 2.1; Chapter 3).

Likewise, the lacuna of learning outcomes for personal, social, moral, and civic development in these performance reports is problematic (Chapter 3). If the Spellings Commission had its way and currently available standardized tests were used to index learning, the diversity of campus missions and corresponding curricula would be threatened; narrowing college missions and curricula is not the solution. Narrowing flies in the face of what the public and educators recognize are highly valued college outcomes (see Chapter 2). To say, as does the ETS report on accountability (Dwyer, Millett & Payne, 2006), that measures of what ETS terms "soft skills" today are threatened by teaching to the test, and so cannot be measured, is unacceptable. The same thing was said some years ago of measuring such outcomes in K-12 mathematics and science education (Shavelson, Carey, & Webb, 1990). It was unacceptable then, and the situation has not substantially changed today. These college outcomes are simply too important to ignore; substantial resources should be allocated to devising credible ways to overcoming measurement limitations. One possibility is suggested by the Collegiate Learning Assessment. Some of the CLA's performance tasks involve issues of moral judgment, of trade-offs between equally desirable outcomes involving social and personal impact, and the like. Perhaps this approach might be expanded so that moral, social, civic, and personal outcomes are recognized as equally cognitively demanding, plus some, and highly regarded. The measurement limitations should not narrow college outcomes in an accountability system. The unintended consequences that follow are unacceptable.

Changing State Role in Assessment and Accountability: Clash of Cultures

Over the past twenty years, states have moved from providing campuses more institutional assessment autonomy to providing them less, from focusing on internal quality improvement to focusing on compliance, and from assessment for improvement to assessment for accountability. In this shift, we have seen emerge an increasing demand by actors responsible for ensuring quality education—policy makers and state higher-education board members—for more transparency in campuses reporting on their performance. Reputation and selectivity are no longer adequate assurances in light of increases in the number and diversity of students entering colleges, tuition costs, need for remediation, and decreases in graduates' performance, at least as measured by NAALS. Likewise, consumers (see Figure 6.1) have called for more and better comparative information among campuses.

In contrast, college leaders and faculty have a culture of shared governance. Faculty are responsible for curriculum and teaching, administrators for running the academy (see Figure 6.1). While faculty and administrators debate governance issues fiercely, they are pretty much united in their culture of shared governance when confronted with external accountability by those outside the academy.

These "cultural conflicts" have led policy makers and consumers to distrust campus leaders and to claim that accreditation as currently practiced does not meet their needs. The fundamental criticism of accreditation—an accountability mechanism created by colleges and universities but serving a key accountability function for the federal government—is that comparative information among campuses on a reasonable set of important indicators has not been forthcoming. An accreditation thumbs-up or thumbs-down is no longer satisfactory to consumers. Moreover, the claim that accreditation information is used by campuses for improvement is beginning to fall on deaf ears.

State policy makers and higher-education boards have felt the sting of "information asymmetry" (Chapter 6). Neither they nor parents and students have adequate information for making comparative decisions among campuses and acting on those decisions for the purpose of allocating budgets, sanctioning or rewarding performance (policy makers), or making choices among campuses (parents, students, and those government and private-sector organizations seeking research and training). The states' vision, then, is one of summative accountability providing comparative information to policy makers and higher-education staff for top-down oversight, and to parents and students and other "customers" to inform bottom-up demand (see Figure 6.1).

However, campus leaders, in turn, distrust policy makers. Performance indicators are typically just numbers; only when they are interpreted to fit into some plausible, culturally supported narrative—e.g., "Colleges are failing our students and the public"—do they come to have meaning and impact. As pointed out in Chapter 7, such accounts have the potential to mislead and do a great deal of mischief before course corrections can be made. When policy makers put their own partisan political spin on such indicators, ignoring context with sound bites and often negative statements accompanied by simplistic policy solutions, campus leaders rightly recognize that the well-being, and even the existence, of their institutions could be in jeopardy.

Some have called the situation a crisis in confidence and commitment (e.g., Naughton, 2004). State officials are not confident that their campuses are providing the quality of education that the officials have, in the past, assured the public of; their commitment of financial and other support has dwindled substantially. Campus leaders distrust state officials' political spins and quick-fix policies that could negatively affect their campuses. Their commitment has correspondingly decreased in states with rapidly increasing enrollments and rapidly decreasing financial and political support. Is there a common ground? If so, what is it? At one time, state higher-education boards were supposed to serve a buffer function. Today, this does not appear to be the case. A common ground needs to be found. In the final chapter, we will return to this theme and present possible alternative paths for progress.

Performance Reports and Report Cards: Instruments for Reform

The good news, then, is that states have stepped up and demanded that campuses account for their performance. In many states, the public, policy makers, and educators now have a wealth of information available, and direct measures of student learning are beginning to make their way into those indicators.

The bad news is that in many states the public, policy makers, and educators have a wealth of information available—an overwhelming amount. Much of the information has not been synthesized adequately, and some of it is not always the kind on which to make informed decisions, especially for campus improvement or college attendance. The challenge to states and to those who design accountability systems is to collect and report, as simply as possible, information that can be used for educational improvement (formative function of accountability) with summary information that provides comparative information to policy makers and consumers of higher education. Misalignment of these two is likely to be costly and lead to negative, unintended consequences (Linn, 2000).

Report cards are one possible policy instrument for simplifying and conveying information to responsible state officials, consumers, and education leaders. Report cards have the potential for stimulating change and improvement. For example, Gormley and Weimer (1999) provided a rationale for and evidence that report cards stimulated considerable improvement in the HMO health care sector.

The appeal of report cards such as *U.S. News*' college rankings lies in their simplicity and comprehensibility. At a glance, the reader sees and can readily interpret rankings of campuses overall and on a small set of readily understood categories. These rankings noticeably affect campus behavior, but often this behavior is more symbolic than substantive (e.g., Diver, 2005; McDonough et al., 1998; but see Ehrenberg, 2002). NCPPHE's state-by-state higher-education report card provides an example of what a state report card might look like (although not all categories would necessarily be the same). NCPPHE takes a large amount of data, forms a set of indicators for each of its six categories, and gives weights to each indicator in getting a category score that is reported as a grade (A–F and incomplete).

The states have not gone as far as producing a true report card. Moreover, it is not clear whether moving in this direction would encourage campuses within a state to improve their performance substantively, to respond symbolically by massaging the numbers, or even to face going out of business perhaps in a region where it is the only provider. Given the complexity and number of outcomes balanced by higher-education institutions and the wide variety of missions and students served, the simplicity of report cards may do more mischief than good. Indeed, although NCPPHE's true report card has gained the attention of state policy makers (sometimes in protest), it has not been transformative. I suspect this might be so because the state as a whole may not be the best unit of analysis, given the heterogeneity of institutions within each state.

The benchmark indicators reported by Texas, and many other states, reflect the current compromise between campuses and states; neither strong positive nor strong negative consequences have emerged. However, synergy between state indicators of performance and accreditation's demand for learning outcomes has moved campuses to change, and in more than just symbolic ways. Perhaps some combination of mechanisms, then, might move campus improvement forward in a positive way, a topic to be taken up in the last chapter.

Appendix A

A coding scheme was used to catalogue information about state higher-education report cards and classify the reports' performance indicators (see Table 8.4). Judgments were made as to the performance indicator *type*—input, process, output, or outcome—based on definitions by Gormley and Weimer (1999). Critical to the analysis, key words were assigned to each indicator (e.g., faculty, research, or learning). A duplicate coding of eight states, conducted independently by two graduate students, tested the reliability of data coding. This check showed nearly 95 percent agreement on all coding; discrepancies were primarily related to the level of aggregation of particular performance indicators (i.e., whether an indicator was coded as one system-wide indicator or as two indicators separately reporting two- and four-year sectors).

Table 8.4. State Higher-Education Report Cards Database: Information Collected

State Report Card Information

- State higher-education agency or board
    - agency or board name
    - agency or board URL
- Accountability program
    - program name
    - program mandate origin (agency/board, legislature, governor, combination, other)
    - program mandate description (including enabling legislation or policy order)
    - program model (whether absolute, relative, or approximate performance expectations are defined)
    - program's ordinal system (whether "grades" or other rankings are used)
    - program's budgetary implications
- Report card
    - report title
    - report date
    - report URL
    - report addressed to or produced for whom
    - report addressed from or produced by whom
    - other notes (including frequency of updates, information on changes, etc.)

Performance Indicator Information

- Performance indicator description
    - indicator name
    - indicator description
    - indicator key words
    - indicator type (input, process, output, or outcome)
    - indicator reporting form (number, percentage, rank, grade, etc.)
    - level of aggregation in reporting (institution, system, sector, and/or statewide)
    - broader goal or outcome under which indicator falls in report
    - who defined indicator (legislature, board, institution)
- Performance indicators related to learning—additional information
    - whether a direct or indirect measure of learning
    - cognitive outcome measured (from Shavelson and Huang [2003] framework)
    - if direct measure, instrument(s) used

SOURCE: R. Shavelson.

Appendix B

Table 8.5. State Higher-Education Report Cards

State	Report Card Title	Year
Arizona	Arizona University System 2000 Report Card	2000
California	Performance Indicators of California Higher Education 2001	2002
Colorado	Performance Funding Process and Quality Indicator System for FY 2001–2002	2001
Connecticut	Higher Education Counts: Accountability Measures for the New Millennium (vol. 1)	2001
Florida	State Universities' Accountability Report	2002
Hawaii	University of Hawaii Institutional Effectiveness Report	2000
Kentucky	Key Indicators of Progress Toward Postsecondary Reform	2002
Louisiana	Trend and Statistics in Louisiana Public Postsecondary Education: 2000 Accountability Report	2000
Missouri	Striving for Excellence—Progress Report 2002	2002
New Jersey	Higher Education in New Jersey: The Sixth Annual Systemwide Accountability Report	2002
New Mexico	Aiming for Excellence: An Accountability Report on New Mexico Public Higher Education	1999
North Carolina	Accountability Overview and Report on Campus Visits in Academic Year 2001–2002	2001
North Dakota	Creating a University for the 21st Century: 2nd Annual Accountability Measures Report	2002
Ohio	Profile of Student Outcomes, Experiences, and Campus Measures	2002
Oklahoma	Report Card on Oklahoma Higher Education	2001
Oregon	Measuring Our Performance, Planning Our Success	2001
South Carolina	A Closer Look at Public Higher Education in South Carolina	2003
South Dakota	The State of Public Higher Education—1998	1998
Tennessee	The Status of Higher Education in Tennessee	2001
Texas	Texas Public Universities' Data and Performance Report	2002
Utah	Biennial Assessment and Accountability Report 2000	2000
Virginia	Reports of Institutional Effectiveness	2002
Washington	Performance Accountability: 1999–2000 Academic Year Review and Recommendations for 2001–2003	2000
West Virginia	West Virginia Higher Education Report Card 2002	2002
Wisconsin	Achieving Excellence: The University of Wisconsin System Accountability Report 2000–2001	2001
Wyoming	University of Wyoming FY 2000 Performance Report to the Governor	2000

SOURCE: R. Shavelson.

9 Higher-Education Accountability Outside the United States

UP TO THIS POINT, assessment and accountability as they are conceived and practiced in the United States have been scrutinized. This chapter steps outside the United States to see what other countries are doing to hold their higher-educations systems accountable. More specifically, major trends in accountability in higher education internationally are characterized, drawing largely on the European experience. As will be seen, other countries approach accountability in a somewhat different manner than our states (although many of the same tensions exist). Other countries employ a version of accreditation but then incorporate total quality management approaches into what they call "quality assurance." And, indeed, some U.S. accrediting agencies and states are following their lead and beginning to incorporate quality assurance practices, as well.

This chapter provides a broad overview of quality assurance by first exploring the rise, context, and objectives of quality assurance, then by taking a closer look at three oft-implemented types of quality assurance programs—academic audit, subject assessment, and research assessment. The chapter concludes by considering the emerging role of multilateral organizations and the internationalization of quality assurance in higher education. The aim is to offer insight into how the United States might evolve its assessment and accountability systems, balancing academic, governmental, and consumer expectations and demands.

The Rise of Quality Assurance in Higher Education Worldwide

In the past two decades, universities worldwide have experienced historic changes—massive increases in the number and diversity of students in Europe (Alexander, 2000; El-Khawas, DePietro-Jurand & Holm-Nielsen, 1998); tightening of public funding with resultant overburdened facilities, staffs, and resources (e.g., libraries, scientific equipment; Alexander, 2000); internationalization and greater competition (Dill, 2001) with reduced government support; and an expansion of higher-education aims to include diverse student needs, public service, and life-long learning (Dill, 2000b; Floud, 2006). In this rapidly changing environment, as at the turn of the last century and after World War II (see Chapter 6) in the United States, concerns have arisen about the balance between equity and excellence (Dill, 2003b) and about how to ensure and improve academic standards in research and student learning (Dill, 2003a). As informal quality assurance—professional authority—alone no longer holds sway (Alexander, 2000), government actors have sought to ensure quality in addition (Lewis, 2004), going beyond the more traditional concerns of access and cost (Dill, 2003a).

Comprehensive quality assurance began in the mid-1980s in response to these changes and the possibility of quality dilution. European governments began creating agencies and systems to evaluate the quality of higher education.[1] In 1985 the French government established the first national quality evaluation agency, the Comité National d'Evaluation (CNE), and Dutch universities set up the Association of Universities of Professional Education. In 1989 the Association of Universities in the Netherlands was created to oversee quality assurance in Dutch universities (Lewis, 2004). In Hong Kong, the Netherlands, and the United Kingdom (UK), quality assurance was initially developed for the nonuniversity sector of higher education because of quality concerns about these "less esteemed institutions," but it quickly became apparent that systematic evaluation of the university sector would be useful, as well (Lewis, 2004). By 2000 almost all countries in the European Union (EU), as well as many countries in Africa, Asia, and South America and a number of U.S. states, were experimenting with new forms of academic quality regulation (Dill, 2003b). According to Lewis (2004), fifty-six countries worldwide have established a reasonably comprehensive national system of quality assurance or are in the process of developing such a system.

To see how quality assurance provided a reasonable compromise or solution to the accountability challenge, consider the three forces shaping the behavior of higher-education institutions—professional authority, state authority, and the market (see Chapter 6; Clark, 1983; Burke & Associates, 2005). Policy makers turned to quality assurance as a way to maintain their country's oversight role and hold higher-education institutions, in all their diversity, accountable. In return for increased autonomy through reduced governmental control over budgets and programs (at least rhetorical autonomy; see Floud, 2006), colleges were to be held accountable within a framework of government priorities (Dill, 2001). In this way governments sought to increase economic efficiency, quality of outcomes, and accountability (Godegebuure et al., 1994; Lewis, 2004). Quality assurance, then, maintained government influence in a new environment in which the forces of competition and consumer demand significantly influenced the behavior of higher-education institutions.

As a case in point, consider Denmark. This country experienced a massive increase in the number of students applying for higher education in the past two decades of the 20th century. This led to concern that with expansion, academic quality would decline. This concern was deepened by constraints on public spending, triggering an increased focus on efficiency and effectiveness. In return for more autonomy to decide how to allocate resources internally, programs had to be evaluated by a new national agency, the Centre for Quality Assurance and Evaluation of Higher Education (since 1999, the Danish Evaluation Institute [EVA]). Furthermore, Denmark's and the EU's international commitments meant that Denmark had to ensure a certain level of quality in its academic programs as a member of a larger community (Stensaker, 2003, 2004).

Mechanisms for Quality Assurance

Quality assurance programs adapted Demming's total quality management approach to education with its focus on quality processes. These processes are "*organized activities dedicated to improving and assuring education and research quality. They systematize a university's approach to quality instead of leaving it mainly to unmonitored individual initiative*" (Massy, 2003, p. 159; italics in original).

Three mechanisms have commonly been used for quality assurance: academic audits, subject or program assessments, and research assessments. Quality assurance is described generally below, and then each mechanism is described in turn, exemplifying and contextualizing these mechanisms with examples from specific countries and cross-country comparisons.

Commonality and Variability Among Forms of Quality Assurance

Regardless of the audit mechanism, quality assurance tends to follow a similar process model (e.g., European Association for Quality Assurance in Higher Education, 2005; for more on this general model, see Lewis, 2004; European Network for Quality Assurance, 2003; Brennan & Shah, 2000). The commonality among quality assurance programs grew out of wide-scale borrowing of ideas and procedures, and from the traditional academic review process, which included self-review and external, expert teams (e.g., El-Khawas, DePietro-Jurand & Holm-Nielsen, 1998). However what is evaluated and how the evaluation is used differ among the mechanisms.

Commonalities among countries' quality assurance processes, El-Khawas, De-Pietro-Jurand & Holm-Nielsen (1998) suggested, arose from wide-scale cultural borrowing in quality assurance programs. The authors also pointed out that the programs have much in common because they are a modification of the traditional academic review process, which often includes self-study and input from external academic experts.

Quality assurance procedures, however, vary as to (1) funding and control of the agency conducting the evaluation; (2) the unit evaluated (a program, a course of study, or the institution); (3) whether comparative reports or just general results are made public; and (4) whether there is a form of summative grade or consequence of the report (Lewis, 2004). For example, many quality assurance systems across Europe have comparable elements but vary on funding and whether they have a program or an institution as the focus of review. Governments fund quality assurance agencies, but more than a quarter of such agencies are funded indirectly by the government through higher-education institutions (European Network for Quality Assurance, 2003). Differences across units are even prevalent. For example, Denmark, the Netherlands, and Portugal have focused on academic reviews; whereas France began with institutional evaluation devolving to both institutional and program reviews. Some universities in Germany adopted institutional audits; others adopted institution-wide reviews. In the UK, institutional, program, and research reviews have been conducted.

These differences across Europe highlight one of the most significant differences in quality assurance programs. When the focus of quality assurance is on the institution, such as in academic audits, the principle is to examine and support institutions in ensuring the quality of their programs (Lewis, 2004; Brennan & Shah, 2000). In contrast, program reviews and subject assessments judge the quality of a program (Lewis, 2004). These judgments may have consequences for an individual department in the form of accreditation, funding, public esteem, or some combination.

Program review appears to be more widely used than institutional review (European Network for Quality Assurance, 2003). Program and subject reviews have been particularly popular in smaller countries, such as the Netherlands and Denmark, because it is possible to review all the programs in a given discipline in a short period with a single team of external peers (Lewis, 2004). An international survey of quality agencies revealed that while improvement was the first objective of quality assurance agencies, accountability and accreditation were second (Lewis, 2004). Furthermore, quality assurance agencies in Europe are now facing new demands, such as providing some sort of evidence of quality, as institutions must now comply with the requirements of the Bologna Process (for more on this, see New Force for Quality Assurance: The Bologna Process).

Impact of Quality Assurance Systems

The impact of quality assurance has varied across different types of systems and countries. El-Khawas, DePietro-Jurand & Holm-Nielsen (1998) argued that these programs resulted in institutions focusing more intently on issues related to effective teaching and learning. However, the impact depended on what was included in the quality assurance system. For example, if degree completion rates were included in the system, more attention was paid to student services and advising (El-Khawas, DePietro-Jurand & Holm-Nielsen, 1998). If the system focused on the institution, institutional management and strategic planning improved (Brennan & Shah, 2000). This said, it is hard to know if these were substantive changes, because often they were found through reports published by the institutions themselves.

There have been negative consequences, as well. Quality assurance systems may lead to excessive paperwork and "compliance" behavior—making improvements just to satisfy the assurance program (El-Khawas, DePietro-Jurand & Holm-Nielsen, 1998). When comparative results are reported, often there are few surprises; reputational rankings provide roughly the same information. Furthermore, quality assurance programs can be difficult to sustain, as they depend on political support; they may not survive leadership changes.

Quality assurance programs have, not surprisingly, intensified tension between policy makers and higher-education administrators and faculty (Alexander, 2000; Floud, 2006; Crosier, Purser & Smidt, 2007). This is partially because quality assurance mandates often come at a time when higher-education institutions are expected to do more with less. Furthermore, as we have seen, governments and higher-education administrators and faculty have different interests (see Chapter 6). Governments focus on summative accountability and often prefer to use indicators that show institutional efficiency, consumer satisfaction, graduates' career success, and value for money; they also often seek to compare institutions' productivity and performance. University administrators and faculty focus on formative accountability and prefer measures that reflect their own institutions' specific missions; they also often want to use reporting only in a noncompetitive manner for improving performance.

Initial resistance to change and defense of academe's traditional methods of quality assurance have waned, and, overall, academics eventually conceded that the new pressures on higher education (e.g., large-scale massive growth, "massification," and fiscal constraints) have made external methods of quality control an emerging consensus (Crosier, Purser & Smidt, 2007; Floud, 2006).

Types of Quality Assurance Mechanisms

Under the umbrella of quality assurance can be found three common approaches: *academic audits*, which have an institutional focus on teaching and learning; *program assessments*, which have a departmental focus on teaching and learning; and *research assessments*, which have a focus on research productivity and quality.

Academic Audits

Academic audits focus on the *organized processes and procedures* that a higher-education institution uses to ensure its academic standards. Unlike accreditation, an audit does not seek to review an institution's activities or programs. Instead, an audit evaluates the processes an institution has put in place to ensure quality. What procedures, for example, does the institution have to ensure that the standards it has created for itself are met (Dill, 2003)? The focus of an academic audit, then, is on quality work rather than quality per se (Massy, 2005).

Audits evaluate whether institutions and their faculties honor their public responsibility to monitor academic standards and improve student learning (Dill, 2000a,c). Academic audits thus offer a measure of public accountability by providing assurance that universities are serious about academic quality, even when subject to increasing market pressures and less direct government control (Dill, 2003). Furthermore, note that the focus of the audit on institutional quality assurance processes may be a more appropriate form of accountability than a focus on summative outcomes, given the evolution of higher-education institutions as self-regulating learning organizations (Dill, 2000b).

The academic audit follows a general model. In this case, it has an institutional focus, aimed at quality processes. Academic audits include a self-evaluation or submission of institutional documents related to quality processes, a peer review and a published report, and some form of follow-up (European Association for Quality Assurance in Higher Education, 2005; see also Dill, 2000a,b; Massy, 1997, 1999). Academic audit programs differ in composition and continuity of external review teams, distribution of reports, and type of follow-up activities.

Self-Evaluation.   The first stage of the academic audit process is the audit submission, in which institutions are required to prepare and submit documents describing their quality processes. These institutional submissions have evolved over time as teams gained a better understanding of what kinds of information is effective in the review (Dill, 2000b). Initially, the submissions were open ended, often resulting in a mountain of documents. This was partially a result of institutions themselves being unclear as to what exactly was being reviewed. Over time submissions devolved into a short, thoughtful account of quality assurance processes (a self-study) that informed both the institution itself and the external auditors, the audit team (Dill, 2000b).

External Peer Review.   The second stage of the academic audit process involves an audit team visiting the site. The team represents an external review body that receives the audit submission. In all countries audit teams typically include senior-level academics; sometimes one or more members are drawn from other countries. These teams appear to be uncontroversial and receive little criticism, most likely due to the tradition of the academic review process that preceded external quality assurance mechanisms. Yet each team reflects a country's unique traditions.

The audit team reviews the institution's submission prior to the site visit and holds a meeting to identify significant issues and decide whether additional written materials may be necessary, as well as to develop an agenda for the visit. Once on site, teams spend anywhere from a day and a half in Hong Kong to four days in the UK reviewing the institution. Typically, the agencies responsible for conducting the audits organize preparatory meetings with the institution to introduce audit team members and answer questions about the process.

To ensure quality, teams look at institutions for evidence of a "culture of quality," in which effective interaction is seen across differential institutional levels (e.g., Crosier, Purser & Smidt, 2007; Stensaker, 1999a). Site visits in both the UK and Hong Kong, for example, look for this culture. In the UK this is done by tracing a particular issue, such as design of curriculum, through the different levels of the institution to examine the process's effectiveness. In Hong Kong, the audit team first reviews quality processes at the institutional level. Then it focuses on academic units selected by the team for discussion with students and faculty about quality assurance processes. These approaches seem more effective than a superficial audit visit with a set of various institutional actors without particular focus (Dill, 2000a).

Audit Report.   After the site visit, the audit team drafts a report for the institution. The report's creation is similar to other processes in higher education—team members draft segments, and the overall process is coordinated by the audit chair. Usually, the report is viewed and commented upon by the institution prior to publication.

In all academic audit systems, *publication of the audit report is viewed as one of the most significant forms of accountability* resulting from the audit (Dill, 2000b). Audit evaluations indicate that publication of the institutional report increases the importance placed on the process by the institutions (e.g. Brennan, de Vries & Williams, 1997).

Follow-up Activities.   After the report's publication, follow-up activities often take place. There is a broad range of such activities, which include continued discussion and workshops with quality assurance organizations and progress reports.

Audit Impact.   Literature and case studies on academic audits reveal generally positive outcomes associated with the process. Dill (2000c) described the overall outcomes of audits as assisting universities to better approximate "learning organizations" by developing capacity and knowledge transfer for continuous improvement of academic activities. Specifically, audits helped make improving teaching and student learning an institutional priority (Dill 2000a,b). *The publicity generated through the audit process and the published report placed external pressure on the institutions for change, leading to active discussion of how to improve teaching and learning.* This was especially strong in Sweden and Hong Kong, where institutions and departments were encouraged to contribute to the process (Brennan et al., 1999; Stensaker, 1999a). The audit process also makes clear that the responsibility for improving teaching and learning lies at all institutional levels, even though the audits often revealed that many institutions avoided taking responsibility for such activities (see Massy 1997, 1999). Overall, then, the audit appears to set in motion a process of self-reflection and continuing attention to quality (Henkel, 2000). Indeed, external attention generated by the audit enables large and complex universities to bring about positive changes in teaching and research (Henkel, 2000).

Academic audits have limitations. Both the academy and the audit teams require a considerable amount of time to learn audit processes. Indeed, when audits were initiated, neither auditors nor those being audited had clear conceptions of what constituted an academic quality assurance process (Dill, 2000b). Both groups reported confusion as to the difference between academic objectives, and

outcomes and processes. In some cases, with experience, this confusion was recti-
fied. For example, it became clear that in order to achieve maximum effectiveness, auditors and academics found that audits needed to have a narrow focus on
quality processes related to teaching and learning at the academic-unit level for
change to take place. In another example, England's audit was criticized because
it seemed to involve only a small minority of academic staff, with only trickle
down to other members of the faculty, rather than the ideal of involving every academic (Henkel, 2000), a concern addressed in subsequent audits.

Australia's audit process had an unintended consequence, as it appeared to
lead to a "game mentality." Universities focused on using the audit process to look
good and be placed in the highest tier. It appeared that university rankings were
more important than improving quality or even receiving additional grant
money. To this end, overseas consultants were hired to prepare the audit portfolio,
and the university provided coaching to university staff and faculty to impress reviewers. At least initially there was a decline in the diversity among institutions, as
all tried to act like the older institutions, which received the highest rankings
(Massaro, 1997).

The academic audit does not necessarily change some of the fundamental internal challenges universities face in improving teaching. Even if there were more
thought given to quality of teaching, this did not change incentives—institutional
and individual academic reputations and funding continued to be related to research records (Henkel, 2000). Moreover, the emphasis on process—as opposed
to outcomes—made it difficult to justify the academic audit to successive governments and the public (Dill, 2000c; see Chapter 7 on process-outcome trade-offs in
accountability). The guiding principle behind audits—that improvement in quality assurance processes related to teaching and learning will lead to improved
academic outcomes—is extremely difficult to prove; audits may be politically un-
sustainable in some countries.

Subject Assessment

Subject assessments are carried out by external agencies and focus on the
quality processes that an academic department uses to monitor, feedback, and
improve teaching and learning. The first such assessment was carried out by
the Association of Dutch Universities (VSNU) in the late 1980s; it has greatly
influenced quality assessment practices in other countries (Brennan & Shah,
2000).

In a subject assessment, graded academic-quality judgments are typically
made about academic programs (Dill, 2003, 2000b). Subject assessments have

been used in Denmark, the Netherlands, and the UK and to a more limited extent in Mexico. Similar programs based on a Dutch model have been used in Flanders, Belgium, and Lower Saxony, Germany. These programs appear more likely to be found in smaller countries (or states), as it is easier to conduct a nationwide assessment and to compare all programs in a particular discipline (EVA, 2003).

The subject assessment closely follows the general quality assurance model, including self-study, external review, public report, and follow-up. To characterize the subject assessment, consider Denmark. The Danish Evaluation Institute conducted a preliminary study to identify programs to be included in the assessment and established objectives for the assessment.[2] Up to ten programs would typically be reviewed, and information was collected on the following: management, organization and content, methods of teaching, student progression, internationalization, and, in some cases, link with national policy objectives.

In the first step in the subject assessment the department drafts a self-evaluation following the EVA's detailed protocol. While the unit is in the process of completing the self-evaluation, EVA sends a comprehensive survey on the program's quality to users (students, graduates, or employers). The survey is meant to provide additional perspectives on the departments and the subject field as a whole.

In the next step, an external committee of experts visits the department, focusing on academic content (Brennan & Shah, 2000). The external committee typically gathers information by interviewing academic staff, administrators, and students. The committee's work emphasizes sound methods and observer triangulation as part of the process (Stensaker, 2003, 2004). The same committee usually visits all of the study programs within the country. Research in Denmark, however, suggests that as the number of programs increases, institutions perceive lower benefit (Stensaker, 2003, 2004).[3]

The third step in the Danish assessment process is the findings report. Following the external visit, the expert committee drafts a report presenting both an overall perspective on the quality of the programs at a national level and separate analyses of each of the departments. Before publication, the draft version is provided to the departments at a conference, where issues related to the report are discussed. The final report on the quality of the programs is made available to the public and includes the self-evaluation report and the survey results. Public release of the report is often covered in the newspapers and is sometimes the subject of significant public debate (Stensaker, 2003, 2004).

Note that, in contrast to academic (institutional) audits, subject assessment reports provide some form of judgment about program quality. For example, the goal of the assessment in the Netherlands is accountability and improvement. As a result, the final report provides indicators of the quality of each of the programs assessed and how the programs might be improved.

The fourth step is follow-up. The Danish National Education Councils have responsibility for following up to see if departments have moved to address the reports' recommendations. However, neither the institutions nor the departments are mandated to follow the recommendations as long as the department has sound reasons for not doing so (Stensaker, 2003). Brennan and Shah (2000) suggested that, as a result, the typical effect of the Danish assessment is to change institutional cultures and increase motivation for focusing on improved teaching and learning.

However, follow-up and consequences related to the subject assessment vary widely from country to country. The consequences can range from recommendations for improvement in Mexico to bad press in Denmark, to eliminating programs from a recognized list of programs, to modest funding allocation changes in the UK. In the Netherlands, for example, the assessment has more of a control orientation than in Denmark (Stensaker, 2003; Brennan & Shah, 2000). The inspector of higher education may take action if a program experienced a poor assessment. The inspectorate would further investigate the institution, which could result in the department being removed from the recognized list of funded programs. In reality, in the 1990s only a few programs were investigated by the inspectorate, and none of the programs was closed as a result of the investigation. The institutions were seen as making satisfactory progress toward improvement.

The UK's subject assessments in the 1990s were oriented more toward evaluating different programs than initiating improvement processes in the institutions (Brennan & Shah, 2000). Subject assessment included linking some modest funding to judgments about quality of teaching and learning (Alexander, 2000). In the UK, then, a summative judgment was made of the program. The outcome could lead to a change in the status or reputation of the program.

A number of positive consequences have emerged from the subject assessment process. In the UK, research on the effects of subject assessments shows that they increased concern for teaching and learning among university faculty (Henkel, 2000). They also appeared to have increased communication and collaboration among faculty on teaching activities and the development of mechanisms within universities to ensure faculty accountability for quality (Henkel,

2000). In Denmark, an impact study indicated that the program assessments continued to influence Danish higher education even in the second round of evaluations (Stensaker, 2003). Moreover, university faculty and staff continued to have a positive view of the subject assessments, possibly because of the absence of a performance indicator system (Stensaker, 2003). Finally, actions were taken on about 60 percent of the expert committee's recommendations.

The typical result of the subject assessment is increased dialogue and reflection at the institution (Massy, 1999; Stensaker, 1999a,b). This often triggers changes in curriculum structure or teaching methods. There does not appear to be a decline in the effect of the subject assessments as institutions learn the process and "tricks" that might be used to look good. Stensaker (2003) argued that because the evaluations mainly stimulate dialogue and reflection, "strategic" behavior by institutions might be less likely.

The overall effect of subject assessments appears to be fairly limited, and this quality assurance mechanism has a series of limitations. For example, subject assessments are time consuming and expensive (Stensaker, 2003; Henkel, 2000), and small countries may not have enough experts to allow for peers to review in all subjects (Dill, 2003). This is especially true as universities rapidly develop interdisciplinary programs. For example, in Denmark, subject assessments have not focused as heavily on ensuring quality in new study programs. As a result, Stensaker (2003) suggested that the system is more oriented toward a general form of accountability in a relatively stable system than toward one characterized by rapid change. One consequence is that students and public authorities have limited information about programs. As universities develop their own, more sophisticated systems for management and evaluation, external subject reviews may be seen as superfluous and unproductive (Dill, 2003); indeed, high-level university leadership in Denmark, the Netherlands, and the UK have called for institutional control of program review (Dill, 2000a,b). And as we shall see, ministers of education in European countries have gone on record placing primary responsibility for quality assurance on the institutions themselves (Crosier, Purser & Smidt, 2007).

In addition to broad limitations, there are also some country-specific critiques of the subject assessments. Critiques of the Danish assessment (Stensaker, 2003) are particularly instructive and may be summarized as follows:

• lack of follow-up and incentives for institutions to follow recommendations
• initially, a lack of focus on quality *processes* in place for program improvement and more of a focus on traditional academic content

- initially, a top-down procedure with lack of program input into the process for program improvement purposes
- a tendency to separate institutional leaders from program leaders in the review process

Denmark continued its systematic subject assessment programs but introduced new forms of evaluation at different institutional levels, as well as institutional audits. These programs sought to maintain the dual goals of accountability and improvement (Kristoffersen, 2003).

In the UK, there was a sense that the assessment was just more paperwork that had to be completed, and that it did not provide substantive improvements (Henkel, 2000). In addition, there was a feeling that the assessment had orthodoxies for what represented quality teaching that did not necessarily improve student learning (Henkel, 2000).

Subject assessment programs, like academic audits, rarely retain the same form for a long period of time. In the UK, the Quality Assurance Agency moved away from a comprehensive application of program review, but institutions were still required to demonstrate that they were in compliance with subject benchmarks. Lewis (2004) suggested that this change showed how a government can maintain some leverage on curriculum without engaging in a full-fledged program review.

In the Netherlands, the assessment evolved into a more outputs-based assessment through the introduction of accreditation. This change came about in conjunction with the introduction of the bachelor-master structure in Dutch higher education and the need for a formal quality label as part of the Bologna Process (in which European countries have agreed to have an open education area in Europe by 2010). Programs now must be accredited to receive funding by the state, to have their diplomas recognized, and for students to receive financial loans (EVA, 2003).

Research Assessment Exercise

In the mid 1980s, the UK and Mexico introduced Research Assessment Exercises (RAE), which used research quantity and publication-source quality indicators to judge departments (e.g., Brennan & Shah, 2000). In the 1990s Hong Kong followed suit (e.g., French et al., 1999, 2001; Massy, 1997). In the first part of this decade other countries in the commonwealth, including Australia, Ireland, and New Zealand, developed research assessment exercises. The purpose of these assessments was to provide incentives for higher-education institutions to produce high-quality research, strengthen their research culture, and improve performance management systems (Massy, 2005). In addition, these programs sought to allocate resources to institutions and departments that exhibited high levels of research intensity.

Here we focus on the UK, as it is perhaps the most instructive case. The Research Assessment Exercise was introduced during massification, while at the same time the government was reducing higher-education expenditures. The RAE was viewed as a way to strengthen international competitiveness and protect the quality of research in Britain's major universities by channeling scarce funding to institutions and departments with high-quality research (Roberts, 2003). Henkel (2000) described the RAE as a new form of academic evaluation that changed processes of peer review into a comprehensive national assessment—a single periodic and highly public event that linked research resources for four to five years to a simple formula. Alexander (2000) described this as a form of performance funding (see Chapter 7) in which the government determined departmental research budgets based on performance indicators, including a measure of output (number and quality of publications), a measure of impact (the number of citations), and peer review.

While the program in the UK began in the 1985–86 academic year, it was fully institutionalized by 1992, as all higher-education institutions wishing to receive funding had to participate. By 1996 the exercise had changed to assess the work of each individual researcher in subject groups rather than assessing the work of the subject group as a unit (Henkel, 2000). To this end, each department submitted a list of active research staff, along with a list of publications, the number of research students, and external research funds received by each staff member, as well as an outline of future research plans. An external panel of peer reviewers evaluated the submissions. Quality of publication was the most important criterion, and departments were given a grade ranging from one to five stars.

Performance on the RAE determined almost all of the allocation of research funds by the Funding Councils. The two lowest grades did not have money attached to them. Each grade above the minimum received a reward with a 50 percent higher reward per grade above the minimum. As a results, changes in grades had real consequences for institutions; the funds could make a significant difference in research income (depending on the subject and the institution). This process stratified institutions and departments tangibly as well as symbolically, because the RAE signaled the best research departments to other funding sources, as well as the government. Research went from individual responsibility to one of significant departmental interest and had major consequences for individuals who were not considered research active (Henkel, 2000).

The RAE has had perhaps the clearest set of consequences of any of the forms of quality assurance considered here. Henkel (2000) argued that research assessment became one of the most important influences on academic institutions, both because of funding allocations and because of how it accorded status in a way that was comprehensible to the public. The RAE compelled institutions to think more strategically, creating goals, structures, and staffing to maximize research-related funding. This led institutions through their senior leadership to increase the level of effort on research, including incentives and support structures for research.

The RAE proved successful in selectively allocating limited research funds (Boston, 2002). Traditionally strong universities—Cambridge, Oxford, University College London, and Imperial College—received almost 25 percent of available funds. This meant that although some universities received £50–60 million annually, many other universities—especially former polytechnics that were granted university status in 1992—received less than £1 million. In other words, the RAE process concentrated research support, and this led to the closure of some lower-rated departments (Henkel, 2000). It is important to note here that even in countries committed to the RAE process, such as the UK, the proportion of funds allocated using the RAE has decreased over time, while the proportion allocated on a competitive basis similar to that of the U.S. system has increased (Dill, 2003).

The Research Assessment Exercise has its limitations (e.g., Roberts, 2003). It has been seen as encouraging "gaming the system" to look good, as creating uncertainty in sustaining research programs, as an administrative and fiscal burden, and as an insensitive instrument for distinguishing among top (old) universities (e.g., Roberts, 2003). In the research arena, scholars found that the RAE limited the diversity of research in some disciplines by limiting accepted research to a small number of journals (Henkel, 2000; French et al., 1999; French, Massey & Young, 2001). In addition, it was seen as encouraging short-term, discipline-based research projects to the detriment of long-term research and scholarship. Moreover, there was little credit given to nontraditional outputs or publications in other venues (French et al., 1999). Not only did RAE place some limitations on research, it devalued teaching even further, because the institution's reputation and at least some portion of its funding rested on research success (Henkel, 2000). Finally, there was little recognition given to the scholarship of teaching (French et al., 1999).[4]

In the policy arena, the RAE has had its ups and downs. At one time (spring 2006) it was on the brink of elimination. But it was resurrected into a fully revised exercise in 2008, following Sir Gareth Roberts's (2003) report recommending changes. The 2008 RAE makes several significant changes to the last (2001) exercise, including distinguishing research intensive universities from others; using a profile of scores awarded to characterize an institution's performance rather than a single score; and making explicit the criteria in each subject to assess applied, practice-based, and interdisciplinary research as appropriate (www .rae.ac.uk/aboutus/changes.asp). Not surprisingly, however, the (London) *Times* summed up the profile and reported overall scores in league tables on December 18, 2008.

While the UK and Hong Kong have had research assessment systems for years, these programs have more recent histories in Australia, Ireland, and New Zealand. Ireland began its program in the late 1990s, when the Higher Education Authority introduced the Programme for Research in Third Level Institutions. As with the other programs, the idea was to enhance research capacity. This program, however, also emphasized interdisciplinary and inter-institutional collaboration, as well as increasing the quality and impact of research on teaching and learning (HEA, 2003). New Zealand introduced the Performance-Based Research Fund in 2004, focusing on research quality and improvement and moving away from a program that allocated funds based on student enrollments. The fund sought to provide incentives to increase the quality of research and support "investigator-initiated" research without undermining training or research for degree programs based on standardized and transparent information on research productivity (Ministry of Education, 2004).

New Force for Quality Assurance: The Bologna Process

For most of the twentieth century, European higher education was typically provided on a national or subnational basis to local students. Forces of globalization have changed this. Students are mobile, increasingly seeking out the best available education. Consequently, higher education is changing. Many universities based in one country offer degrees in another; others offer Internet programs.

Regional and global trade agreements further promoted the movement of services and individuals across national borders. Countries in Europe are striving to create a higher-education area by 2010 via what is known as the Bologna

Process. This creates the need for standardization and recognition of degrees across the European area and beyond (see Adelman, 2008, for overview). It also creates internal (student mobility, international marketing and export of higher education) and external (international trade agreements and organizations) pressures for quality assurance (Campbell & van der Wende, 2000).

In the United Kingdom, for example, the Quality Assurance Agency was charged with ensuring that the academic standards for collaborative transnational programs were equivalent to those at the home institution and the national subject benchmarks. And the higher-education institution granting the degree was responsible for the academic standards of all degrees given in its name. Moreover, some recipients, such as Hong Kong, Israel, Malaysia, and South Africa, required accreditation of transnational programs. Indeed, the accreditation requirement has become more difficult with the addition of online provision of courses.

Examining one internationalizing pressure—student mobility—revealed many of the changes occurring in quality assurance while also indicating some of the challenges (El-Khawas, DePietro-Jurand & Holm-Nielsen, 1998). When students enrolled in a new degree program, their previous course of study had to be evaluated and a decision made as to the level (e.g., master's or doctoral) at which the student should be placed. Quality assurance agencies, then, had also to address assessment and monitoring challenges that arose as increasing numbers of students sought to complete a degree or component of a program in another country (El-Khawas, DePietro-Jurand & Holm-Nielsen, 1998). Partly in response, European quality assurance agencies have been linked by the creation of the European Network for Quality Assurance in Higher Education (ENQA). This signals a trend. In partnership with other agencies, quality assurance agencies worldwide are taking a significant role in the development of national qualification frameworks that specify attributes that are expected of a degree holder at a specific level of education (Lewis, 2004).

One possibility for improving quality assurance is through stronger linkages written into reciprocal agreements among countries through trade and other international bodies. For example, the Washington Accord recognized the need for quality assurance in an agreement among engineering organizations by setting criteria for the equivalence of national accreditation programs for first professional degrees in Australia, Canada, Hong Kong, Ireland, New Zealand, South Africa, the UK, and the United States. Each country defined its own approach to quality assurance for entry to graduate programs and initial professional recognition. The Accord recognized each of these as valid, and observer visits and information exchanges were used to confirm continuing quality (Campbell & van der Wende, 2000).

Internationalization is clearly changing the face of higher education, and in turn there are new conditions that quality assurance must address. Paramount to these challenges is the Bologna Process (e.g., Floud, 2006). The Bologna Process reflects the evolution of quality assurance in higher education in the context of major initiatives and changes taking place in multilateral and international organizations. We note in passing that the World Trade Organization's General Agreement on Trade and Services may also significantly affect higher-education accountability worldwide (see Campbell & van der Wende, 2000; Robertson, Bonal & Dale, 2002; Rose, 2003).

In June 1999, education ministers of twenty-nine European countries signed the Bologna Declaration calling for the creation of a voluntary European Higher Education Area (cross national integrated system of higher education) to be completed by 2010. The idea was to increase the "compatibility and comparability" of European higher-education systems. Today the Bologna Process, an agreement among education ministries and universities and colleges of forty-five European countries, is at its core a commitment "to adopt the three-tiered degree structure of bachelor's, master's, and doctoral degrees. Underpinning these degree structures are agreements about quality assurance, student mobility, new ways of measuring student achievement, and the relationship between teaching and research" (Floud, 2006, p. 9). This is perhaps the most extraordinary step taken in European higher education—to try to coordinate the diversity of higher education in so many countries.

All countries participating in the European Higher Education Area must ensure a certain level of accountability, raising higher-education institutions' awareness of the potential benefits and challenges of quality assurance processes (Crosier, Purser & Smidt, 2007). Now there is a constructive discussion among institutions, quality assurance agencies, stakeholders, and public authorities, based on the agreement at the Berlin 2003 education ministers' meeting: "The primary responsibility for quality assurance lies with each institution itself and this provides the basis for real accountability of the academic system within the national quality framework" (Crosier, Purser & Smidt, 2007, p. 55). This agreement laid the foundation for adopting European standards and guidelines for internal and external quality assurance adopted at the ministers' conference in Bergen in 2005 (www.bologna-bergen2005.no/Docs/00-Main _doc/050221_ENQA_report.pdf).

One element of the process is to stimulate European cooperation in quality assurance by developing comparable criteria and benchmarks (Campbell & van der Wende, 2000). The Bologna idea of quality can be seen in the framework set up for the European Credit Transfer System (Kohler, 2003). Programs must have the following elements: (1) a coherent curricular design; (2) teaching that is coordinated with goals of student outcomes; (3) examinations related to outcomes; (4) transparency for students, stakeholders, and the general public; and (5) a means test that ensures adequate resources, including staff, books, and classrooms (Kohler, 2003). Institutions must ensure that the criteria for program quality are met by, for example, establishing basic program structures following the Bologna Agreement; ensuring program compatibility with this structure; and ensuring implementation, including providing adequate resources and monitoring results (Kohler, 2003).

Internal Accountability

As of summer 2007, European quality assurance mechanisms were being internalized by higher-education institutions. Academic program evaluations were carried out by 95 percent of participating institutions, and 72 percent carried them out regularly. Site visits confirmed that quality assurance mechanisms were in place and used at these institutions (Crosier, Purser & Smidt, 2007). Moreover, research and individual staff teaching were regularly evaluated in about 65 percent of institutions. This said, student learning services were lagging—regularly available at only 43 percent of institutions (Crosier, Purser & Smidt, 2007, p. 56). Simply put, "a significant development in . . . quality assurance . . . has been a growing focus on quality culture" (Crosier, Purser & Smidt, 2007, p. 58).

External Accountability

The main form of external quality assurance is a version of accreditation (Stensaker, 2003; Campbell & van der Wende, 2000), a means of ensuring required minimum standards of quality for students, employers, and society. For example, Germany now has an accreditation council for its bachelor's programs. In addition, the process puts pressure on countries where quality assurance systems do not exist or do not seem transparent to develop systems that will be acceptable to other countries in the Bologna Process.

The development of mutual trust across all the countries in recognizing quality assurance and accepting programs across the entire higher-education arena is an ongoing challenge. This can be seen from the institutions' perspective. In its report

(*Trends V*) to the education ministers at its spring 2007 meeting in London, the European University Association identified external accountability as its key issue (Crosier, Purser & Smidt, 2007, p. 77): "Many higher education systems are currently being held back from Bologna implementation—and thus from offering improved services to students and society—by national QA systems that are costly, offer no evidence of overall quality improvement, and stifle the institutions' capacity to respond creatively to the demands of evolving European knowledge society."

Reprise

Countries outside the United States approach accountability—typically called quality assurance—somewhat differently than we do. Whereas U.S. higher-education accountability focuses on multiple input and output indicators (now including direct and indirect measures of student learning), other countries focus on "quality processes." These are organized processes dedicated to improving teaching and learning that are existent within an institution. The focus of quality assurance is not on outcomes but on organizational structures and activities dedicated to monitoring teaching and learning, and acting for improvement purposes. Quality assurance, then, focuses on the culture of evidence within an institution and on the use of that evidence for continual improvement, a key characteristic of a "learning organization." Consequently, other countries' approaches to accountability might well inform future accountability in the United States.

Other countries widely share a four-stage quality assurance review process. The first stage is a self-review following external guidelines. The second stage is a site visit by an external team of experts building on the self-review. The third stage is the drafting of, institutional commenting on, and publishing of the review findings. And the fourth stage is follow-up, in which an external (typically governmental) agency verifies or even assists in the implementation of the review findings and recommendations.

One or any combination of three quality assurance mechanisms may be employed within a country. The first is the academic audit in which the review focuses on quality processes and their structure, with the goal of improving teaching and learning processes throughout the institution. It is the most comprehensive of the three. The second is the subject assessment, which focuses on teaching and learning processes in subject-matter programs or departments (e.g., history). It typically compares an academic department across a country's universities through rankings, scores, or score profiles. Such assessments may have direct financial impact through governmental allocations or indirect impact through market forces. The third quality assurance mechanism is the Research Assessment Exercise. It focuses on research productivity and quality. It differs from the academic audit and subject assessment in that it focuses on outputs far more than on processes. The exercise ranks, scores, or profiles research performance across institutions and may be used as a means of allocating scarce research funds.

The academic audit seems to be the most relevant of the three quality assurance mechanisms for U.S. higher-education accountability. The reasoning goes as follows: Academic departments in U.S. colleges and universities have traditionally been reviewed by external teams every six to eight years. Moreover, external agencies such as the National Academy of Sciences periodically evaluate and report rankings of academic departments. Finally, an institution's research quality and funding are accounted for through a competitive process of peer review, with the federal government being the major player. In essence, competition provides the accountability mechanism for U.S. research productivity and quality.

The following characteristics of the academic audit have particular appeal as a basis for thinking about U.S. higher-education accountability: First, the audit focuses on quality assurance *processes* and not comparisons of institutional outputs. Such a focus seems particularly well adapted to the wide diversity of higher-education institutions in the United States and consistent with the academic culture. In academic audits, institutions define their goals consistent with their missions. They put in place quality assurance mechanisms, including learning assessments, to monitor and feed back information for improving teaching and learning. And the institution is held externally accountable for meeting its goals in a rigorous manner by an external team of experts.

The second reason the academic audit appeals is that the institution is held accountable for linking its quality assurance processes up and down the institution—from the president and provost to the deans to the department chairs to the faculty and to the students. For example, it is not uncommon for an audit team to *randomly* determine, a short time before its site visit, several departments for an in-depth review of their quality processes. The time between identification and visit is too short for departments to "fake" quality teaching and learning processes. Breaks in organizational quality-process linkages raise questions about the adequacy of the processes and the quality of the education provided by the institution.

A third reason for the attractiveness of the audit is that, unlike current accreditation findings in the United States, the audit findings and recommendations are made public so that policy makers, bureaucrats, and consumers, as well as the institution itself, have access to information about quality processes. In this way these entities can judge the extent to which the institution embraces a culture of evidence in the form of a learning organization and the extent to which it is meeting its own goals.

This said, the forces impinging on U.S. higher education—professional authority, governmental authority, and the market—also impinge on other countries' higher-education institutions. However, the nature and focus of these forces are somewhat different. Specifically, tensions between professional and governmental authority are clearly evident in the Bologna Process, for example. I suspect this arises, in large part, because of the differences in funding higher education in the United States and other countries. Unlike the U.S. government, most other countries' governments are largely responsible for funding higher education directly. Consequently, throughout the twenty-year history of quality assurance in Europe, externally imposed quality assurance through government-sponsored, external agencies has had a large impact on colleges and universities. Moreover, with increased internationalization of higher education, even more governmental oversight is expected to ensure quality on the one hand and competitiveness in the marketplace on the other.

With all this pressure, however, professional authority has continued to challenge governmental authority. Nowhere is this challenge playing out more than in the Bologna Process, in which the ministers of education of European nations endorsed the notion that, ultimately, responsibility for quality assurance rests with the higher-education institutions. Nevertheless, governments continue to exert great authority in quality assurance reviews.

10 Learning Assessment and Accountability for American Higher Education

LEARNING ASSESSMENT AND ACCOUNTABILITY visions and practices, not surprisingly, vary tremendously in the United States and elsewhere. In the United States, students, parents, and the public rely heavily on comparative, largely reputational information among campuses, available from college rankings such as those published by *U.S. News*. State policy makers across the nation require some form of performance reporting, often as higher-education indicators. Higher-education professional organizations have begun to report their own indicators, as well. And colleges and universities rely on external accreditation and internal assessment and accountability mechanisms to warrant their performance quality externally and monitor their performance internally. Internationally, many countries rely on the academic audit, which takes a different accountability turn from that commonly seen in the United States. The audit examines goals and organizational structures and processes that are in place to monitor, provide feedback, and progressively improve student learning and other outcomes within the college or university. And, unlike U.S. accreditation, detailed academic audit reports are issued, so that the public can compare colleges and universities as to quality processes and progressive improvement.

In this final chapter, what is known about learning assessment and accountability mechanisms is brought together, and strengths and weaknesses are briefly reviewed. Three learning outcomes are given priority: achievement in the academic major, achievement of broad cognitive abilities, and competence in broad individual and social responsibilities. The challenge, of course, is to find adequate direct measures where applicable; the Collegiate Learning Assessment serves as an exemplar. Then a set of principles is set forth that should be considered in the design of an accountability system, including the need for multiple learning out-come indicators, alignment of formative and summative functions of assessment and accountability, and co-accountability between higher-education leaders, pol-icy makers, and clients. Finally, one possible vision of an accountability system that fits these principles is sketched out. As the saying goes, there is nothing new under heaven and earth, and so it will be the case here. The vision of accountabil-ity, however, will be patterned somewhat differently from previous visions (e.g., Graham, Lyman & Trow, 1995; Dill et al., 1996).

Vision of Learning Assessment and Accountability in a Nutshell

It is quite possible to get lost in the trees of this chapter and come out without a vision of the forest itself. Before venturing into the forest, this chapter's vision is outlined here. Imagine a triangle with one vertex a new form of *accreditation*, a second vertex an *assessment* of learning quality, and the third vertex an *aca-demic audit* that assures stakeholders that the campus has in place the processes to ensure improvement and that the assessment results (vertex 2) show that the campus is improving (or not).

Accreditation would serve several functions. It would be responsible for or-ganizing, carrying out, and reporting *publicly* detailed findings of the academic audit. Accreditation would, as it does now, consist of regional agencies (given the number of colleges and universities and their regional distribution in the United States) overseen by a national agency. Each agency would have a board composed of a majority of academic leaders and a balance of policy makers and other stakeholders (say, a 55–45 percent split). Reports of audit findings would have to be approved by the board before they could be issued publicly. In this way, co-accountability and protection from political spins would be inten-tionally built into the accountability process.

The *assessment* vertex would focus on institutional and program/major *qual-ity*. The assessment would be carried out by the campus and include external learning assessments (e.g., the Collegiate Learning Assessment) to benchmark performance. The assessment would set high standards for outcomes, which must include learning in the academic major, learning in general or liberal education, and learning of individual and social responsibility (along with other indicators of quality). Direct measures, to the extent possible, along with other measures would be taken, analyzed, and fed back to appropriate units. Units would use this information to hypothesize or conjecture how to improve student learning, ex-perimentally test these conjectures, and choose an appropriate course of action and monitor progress (in the next assessment phase).

The *audit*, carried out by the accrediting agency in a manner described in Chapter 9, would focus on the rigor of outcomes set by the institution, the quality of the processes it has in place for improvement, and the extent to which it is progressing toward its goals. The findings of the audit, not the assessment, would be mandatorily reported to the public. The report would permit comparison among colleges and universities. And it would be up to the campus as to whether it wanted to report the results of its assessment externally, perhaps in the Voluntary System of Accountability's College Portrait (see Chapter 6).

Assessment of Learning

Increasingly, U.S. colleges and universities are being pressured to assess learning and to do so directly, as well as indirectly (see Chapter 2). There is considerable pressure from the policy community and from some higher-education associations. Recently, countries belonging to the Organization for Economic Cooperation and Development (OECD) have been pressured to measure learning directly and comparatively. As of this writing, the OECD is planning a pilot study to collect direct measures of student learning (most notably using the Collegiate Learning Assessment; see Chapter 4), with the goal of producing comparative information not necessarily country by country but possibly by college and university (www .oecd.org/edu/ahelo).

Learning Outcomes

Three learning outcomes stand out. The first outcome would be students' learning in the majors. This outcome transcends individual courses; faculty already assess course learning. Rather, it would focus on a summary picture of what students have achieved in the major overall. By "achieved" is meant the declarative, procedural, schematic, and strategic knowledge and reasoning and problem solving capacities that students have developed in a major (see Chapter 2).

Measurement of these outcomes in the majors has proven to be illusive and difficult for several reasons. One reason is that faculty within a discipline do not necessarily agree on specific outcomes or on how to measure them. Moreover, academics and policy makers do not agree as to whether assessment of this learning should be carried out within a campus for formative improvement purposes (see Chapter 5) or carried out externally so that comparisons among departments across campuses could be made for both formative purposes (benchmarking and improvement) and comparative purposes (choosing among departments) (see Chapter 6). One potentially fruitful avenue might be a CLA-type assessment for majors (see Chapter 3) that might serve both accountability functions. In this

case, the focus would be less on particular content knowledge that typically is assessed in courses and more on the kinds of schematic and strategic knowledge
and reasoning that a particular discipline seeks to develop in its students and that
distinguishes one discipline (e.g., history) from others (e.g., chemistry, political
science).

The second learning outcome falls in the area of broad reasoning and communicating abilities (see Figure 2.1). By this is meant the ability to think critically,
reason analytically, solve problems, and communicate clearly and concisely. Measurement of this outcome has advanced (and retreated) over the past hundred
years, but currently a number of measures are regarded as viable alternatives for
measuring student learning and are currently in use across a large number of
campuses. Three such learning assessments that are well known and well used are
the Measure of Academic Proficiency and Progress (MAPP), the Collegiate Assessment of Academic Proficiency (CAAP), and the Collegiate Learning Assessment. The first two assessments grow out of a behavioral and psychometric
tradition and are largely multiple-choice tests. The last grows out of a rationalist
(cognitive) and sociohistorical tradition and is characterized by constructed
responses to complex problems. This book has featured the CLA, as it is new, innovative, and possibly a signal as to the next generation of college learning assessments.

The third learning outcome has typically been dubbed "noncognitive skills"
or "soft skills," neither of which is an apt or fair description of outcomes that involve the integration of cognition, volition, and emotion. A more apt label for
these outcomes might be the AAC&U's designation: "individual and social responsibility." The AAC&U-envisioned outcomes are civic responsibility and engagement, ethical reasoning, intercultural knowledge and actions, and propensity
for lifelong learning (AAC&U, 2005). My colleagues (Matt Bundick, Dick Hersh,
Amy Kurpius, Daniel Silverman, Lynn Swaner) and I have been working on a
somewhat different but overlapping set of "responsibility" outcomes that include
identity, resilience, emotional competence, and perspective taking and acting.
The last of these outcomes includes most of the AAC&U outcomes.

The three outcomes—knowledge, broad abilities, and responsibility—when
considered together and supported by a college's environmental ecology, create
what might be thought of as transformational learning outcomes. To achieve
these outcomes the "whole student" has to be involved in learning (Figure 10.1).
This view of learning leads to an overarching outcome, one of a student flour-
ishing or thriving in the sense, not just of the absence of "problems," but in the

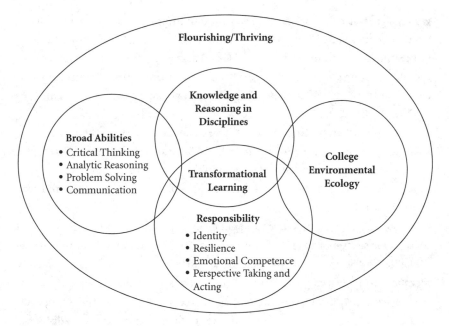

Figure 10.1 Learning outcomes.
SOURCE: R. Shavelson.

sense of positive well-being, with the knowledge, broad abilities, motivation, and emotions that, together, create a positive outlook on and high potential for a purposeful and meaningful life.

Learning Assessment

Measurement of learning outcomes is challenging. The focus here is on "cognitive" outcomes—knowledge and reasoning and broad abilities—because such measures have been developed fairly extensively (see Chapter 3). However, before turning attention to the assessment of these outcomes, a few words about responsibility outcomes seem warranted.

Assessment of Responsibility Outcomes.   The learning outcomes model in Chapter 2 (Figure 2.1) identifies responsibility outcomes as important and at the level of broad-ability cognitive outcomes. Nevertheless, as pointed out in Chapter 3, assessment of responsibility outcomes is challenging because most such measures, due to their self-reporting nature, are coachable and open to socially desirable responding, and so are "fake-able." Consequently, a great deal of developmental work is needed here. This said, not to measure these outcomes would signal that they are not valued or are unimportant, and they most likely would not be attended to in the undergraduate curriculum. Given the trade-off—to measure or not to measure individual and social responsibility outcomes—an evolutionary view seems appropriate: Begin to measure these outcomes now, and evolve the measurement of these outcomes through a concerted research and development effort.

Typically, self-reporting measures have been used to gauge these outcomes; such measures are limited for the reasons given above and more. Nevertheless, they provide a starting place and thus should be incorporated into learning assessment systems. This would be a first step in evolving more reliable, valid, and useful measures.

Some alternatives are currently under development. For example, to avoid some of the self-reporting pitfalls, one possible tack—a tack taken by the Educational Testing Service (ETS)—would be for "significant others," such as faculty members, to rate students on some of these outcomes. The GRE plans to assess these outcomes by having three or four faculty recommenders or student supervisors evaluate a student's knowledge and creativity, communication skills, team work, resilience, planning and organization, and ethics and integrity on a scale from one to five. The assessment will produce a Personal Potential Index (scheduled for July 2009). Of course, the big questions are (1) Would faculty/supervisors be willing to do this? (2) Do faculty/supervisors have access to the information about the student needed to provide valid ratings? and (3) As many other responsibility outcomes are not amenable to this procedure, how will they be assessed?

Still another possible way to measure some of the responsibility outcomes (e.g., emotional competence, perspective taking)—one that provides a direct measure of learning—was suggested in Chapter 3. Imagine a CLA-type task in which the student is given an "in-basket" of information (scientific reports, newspaper articles, opinion editorials, statistical and economic data) and asked to review and evaluate arguments made by local environmentalists and the business community for and against removing an old dam and recommend a course of action. On the basis of their review and analysis, students would be asked to outline the personal, economic, political, social, and ethical pros and cons of removing the dam and to arrive at a recommendation for a course of action. While there would be no single correct answer, the quality of the students' reasoning and justification—the application of some of their social responsibility skills—could be judged. Of course, questions of validity immediately arise and would need to be addressed. For example, would the CLA-type task capture students' actual deliberations and actions in the sense of what they would normally do, or would it just measure, once again, maximal performance in response to a cognitive test?

Assessment of Broad Cognitive Abilities.   "Broad cognitive abilities" refers to students' capacities to think critically, reason analytically, solve problems, make decisions reasonably, and communicate ideas clearly and concisely in broad domains characterized by the labels humanities, social sciences, and natural or life sciences. These are integrative abilities in the sense that they are broadly applicable to life situations, and disciplinary preparation and course-by-course preparation are too narrow, alone, to prepare students for these outcomes. At present, in most institutions they are built up haphazardly over the course of experience in college. By measuring these outcomes as part of learning assessment, college curricula, teaching, and learning might shift to address these outcomes coherently.

In contrast to individual and social responsibility outcomes, there are a myriad of broad ability measures available, most notably CAAP, CLA, and MAPP. Typically, they are externally developed measures of learning capable of providing a signal to campuses as to how well students perform relative to benchmark performance. Consequently, these learning assessments focus primarily on the summative function of assessment. CAAP and MAPP differ considerably from the CLA in philosophy (component task vs. holistic tasks), unit (student vs. program/school), format (multiple choice vs. constructed response to performance tasks), administration (paper and pencil or computer-adapted vs. Internet), scoring (student subtest scores vs. program/school scores and value added), and interpretation (separate abilities summed to reflect the whole vs. complex integrative abilities and value added) (see Chapters 3 and 4). Of course, as one of those responsible for developing the CLA, my biased recommendation should be obvious.

Alternatively, these abilities can be and are measured by campus-constructed measures, such as those developed at Alverno College (see Chapter 5). Homegrown learning assessments benefit from being more closely tied to the college curriculum than externally developed assessments. Such measures thus contribute to the formative function of assessment. However, typically, students' performance on such measures cannot be benchmarked against students' performance at other institutions. The question of how good is good enough, then, is difficult to answer.

The measurement of broad abilities is not an either-or issue. Some combination of internal and external assessment seems appropriate. External measures provide an answer to the question of how good is good enough; internal measures should provide diagnostic information for improvement. Both types of measures provide information when used as outcomes of campus experiments in improving students' broad cognitive abilities.

Knowledge and Reasoning in the Major.   Outcomes in the major—knowledge and reasoning in a discipline (declarative, procedural, schematic, and strategic; see Chapter 2)—are uncontested; they are the "bread and butter" of a college education. What the outcomes within a discipline should be and how to measure them, however, *are* contested. They are so contested that the development of disciplinary learning outcome measures has been largely left to individual faculty (course grades, examinations) and individual departments.

External attempts by testing companies to provide measures of these outcomes have, historically (Chapter 3), met with limited success; measures have come and gone—mostly gone (e.g., GRE Area Tests). Nevertheless, with renewed interest in college learning outcomes, the "market" has rebounded, and test publishers are gearing up to offer externally developed measures of disciplinary outcomes (e.g., GRE Subject Tests in eight fields).

Internal attempts to measure achievement in the majors have been made in the course of ongoing and emerging campus assessment programs. These measures have taken the form of portfolios, capstone courses, and capstone projects, in addition to off-the-shelf and certification-mandated achievement tests in the discipline or profession (see Chapter 5). The benefit of such homegrown or "certification-grown" assessments is that they are linked to the curriculum, providing a means to monitor student development. And they serve as measures for departmental experiments in improving such learning outcomes. The homegrown assessments, however, are often limited in their technical quality (but see Chapter 5 for exceptions), by their burden on faculty, and by their capacity to benchmark performance against peer campuses.

With this background briefly laid out, the reasonable recommendation would be to combine externally developed and homegrown measures of disciplinary outcomes to provide a means of monitoring, feeding back, and improving teaching and learning. But right now this will not work on a wide scale. For example, the will and capacity to develop high-quality assessments internally is quite limited beyond the end-of-course examination. This said, such an enterprise among a consortium of campuses might prove quite important and productive, not just for assessment purposes but also for curriculum, teaching, and learning in the majors involved. Moreover, external assessments with benchmarking capacity are highly restricted in the majors they measure; these assessments are not widely accepted across departments in those fields. Moreover, developing such assessments externally for the large number of college majors seems a daunting task.

This said, as with the measurement of individual and social responsibility outcomes, the development of assessments in the major should be an evolutionary goal, both for internal and external assessment development. One "audacious" proposal that straddles the internal-external divide goes something like this: Consider the assessment of knowledge and reasoning in history. Why not shape a writing task around, for example, a historical event (real and obscure or fictitious), for which history students would be given a computer in-basket of information and asked to adjudicate among competing interpretations of what happened. It might be possible for disciplinary societies, in this case maybe the American Historical Association, to work with, for example, the Council for Aid to Education to create measures that tap especially strategic knowledge and reasoning within the discipline. In this bridging way perhaps some traction might be gained in moving an assessment-in-the-majors agenda forward (see Shavelson, 2007a,b).

Vision of Learning Outcomes

Assessment of learning should encompass learning in the disciplines and learning that transcends the discipline. Within the disciplines, knowledge (especially strategic knowledge) should be assessed both internally within a college or university (but transcending course-by-course testing and grading) and externally, so that student performance in the campus major can be benchmarked against performance at other campuses.

Cross-disciplinary learning, learning of cognitive and individual and interpersonal responsibility should also be assessed. Measures of cognitive learning should tap critical thinking, analytic reasoning, problem solving, decision making, and communication. Measures of individual and social responsibility should tap identity, perspective taking (including moral reasoning, civic engagement, social and intercultural understanding and action) and resilience, and environmental affordances and constraints on student development. Information about these outcomes, as with outcomes of academic majors, would come from internal and external assessments.

Students and campuses, then, might be characterized by a profile of indicators—statistical aggregates of measures of learning in the majors and learning of broad abilities. Such profiles would be used for both internal improvement and external accountability.

Accounting for Learning

Institutions within a democracy are obliged to account for their actions, and civic leaders have a responsibility to hold those institutions accountable. Colleges and universities are no exception to this rule. Colleges and universities have a responsibility to themselves to account for and improve their performance. Moreover, they have a responsibility to account to clients, such as students and parents seeking the best match for a college education. And, of course, they have a responsibility to civic leaders to account for their performance and assure the public of quality. The question, one that is pursued in the remainder of this chapter, is: How might colleges and universities be held accountable for informing policy makers and clients on the one hand and improving teaching and learning on the other?[1]

In answering this question, a few issues and conflicts need to be addressed, as evidenced in the last four chapters. This is done by setting forth a set of principles for the "design" of higher-education accountability. Next, a brief summary of alternatives for holding higher education accountable is provided. By linking the guiding principles and subsets of previous approaches to accountability, and adding a dash of originality, one possible vision for holding higher education accountable is synthesized.

Principles for the Design of Higher-Education Accountability

In an essay entitled "Accountability of Colleges and Universities," Graham, Lyman, and Trow (1995, p. 9) set forth five principles for holding colleges and universities accountable for teaching and learning: (1) external accountability should reinforce internal accountability, (2) accountability should do no harm, (3) accountability should respect diversity, (4) accountability should be centrally an academic responsibility, and (5) accountability should be a forward-looking responsibility. As will be seen, there is a close correspondence between these principles and the ones enumerated below, albeit the following principles were arrived at independently from the prior chapters in this book.[2]

The first three principles derive from the discussion of learning assessment in the previous section[3] and can be dispensed immediately:

- *Principle 1: Assess Disciplinary and Broad Ability Outcomes* Assessment of learning should include outcomes in the majors and in broad cognitive abilities (critical thinking, analytic reasoning, problem solving, and communication). It should also include broad individual and social responsibilities (e.g., identity, resilience, perspective taking, and environmental supports and constraints).
- *Principle 2: Align and Combine Internal and External Assessments of Learning* Both internally generated and externally provided assessments of learning, closely allied, should be collected and integrated into learning outcome indicators.
- *Principle 3: Characterize Performance by a Profile of Learning Outcome Indicators* Learning outcomes should be conceived and reported as a profile of outcomes, as reflected on cognitive and individual and social responsibility assessments.

As noted in Chapter 6, there is a cultural conflict inherent in the accountability triangle among college and university leaders, policy makers, and "clients" (students, parents, business, and government). Policy makers and clients focus on the summative function of accountability. They seek summary comparative information about the quality of higher-education institutions, the former for assuring the public and the latter for deciding where to matriculate or to invest in research and training. In contrast, colleges and universities focus on accountability for improvement. They are suspicious of and shun comparison. They point to the diversity of their institutions—their missions, student bodies, and the like.

The intensity of this conflict cannot be overstated. Mistrust has evolved; reputations and economic well-being are at stake. This can be seen especially clearly in the Bologna Process (Chapter 9). European governments traditionally have had much more direct involvement in funding and regulating higher education. These governments have built quality assurance agencies to monitor and report publicly on the performance of their higher-education institutions. These institutions have bridled at the oversight and at the "spin" that government agencies put on findings. This has led to considerable conflict, with the resolution that, in the end, quality assurance rested with the colleges and universities.

- *Principle 4: Balance External and Internal Reporting of Accountability Information* Higher-education accountability must strike a balance between the external need to know and the professional responsibility of colleges and universities to regulate themselves.

The conflict reflected by the accountability triangle is mirrored in the distinction between the summative and formative functions of accountability. The summative function provides a summary judgment on the quality of learning at a college or university. This summary judgment is comparative; campuses are distinguished one from another on learning outcomes. The formative function provides information that guides a campus in its effort to improve teaching and learning. That is, the internal assessment of learning, feeding back that information, experimenting with improvements, and monitoring outcomes are all involved in the formative function. Public comparisons are eschewed, although benchmarking among a consortium of colleges and universities, kept private, counts as formative accountability.

• *Principle 5: Align Formative and Summative Functions of Accountability* The formative and summative functions of accountability should not only be balanced (see Principle 4), they should be aligned and mutually supporting. Information for improvement should also be amenable to reporting to external audiences and vice versa.

As pointed out in Chapter 7, education process and output indicators are multiple, multiply caused, and do not speak for themselves. They need to be interpreted to be culturally and socially meaningful. However, herein lies potential accountability mischief, as competing political views vie to "spin" the interpretation of the indicators. The concern for the unintended consequences of political spin is very real in higher-education accountability. It reflects cultural conflict and mistrust, especially between policy makers responsible to their constituencies and higher-education leaders responsible for the quality of their educational programs. Checks and balances are needed in an accountability system to minimize the chance that a single, simple, well-spun interpretation will predominate over other, potentially viable explanations.

• *Principle 6: Incorporate Co-Accountability into an Accountability System* Accountability should be a two-way street in which policy makers hold higher education accountable, and higher education and the public hold policy makers accountable. This function occurs throughout government in the form of, for example, the University of California's Board of Regents or the federal Government Accounting Office. An independent body, jointly appointed by, perhaps, policy makers and higher-education leaders, should monitor and adjudicate claims based on available information.

A notion central to accountability is one of consequences and sanctions for institutions that do not perform within social and cultural expectations. Nowhere are such sanctions more evident than in the current federal No Child Left Behind (NCLB) legislation and practice. However, the sanctions aspect of accountability makes an assumption that may not be realistic for education: that there is a widely available, readily applicable technology that is known to improve education processes and outcomes.[4] There is not (although some believe they have the silver bullet). Rather, improvement is more like what historians David Tyack and Larry Cuban dubbed as "tinkering toward utopia"—progressive improvement that is difficult to see at any particular point. This notion of adjusting based on feedback over time forms the basis of the call for evidence-based decision making and the creation of learning organizations. Experimentation with monitoring, feedback, and change, not quick fixes, is needed to move higher education to higher levels of teaching and learning. Sanctions, then, may not be what is needed. Rather, capacity is needed, and those institutions falling behind expectation may also be the ones with the least capacity. But just how to provide that capacity to these institutions is a challenge, NCLB notwithstanding; it requires a new view of accountability, one with feedback on how to improve processes and outcomes.

- *Principle 7: Provide Informative Feedback to Improve Teaching and Learning* Consequences of accountability should not be sanctions (punishments), which mostly result in symbolic organizational behavior change. Rather, feedback from accountability should focus on organizational improvement through experimentation, progress monitoring, and feedback.

The conflict evidenced in the accountability triangle (policy makers, clients, higher-education leaders) is not solely due to cultural differences. It is also about information asymmetries (Chapter 6). The policy makers and the public seek information that compares colleges and universities; colleges and universities are reluctant to provide that information because of interpretative mistrust, political spin, and the complexity of the information a campus uses to improve its processes. However, a cursory perusal of a state's performance report quickly overwhelms. There is simply too much information for easy comparison. The appeal of reputational ranking systems is that comparisons can be had at a glance—through ranks or grades assigned to complex performance indicators.

- *Principle 8: Report a Profile of Grades Based on Indicators in an Accountability System* Grades like the ones we received in school are an informative, quick way to provide information at a glance. To be sure, they mask a great deal; but, that said, the public and policy makers have the need to know and to know efficiently. Such grades, with extensive backup, are not wishful thinking. The National Center for Public Policy and Postsecondary Education has graded states on a profile of outcomes since 2000 in its state-by-state report card.

Prior Proposals for Higher-Education Accountability

As evident from Chapters 8 and 9, there have been myriad proposals for holding higher education accountable. Accreditation and performance reporting are typical in the United States. Accreditation and academic audits are prominent in other parts of the world. Several prior proposals for higher-education accountability, then, deserve brief mention before turning to the proposal in this chapter.

Accreditation is much maligned, especially by former secretary of education Margaret Spellings' Higher Education Commission. Accreditation sets the bar too low, does not provide detailed performance information to stakeholders, does not provide meaningful comparisons among colleges and universities, is not trustworthy because it is controlled by the very institutions it is intended to hold minimally accountable, and does not have "teeth"— sanctions for poor performance (thought by many to be the way to improve performance). Nevertheless, accreditation has an important role to play in higher education and is currently having an impact on campuses by getting them to focus on student learning outcomes. Moreover, accreditation, when combined with state policies for improving higher education, serves as significant motivation for change. So accreditation alone is inadequate. But throwing the baby out with the bathwater is equally indefensible. As will be seen, accreditation does have a role to play.

Several proposals for U.S. higher-education accountability have focused on professional self-regulation. Two stand out. About fourteen years ago, Richard Lyman (former president of Stanford University), Patricia Graham (former dean of the Harvard Graduate School of Education and president of the Spencer Foundation), and Martin Trow (former director of the Center for Studies in Higher Education at the University of California, Berkeley) wrote a brief treatise on higher-education accountability, stressing the importance of institutional self-regulation. This tack, perhaps not surprising, as all three were higher-education leaders at the time, was prescient: To ignore the importance and power of higher-education self-regulation would be fatal. The same conclusion was reached later in the EU's Bologna Process (Chapter 9).

Graham, Lyman, and Trow (1995) conceived an accountability system that focused on institution-wide internal processes whereby faculty and administrators, together, assessed the quality of academic programs with the goal of improving teaching and learning. They noted optimistically that the proposed system of accountability "will not operate properly unless institutions first nurture a climate of critical self-inquiry where candor and criticism can flourish and where each unit is allowed to express its own mission, its strengths, and its weaknesses" (p. 7).

They went on to say, "This improved internal accountability [formative function of accountability] can lead to better external accountability [summative function] through audits" (p. 7). The role, then, of accreditation would be to audit these internal processes and report on improvement (or lack thereof). Accreditation agencies would report on the extent to which processes were in place on a campus to collect, provide feedback on, and monitor progress toward goals set by the institution.

Moreover, new external accountability mechanisms should focus on ensuring the presence and effectiveness of internal accountability processes. External audiences, then, would have evidence of internal quality processes and the extent to which the institution was moving toward its goals, along with financial audits and the like. They viewed alignment of internal and external accountability in such a system as essential, and college and university trustees would stand at the juncture of the two.

Dill et al. (1996; see also Dill, 1997) built upon Graham, Lyman, and Trow's ideas, enumerating three pieces of the accountability puzzle: accreditation, assessment, and audit (see Chapter 9). They agreed with Graham, Lyman, and Trow (1995) that "the most needed reform is the renewal of *internal* mechanisms for quality assurance" (p. 18, italics in original) and viewed accreditation and academic audit as a "necessary component[s] of this reform" (p. 18).

According to Dill et al. (1996), accreditation, carried out by an external agency, should serve to determine whether a campus or program met threshold quality criteria based on a combination of campus self-review, performance indicator, and peer review. It should validate the appropriateness and rigor of campus-defined outcomes and determine whether the resources needed to attain them were in place. It should compare observed performance against a set of campus-established criteria. And, finally, drawing on the international perspective, accreditation outcomes should be *published*—"such publication is necessary for accreditation to perform its certification function" (p. 21).

Accreditation, however, is insufficient by itself to bring about the teaching and learning reform envisioned by Dill et al. (1996). A second necessary ingredient is assessment, the internal mechanism for setting outcomes and measuring and evaluating the extent to which the institution or program is moving toward them. Assessment might be carried out by an outside agency, an institutional consortium, or the institution itself. It typically focuses on the program or department and combines performance indicators, self-study, and peer review. The outcome of the assessment is "graded judgments about academic quality levels rather than binary judgments relative to threshold standards" (Dill et al., 1996, p. 21). These judgments are typically made public so that institutional comparisons can be made.

While the assessment focuses on teaching and learning quality, the academic audit focuses on the "processes that are believed to produce quality and the methods by which academics assure themselves that quality has been attained" (Dill et al., 1996, p. 22). Academic audits focus on the institution and drill down to the department and individual instructors to ensure that an institution's chosen standards are being met. "Audits . . . follow 'audit trails'—three or four extensive investigations undertaken on a sampling basis by looking at records and interviewing faculty members, staff, and students at the subject level." For example, they might focus on curriculum design (design processes, review, and improvement), pedagogical design (decisions about teaching methods and improvement), implementation quality (processes to monitor, review, and reward performance), outcome assessment (to monitor performance and link it to teaching and learning), and resource provision (evidence of adequate human, financial, and technical resources when needed). Audit findings are always made public.

Dill et al.'s (1996) vision of accountability, then, is premised on professional self-regulation. The central mechanism for quality assurance is "collegial peer review and evaluation" (p. 19) that is made public. In sum, "what is needed is a coordinated program of self-regulation that would require all postsecondary institutions to allocate faculty time and other resources to academic quality assurance activities as a fundamental business requirement" (p. 20). The federal government is unlikely to pull this all off successfully. Rather, Dill et al. (p. 25) "believe that the well-established system of regional, voluntary self-regulation [accreditation] offers the best potential vehicle" for quality assurance with oversight from a central, high-level accreditation board.

In contrast to the visions of accountability provided by Graham, Lyman, and Trow (1995), Dill et al. (1996), and the principles above, stand the former

U.S. Secretary of Education, Margaret Spellings, and her Higher Education Commission. The secretary and her commission see a central role for the federal government in holding higher education accountable (see Chapter 1). As in K-12 education, but (arguably) with a bit more flexibility, the federal government would set standards and insist upon the use of common, externally provided measures of students' learning (CLA and MAPP, specifically) to monitor performance toward those standards. Progress would be made public so that policy makers and clients could compare campuses on the same yardstick; market forces would sanction campuses that did not measure up.

A strong federal role is unlikely to work. Cultures clash, campuses and external regulators distrust one another, and the potential for mischief and spin abound. Colleges and universities have been remarkably resilient to external attempts to regulate them. Witness the recent emergence of higher-education associations entering the self-regulation game alongside accreditation and even moving to a voluntary system of accountability with comparisons of campuses on external learning assessments to fend off federal intrusion (Chapter 1). Moreover, such oversight requires a substantial financial commitment from federal and state governments that in good economic times is there but in bad times is not—witness some states' attempt at performance funding (Chapter 8) and the recent history of learning assessment demands (Chapter 3).

Some middle ground, between government involvement and professional self-regulation, seems appropriate and even necessary. That is, the evidence is pretty clear (Dill et al., 1996, present it concisely) that, without external impetus, most campuses are unlikely to self-regulate beyond current-day accreditation, with all of its limitations. And federal (and state) intrusion into higher education has been and will continue to be met with resistance. What has seemed to work in the United States to date is a synergy between professional self-regulation and government policy. For example, the federal government insisted that accrediting agencies (which the federal government accredits, kind of) focus on student learning and not just on inputs and processes. Accrediting agencies complied and, in combination with state policies and professional organizations moving to head off external regulation, have moved the learning assessment and accountability agenda forward. But not forward enough.

To move forward, a vision is needed. Graham, Lyman, and Trow (1995) and Dill et al. (1996) were on the right track in the sense that what they proposed jibed with many of the design principles enumerated above. They have laid out the general framework for assessment and accountability endorsed here. There are a few details to be added or changed to reflect what has been learned and accomplished in the past ten-plus years, but a large part of the work outlined in this chapter has been accomplished.

A Vision of Learning Assessment and Accountability

Higher-education accountability would have three components: accreditation, academic audit, and assessment. With a few adjustments, the first two components would look very much as described in the last section. The assessment component, however, would differ somewhat from that described above because, for example, external mechanisms (e.g., the National Research Council) currently exist for evaluating and comparing academic departments.

In the vision of the assessment component described below, assessment would not be focused only on departments and programs. Rather, it would assess student learning at multiple levels of the organization: mastery in the major; competence in broad cognitive abilities across humanities, social science, and science; and competence in personal and social responsibility at the campus level. It would include both externally provided measures of learning outcomes and homegrown measures. And it would feed back performance information and conjectures for improvement and experimentation at all levels—central administration, schools, departments, faculty, *and* students.

Accreditation

Accreditation would have administrative and reporting functions. The administrative function would be akin to national and cross-national agencies in the EU that are responsible for conducting audits (see Chapter 9 for details). Briefly stated, the administrative function would involve orchestration of the academic audit. The orchestration would include specifying information to be included in the campus's self-study; identifying, training, and fielding external peer review teams; specifying topics to be addressed in the review team's report; and specifying the nature and range of recommendations made for campus improvement and mechanisms for monitoring campus efforts to that end.

In its reporting capacity, accreditation would publish the findings of the academic audit publicly—to higher educators, policy makers, clients, and the general public. These reports would give grades to a campus's processes and methods for ensuring improvement in teaching and learning and to the extent the campus had achieved its goals based on objective measures and other indicators. For example, a grade might be assigned as to the rigor of the standards set for students' learning to think critically, reason analytically, solve problems, and communicate clearly and concisely. A grade might also be assigned to the campus as to the rigor of the methods by which it monitors progress on the broad cognitive ability outcome. A grade might be assigned as to the progress made toward goals based on rigorous measures. And, as a final example, a grade might be given for the mechanisms in place to feed back learning assessment information and to monitor progress.

Accreditation would be carried out by regional accrediting agencies, coordinated by an overarching agency, very much like the system that has been in place in the United States for the past twenty years in one form or another. Regional agencies would be governed by boards, whose composition would include representatives from the colleges and universities in the region (administrators, faculty, and students), government officials, and members of the business and general communities in the region. The overarching board would parallel regional boards in composition but at a national level. The majority of board members would be administrators and faculty from the campuses; the balance of the other members would be large—say, 45 percent of the total. The chair of the board would come from higher education; the vice chair from government. Regional agency funding would come from both state governments and the campuses in the region; national board funding would come from the federal government. Finally, the board would have to agree on the interpretation and presentation of findings of the academic audit before they were made public, addressing the political spin source of cultural conflict.

The intent here is to deal directly with some of the well-known criticisms of accreditation, such as the criticism that accrediting agencies are beholden to those they accredit, thereby undermining external confidence. This vision of accreditation also addresses the conflict of cultures by creating boards that include higher-education leaders, policy makers, and clients. It also addresses the criticism that accreditation has "no teeth" by grading campuses and making those grades public. In brief, this conception of accreditation addresses, to some extent, each of the design principles set forth earlier in this chapter.

Assessment

Assessment focuses on the measurement of teaching and learning quality on a campus. It is carried out by the campus and is the heart of the formative function of accountability for the campus. And it forms the evidentiary basis for the academic audit (see the next section).[5]

Assessment can also fulfill, in part, the summative function of accountability if the campus chooses to make public the results of the assessment. In the vision presented here, this is a choice that the campus makes. It is not carried out in response to some external political or professional body. The findings of the academic audit, in contrast, are made public regardless of the wishes of the campus.

In the assessment, learning outcomes would be set forth at the department or program, school, and campus levels, not according to some externally imposed universal set of outcome measures. These would include the campus's version of cognitive outcomes in the major or program and at the school or campus level. Individual and social responsibility would also be assessed at the school or campus level. While the campus sets the outcomes, it is held accountable externally for their rigor. That is, the campus must be able to justify the validity and rigor of these outcomes in the external, academic audit.

These outcomes would be measured by a mixture of externally provided and homegrown assessments. External assessment might be accomplished with *direct measures of learning* such as the CAAP, CLA, MAPP, or some other suitable measure of the campus's choosing. To be sure, other external, *indirect measures of learning* such as the National Assessment of Student Engagement might also be incorporated into the assessment exercise. The value of such measures is that they signal internal campus processes that might become the subject of experimentation and improvement. The external assessment provides the essential function of performance benchmarking. Units on campus need to know how well they are doing, not just in terms of their own standards (as standards need benchmarking, too), but also in terms of how well peer institutions are doing in similar contexts. That is, external benchmarking addresses, empirically, the question: How good is good enough?

Homegrown learning assessments are those built by campuses or perhaps by consortia of campuses. They are closely linked to campus-specific outcomes and curriculum, teaching, and learning. Homegrown assessments, then, should be far more curriculum sensitive than the external measures. They should also be more diagnostic than external measures and be capable of pinpointing problem areas. And they should be more sensitive to the effects of "experiments" for improving teaching and learning than the external measures. This said, over a period of several years the external assessment results—in part serving to audit the internal assessment results—should also reflect the improvement observed with homegrown measures.

For the assessment exercise to fulfill its formative accountability function, the data generated must be analyzed, interpreted, and reported throughout the campus. There need to be organizational structures in place to take that information; feed it back to appropriate units; plan and implement changes in curriculum, teaching, student support, and the like; and monitor progress toward outcomes. These structures include departments, schools, and central administration. They also include campus assessment offices and teaching and learning centers.

Moreover, the information collected during the assessment exercise should be fed back to students and become a meaningful part of their academic programs. All too frequently campus assessment programs stop at the program level, ignoring students (see Chapter 5). The vision here is one of feedback to and action by programs and the administrators and faculty responsible *and* to students as a central part of their academic programs.

Finally, campus incentives, including standards for promotion and tenure, should be in place to reward the "scholarship of teaching and learning" envisioned here, not just symbolically but also substantively. Campus leadership at all levels needs to support substantively the assessment exercise and the quest for campus quality improvement.

Academic Audit

The academic audit would be an externally driven peer review system that focuses on the *processes* a campus has in place to improve teaching and learning quality. The audit does not focus on quality outcomes; that is the function of the assessment exercise. The two are, of course, closely related. As Dill et al. (1996, p. 22) note, the "audit is founded on the principle that good people working with sufficient resources and good processes will produce good results, but that faulty processes will prevent even good people and plentiful resources from producing optimal outcomes."

The academic audit, then, serves to assure policy makers and the public that the campus has strong processes and methods in place and is working to improve teaching and learning. Another way of saying this is that the audit verifies "the effectiveness of the institution's assessment procedures and their implementation" (Dill et al., 1996, p. 22).

The audit should include four steps: (1) self-study, (2) external peer review, (3) report of findings, and (4) recommendations and follow-up for improvement of processes and methods. Discussion of, as well as prior experience with, each step is provided in the prior section and in detail in Chapter 9; that discussion is not reiterated here.

What does need to concern us here is a vision of what to look for when evaluating the quality of an institution's processes and methods for improving teaching and learning. This vision is one of a college or university as a *learning organization* permeated by a *culture of evidence.*

By "learning organization" is meant a campus that changes its structures and functions over time in response to reliable and valid assessment information so as to improve teaching and student learning. By "structures" is meant the governance and information structures that capture this information, feed it back at all levels of the organization, and monitor progress. Governance structures at all levels of the organization are implicated: central administration, with the president and provost directly involved; schools, with deans directly involved; departments, with chairs directly involved; faculty directly involved; *and* students in the loop. At the department level, for example, the focus would be on the design of curriculum and teaching, their implementation, and methods for assessing outcomes and feeding this information back to faculty and students.

Information structures include, for example, a campus assessment office that assists schools and departments (with their corresponding assessment representatives) to collect, analyze, feed back, and monitor assessment information. As we saw in Chapter 5, an assessment office could take various forms. What is key is that the office work both from grassroots enthusiasm and capacity of those involved upward in the organization and from assessment conceptions and methods down the organization—a so-called pandemonium model. Top-down direction of assessment efforts alone seem not to work. Information structures would also include a campus teaching and learning center. Such a center would help interpret assessment information, conjecture ways to improve teaching and learning, and assist faculty with implementing those improvements. The pandemonium model would seem to apply to teaching and learning centers, as well as to assessment centers.

These learning-organization structures are tightly linked from the top of the organization to the bottom. The president and provost would know, would be involved in acting upon, and would even "cheerlead" the assessment effort, making clear to all in the organization that decision making would be informed, significantly, by assessment information. The roles for deans and department chairs would parallel those of the central administrators. Feedback, monitoring, and experimentation would carry to faculty and students.

The functions provided by these linked structures would be oriented to the collection, analysis, and translation of assessment information into conjectures about direct actions that could be taken to improve teaching and learning. These functions would change and improve in capacity over time with feedback from the success of efforts at teaching and learning improvement (or lack thereof).

By "culture of evidence" is meant the use of assessment findings to guide the improvement of teaching and learning. Feedback of assessment findings should lead to conjectures as to how to improve outcomes in a major, in general or liberal education, or in the broad areas of individual and social responsibility. These conjectures would form the basis of "experiments" that compare one or more conjectures against current practice. The results of the experiment would inform action, and the cycle would be repeated.

All this probably sounds fanciful. But there are existence proofs. Different versions of this vision of a learning organization based on a culture of evidence can be found. In Chapter 5, Alverno College, the Student-Centered Learning University, and the Assessment-Centered University each provided exemplars of the vision. Alverno, for example, had an integrated set of learning outcomes encompassing those envisioned here. These outcomes were assessed and fed back to administrators, faculty, and students. Indeed, students knew how well they performed on institutional and departmental outcomes, where they needed improvement, and how to find help to improve. Likewise, faculty and departments were aware of each student's performance and were committed to getting students over the high performance bar.

Although existence proofs can be found, there is, nevertheless, an attitude among many colleges and universities, especially the "elites," that runs counter to the vision painted here. The attitude plays out something like this: "We know what we're doing, and we're doing it about as well as is conceivable. Maybe a tweak here or there is needed, and we attend to that when necessary. If a campus has to assess and audit, it probably means that that campus wasn't good enough in the first place and is unlikely to compete with the likes of us no matter what it does."

Simply put, you have to have the "right stuff." And the elites are likely to remain elite by reputation and resources; they have much to risk by collecting assessment information. Their students are likely to excel because it is well known that high-quality input leads to high-quality output. But there are a few elite universities, including Duke and Harvard, that are assessing, experimenting, and learning. There may be a tipping point, and other elites and nonelites might just decide to follow suit.

Reprise

The vision of learning assessment and accountability presented here for American higher education is one of teaching and learning continuous improvement through the evolution of campuses as learning organizations with progress based on a culture of evidence, experimentation, and action. The vision stresses direct assessment of student learning on cognitive outcomes in the major and in general or liberal education, as well as assessment of individual and social responsibility outcomes, including perspective taking (e.g., intercultural relations, moral development, civic engagement), identity, and resilience.

Campuses would be held accountable by regional accrediting agencies governed by boards that include higher-education leaders (the majority of members), policy makers, and clients (a minority of, say, 45 percent of the board). Regional accrediting agencies would be accountable to a national accrediting agency of similar composition. Accrediting agencies would be responsible for conducting academic audits and reporting the findings of those audits in a readily accessible format to the various interested audiences. These audits would focus on the *processes* a campus has in place to ensure teaching and learning quality and on the extent to which it has met its goals. The audit would be based on the campus's assessment program, which focuses on the measurement of teaching and learning outcomes. The assessment would collect, analyze, and interpret data and feed back assessment findings into campus structures that function to take action in the form of experiments aimed at testing conjectures about improvement. Over time subsequent assessments would also serve to monitor progress made in the majors, in general or liberal education programs, and by individual students.

Similar proposals made over a decade ago have not had the magnitude of impact it was hoped they would have. Policy makers have been skeptical, having been burned in the past, and now seek comparative assessment of learning information. Higher educators are likewise skeptical, as they want to protect their cultures of internal improvement from the whims of political spin and naive improvement fixes in the form of policies and regulations. To some degree, the vision presented here attempts to build on developments over the past ten or so years and to address some of the limitations of prior proposals, most notably attempting to balance the accountability system among higher educators, policy makers, and clients.

Although there may not be room for optimism, given the past, we may make room by balancing the competing demands of the accountability triangle (higher education, government, and clients) while preserving the integrity of professional oversight by higher education itself. There are some signs, from higher-education professional organizations and from campuses themselves, that higher education is coming to recognize that change and improvement, in the form of learning organizations committed to continuous improvement, are in the air of the 21st century.

Reference Matter

Notes

Preface

1. NAEP (pronounced "nape") is the acronym for the federal government's National Assessment of Educational Progress, referred to as "the Nation's Report Card." NAEP tracks 4th-, 8th-, and 12th-grade students' achievement nationally and state by state. The assessment is conducted in mathematics and reading biannually and in other subjects less often.

Chapter 2

I am indebted to Blake Naughton for his research assistance on this chapter. Portions of this chapter have been published in Shavelson (2007a,b) and Shavelson and Huang (2003).

1. This raises concerns about sanctions when colleges do not "produce"—there are multiple causes of a change in a student's performance. It also raises concerns about who gives the account that explains a college's performance—the college, an accreditation agency, or external audiences such as policy makers and pundits. Different spins on performance may ignore the complexity of interpreting performance change and consequently give rise to mischief.

2. There are multiple theories of intelligence. At one extreme Spearman (see Martinez, 2000) postulates a single undifferentiated general intelligence, and at the other extreme Guilford (1971) postulates 128 abilities and Gardner (1983) postulates different, independent intelligences. We do not intend to resolve this dispute (but see Carroll, 1993; Gustaffson & Undheim, 1996; or Martinez, 2000 for treatments). Rather, our intent is heuristic, providing a framework in which to locate debates, as well as achievement tests that have been used in the past to assess student learning.

3. Social Responsibility, not our focus here due to the lack of adequate measures—is integral for assessing student learning in higher education. See "Reprise" at the end of this chapter.

4. For example, the Collegiate Assessment of Academic Proficiency (CAAP), ETS's Tasks in Critical Thinking, the Undergraduate Assessment Program's (UAP's) Area Tests, the Academic Profile (APT).

Chapter 3

Portions of this chapter have been published in Shavelson (2007a,b) and Shavelson and Huang (2003).

1. At about the same time the Pennsylvania Study was conducted, the Progressive Education Association (PEA) launched its Eight Year Study (1930). The study aimed to reform high school education to meet the needs of what had become a disengaged student body. Although both Learned and Wood served as members of the commission for the study (but not as members of the directing subcommittee), this study took a different approach than the Pennsylvania Study with its focus on life skills in both the cognitive and noncognitive domains. The PEA and Eight Year Study, then, challenged the very ideas espoused by the Carnegie Foundation. This difference in views—a focus on declarative and procedural knowledge versus a focus on broad abilities—as we shall see, can be seen in debates about what counts and is measured as learning today.

2. We note the importance of basing assessment on a conceptual framework and not necessarily on the Carnegie Foundation for the Advancement of Teaching's particular conception. This conception was challenged by an alternative vision embraced at the same time by the Eight Year Study (see Shavelson, 2007b).

3. The ubiquitous "Bloom's Taxonomy" grew out of the work of the examiner's office to broaden the measurement of academic achievement. Benjamin Bloom was one of the directors of that office.

4. As noted, the foundation found itself strained by the cost and logistics of large-scale testing in the Pennsylvania and GRE studies. One major contributor to the problem was the cost of scoring, which had become acute by 1939. Large numbers of assistants were needed to score all of the examinations from thousands of test takers. "Langmuir, in charge of that phase of operations, suggested a contract with the International Business Machines Corporation under which the project should rent for its own use punch-card machines and related equipment" (Savage, 1953, p. 297). A year later Learned and Wood hit on a solution through "electro-mechanical means" (Savage, 1935, p. 297) and enlisted the help of Thomas J. Watson, then president of IBM. Watson, a champion of higher education (and trustee of Columbia University) immediately saw the importance of solving the problem, and in 1937 "the International test-scoring machine was ready for contract rental" (Savage, 1953, p. 298).

5. Advanced tests in agriculture, education, and home economics were added in 1946.

6. Incidentally, the reliability of the profile tests was quite high, typically greater than .90 for internal consistency and retest (see Lannholm & Schrader, 1951, p. 9).

7. I served as a consultant to the Council for Aid to Education's Collegiate Learning Assessment. The original Collegiate Learning Assessment included some tasks from Tasks in Critical Thinking.

8. Technically, there are multiple possible explanations that challenge the college-effect interpretation: Some selection must go on between freshman and senior years, with dropouts and transfers that are not perfectly picked up by the ACT or SAT test; simply maturing in the everyday world would provide some of those cognitive skills developed in college; and college is not the only societal mechanism for performance improvement—the same young adults would have developed the same capabilities on the job or in the military. We find the college-effect interpretation the most plausible, but not the only possible, explanation.

9. Indeed, there are many cognitive outcomes, such as moral judgment, we do not assess today, even though some call such outcomes "noncognitive."

Chapter 4

Various versions of this chapter served as the basis for and were informed by several journal articles, including Benjamin, 2008; Klein et al., 2005; Klein et al., 2007; Klein et al., 2008; Shavelson, 2007a,b, 2008a–c. I am indebted to Roger Bolus, senior partner, Research Solutions Group, for providing original CLA data and analyses for this chapter, and to Steve Klein and Roger Benjamin for their comments on a draft of the chapter.

1. The reader can skip this chapter without loss of continuity with the rest of the book.

2. All three of us were former RAND employees. Roger and I both directed the Education and Human Resources program at different times.

3. In order to combine scores from different performance tasks to arrive at an institution-level score, task scores are standardized on an SAT scale.

4. Parts of this section present new, unpublished findings on the CLA. Where published findings are available, the source is cited.

5. Indeed, these various forms of reliability can be integrated into one general framework (Generalizability Theory; see Brennan, 2001; Cardinet, in press; Shavelson & Webb, 1991). However, this introduces more complication than is needed to provide evidence of CLA score reliability here.

6. Klein et al. (2007) have addressed these criticisms extensively, but the latest round of articles in 2008 does not reflect that the authors have read this research.

7. The CLA has found longitudinal studies particularly challenging because of the financial, time, and logistical costs of tracking students over time as they move from one college to another or stop out for some period of time.

Chapter 5

The author is indebted to Dr. Maria Araceli Ruiz-Primo and Dr. Blake Naughton for their assistance with this research and reporting. An early version of this chapter was presented at the Annual Meeting of the American Educational Research Association (April 2006).

Chapter 6

1. At about the same time, William S. Learned at the Carnegie Foundation for the Advancement of Teaching and Ben D. Wood at Columbia College pioneered direct assessment of learning on college campuses in Pennsylvania. This work began seventy-five years of learning assessment in higher education, culminating today in the Collegiate Learning Assessment (for a brief history, see Chapter 3; Shavelson & Huang, 2003; Shavelson, 2007a,b).

2. By "assessment of learning" is meant the use of direct measures of achievement (e.g., certification examinations) and ability (e.g., Graduate Record Examination, Collegiate Learning Assessment, Measure of Academic Proficiency and Progress, Collegiate Assessment of Academic Proficiency) along with indirect measures (e.g., graduation rates, time to degree, employer satisfaction, and civic engagement) that bear on learning outcomes in higher education.

3. By "accountability" we mean evidence requested by policy makers both internal to and external to the academy who have the responsibility for assuring various publics (e.g., students, parents, taxpayers) of the quality of higher-education institutions.

4. In order to dramatize the clash of cultures, I have overemphasized the differences in the goals that each culture seeks. The boundaries are fuzzy, but the differences are real.

5. "Organized anarchies" are organizations characterized by problematic preferences, unclear technologies, and fluid participation. Universities are a familiar form of such anarchies.

Chapter 7

1. For a brief discussion of the etiology of *accountability*, see Wagner (1989).

2. Gormley and Weimar (1999, p. 9) pointed out that, in some cases, inputs have been used as proxies to measure valued outcomes. They said, "Nevertheless, many report cards continue to rely heavily on such techniques. For example, the annual college guide produced by *U.S. News & World Report* gives substantial weight to such input measures as the quality of the student body and faculty resources. Output measures, such as graduation and retention rates, also get considerable emphasis, but outcome measures, such as the alumni giving rate, receive little weight." I do not consider largely reputational rankings as viable accountability mechanisms and so do not treat them in this book.

Chapter 8

Blake Naughton and Anita Suen contributed significantly to the ideas and research reported in this chapter. Much of the material here was reported in Naughton, Shavelson & Suen (2003).

1. A review of the state higher-education accountability reports posted on the State Higher Education Executive Officers' Web site in August 2007 found no appreciable change from what we report here.

2. Although many states published what might be termed "statistical summaries" of higher-education data (e.g., enrollment and completion reports, often by race and degree level), this study focused on state performance reports (report cards and benchmarks) that explicitly tied data to an accountability program. In practice, this meant that performance indicators were tied to valued outcomes, were reported regularly for two or more institutions, and provided at least an implied sense of progression or regression. Reports that simply listed data without a performance context were excluded.

3. This view can be traced directly to NCPPHE's vision of a learning assessment report card, described earlier in this chapter.

4. It is critical to remember that these indicators are those identified for *statewide* performance reporting. Many states mandate or expect institutions to develop additional indicators particular to their missions.

5. The appropriateness of assigning these data as measures of learning is dubious. However, the measures are reported because, to these states, they are interpreted as indicators of learning.

6. On August 10, 2006, the *New York Times* reported, "In an effort to make Texas a magnet for scientific and medical research, the University of Texas is planning a $2.5 billion program to expand research and teaching in the sciences, including medicine and technology" (p. A16).

7. The question of the reliability and validity of the tests used by states to index student learning is another topic in need of consideration but beyond this chapter (see, e.g., Klein et al., 2007; Klein et al., 2003).

Chapter 9

I am indebted to Gayle Christensen for her research assistance on this chapter.

1. Floud (2006) pointed out that, whereas in the United States academic institutions created and support accrediting agencies, in Europe, where most of higher education is government funded, governments created quality assurance agencies.

2. The focus on study programs in Denmark was probably related to the large number of small higher-education institutions and the growing concern that the institutions alone could not be trusted to ensure an appropriate level of quality (Stensaker, 2003).

3. Stensaker (1999b) showed that the perceived benefit of the *self-evaluation* is constant regardless of the number of study programs included in the assessment. In contrast, the perceived benefit of the *external panel visit* and the *report* declined as the number of programs in the assessment increased.

4. Similarly, in Hong Kong, staff at some institutions felt that the criteria for assessing quality were not clear if an individual was deemed research active. Furthermore,

staff felt that more recognition should be given to work done in line with diverse institutional roles and missions, which might include more applied research (French et al., 1999).

Chapter 10

1. The focus here is on the teaching and learning functions of colleges and universities. Their two other main functions, research and service, are not considered but certainly are closely related, as accountability practices in one area will affect those in other areas.

2. Or perhaps unconsciously, as I had read the Graham et al. essay about eight years before writing what follows. Only after writing the principles here did I return to the Graham et al. paper because of its early influence on my thinking about accountability (and my subconscious!).

3. These and other principles below are consistent with Shulman's (2007) seven pillars of assessment for accountability.

4. The sense of indignity that the public felt about the behavior of such organizations as Enron arose because there is a *known technology* that could have been applied and should have been applied to assure the public of honest dealings.

5. The assessment exercise might also form the evidentiary base for departmental reviews that U.S. campuses frequently carry out with an external peer review team every five or six years. With assessment information available, these exercises might go beyond reputation and research productivity and include teaching and learning quality (cf. Dill et al., 1996).

References

Adelman, C. (2008). *Learning accountability from Bologna: A higher education policy primer.* Issue brief. Washington, DC: Institute for Higher Education Policy.

Alexander, F. K. (2000). The changing face of accountability. *The Journal of Higher Education* 71(4): 411–431.

Alstete, J. W. (2004). Accreditation matters. *ASHE-ERIC Higher Education Report* 30(4).

American Association of State Colleges and Universities (AASCU). (2006). Value-added assessment. *Perspectives.* Washington, DC: AASCU.

Association of American Colleges and Universities (AAC&U). (2005). *Liberal education outcomes: A preliminary report of student achievement in college.* Washington, DC: AAC&U.

Astin, A. W. (1993a). *Assessment for excellence: The philosophy and practice of assessment and evaluation in higher education.* Westport, CT: Oryx Press.

Astin, A. W. (1993b). *What matters in college: Four critical years revisited.* San Francisco: Jossey-Bass.

Bailey, S. K. (1974). Education and the state. *Educational Record* 55(1): 5–12.

Baldwin, J. D., and J. I. Baldwin. (1998). *Behavior principles in everyday life.* Upper Saddle River, NJ: Prentice-Hall.

Banta, T. W. (1986). *Performance funding in higher education: A critical analysis of Tennessee's experience.* Boulder, CO: National Center for Higher Education Management Systems.

Banta, T. W. (2007). Can assessment for accountability complement assessment for improvement? *peerReview* (Spring): 9–12.

Banta, T. W. (2008). Trying to clothe the emperor. *Assessment Update* 20(2): 3–4, 15–16.

Banta, T. W. and Associates. (2002). *Building a scholarship of assessment.* San Francisco: Jossey-Bass.

Banta, T. W., and G. R. Pike. (2007). Revisiting the blind alley of value-added. *Assessment Update* 19(1): 1–2, 14–15.

Baxter, G. P., and R. J. Shavelson. (1994.) Science performance assessments: Benchmarks and surrogates. *International Journal of Educational Research* 21: 279–298.

Benjamin, R. (2008). The case for comparative institutional assessment of higher-order thinking skills. *Change* 40(6): 50–55.

Benjamin, R., and M. Chun. (2003). A new field of dreams: The Collegiate Learning Assessment project. *peerReview* 5(4): 26–29.

Benjamin, R., M. Chun, and R. Shavelson. (2007). *Holistic tests in a sub-score world: The diagnostic logic of the CLA*. New York: Council for Aid to Education (www.cae.org/content/pro_collegiate_reports_publications.htm).

Benjamin, R., and R. H. Hersh. (2002). Measuring the difference college makes: The RAND/CAE value added assessment initiative. *peerReview* 4(2/3): 7–10.

Bloland, H. G. (2001). *Creating the council for higher education accreditation (CHEA)*. Phoenix, AZ: Oryx Press.

Borden, V. M. H., and T. W. Banta (eds.). (Summer 1994). Using performance indicators to guide strategic decision making. *New Directions for Institutional Research* 16(2): 82.

Boston, J. (2002). *The purpose of the research assessment exercises in Britain and Hong Kong*. Performance Based Research Fund Technical Working Group.

Bowen, H. R. (1979). Goals, outcomes, and academic evaluation. In A. W. Astin, H. R. Bowen, and C. M. Chambers (eds.), *Evaluating educational quality: A conference summary*. Washington, DC: Council on Postsecondary Accreditation.

Bransford, J. D., A. L. Brown, and L. L. Cocking. (1999). *How people learn: Brain, mind, experience, and school*. Washington, DC: National Academy Press.

Brennan, J., P. de Vries, and R. Williams (eds.). (1997). *Standards and quality in higher education*. Higher Education Policy Series 37. London: Jessica Kingsley.

Brennan, J., and T. Shah. (2000). *Managing quality in higher education: An international perspective on institutional assessment and change*. Buckingham, UK: OECD, Society for Research into Higher Education and Open University Press.

Brennan, R. L. (2001). *Generalizability theory*. New York: Springer-Verlag.

Burke, J. C., and Associates. (2002). *Funding public colleges and universities for performance: popularity, problems, and prospects*. Albany, NY: Rockefeller Institute Press.

Burke, J. C., and Associates (eds.). (2005). *Achieving accountability in higher education*. San Francisco: Jossey-Bass.

Burke, J. C., and H. Minassians. (2002a). *Performance reporting: The preferred "no cost" accountability program*. Albany, NY: Nelson A. Rockefeller Institute of Government.

Burke, J. C., and H. Minassians. (2002b). Reporting higher education results: Missing links in the performance chain. *New Directions for Institutional Research* 112: 1–143.

Burke, J. C., and H. Minassians. (2003). *"Real" accountability or accountability "lite"*: Seventh Annual Survey. Albany, NY: Rockefeller Institute of Government.

Burke, J. C., and A. M. Serban (eds.). (Spring 1998). Performance funding for public higher education: Fad or trend? *New Directions for Institutional Research* 25(1): 97.

Bybee, R. W. (1996). The contemporary reform of science education. In J. Rhoton and P. Bowers (eds.), *Issues in science education*, pp. 1–14. Arlington, VA: National Science Teachers Association.

Callan, P. M., W. Doyle, and J. E. Finney. (2001). Evaluating state higher education performance: Measuring up 2000. *Change* 33(2): 10–19.

Callan, P. M., and J. E. Finney. (2002). Assessing educational capital: An imperative for policy. *Change* 34(4): 25–31.

Campbell, C., and M. C. van der Wende. (2000). *International initiatives and trends in quality assurance for European higher education*. Exploratory trend report. Helsinki: European Network of Quality Assurance Agencies.

Campione, J. C., and A. L. Brown. (1984). Learning ability and transfer propensity as sources of individual differences in intelligence. In P. H. Brooks, R. Sperber, and C. McCauley (eds.), *Learning and cognition in the mentally retarded*, pp. 265–293. Hillsdale, NJ: Erlbaum.

Cardinet, J., S. Johnson, and G. Pini. (In press). *Applying generalizability theory using EduG*. New York: Routledge/Psychology Press.

Carini, R., G. Kuh, and S. Klein. (2006). Student engagement and student learning: Testing the linkages. *Research in Higher Education* 47: 1–32.

Carroll, J. B. (1993). *Human cognitive abilities: A survey of factor-analytic studies*. Cambridge, UK: Cambridge University Press.

Cartwright Young, C. (1996). Triangulated assessment of the major. In T. W. Banta, J. P. Lund, K. E. Black, and F. W. Oblander (eds.), *Assessment in practice: Putting principles to work on college campuses*, pp. 101–104. San Francisco: Jossey-Bass.

Cartwright Young, C., and M. E. Knight. (1993). Providing leadership for organizational change. In T. W. Banta and Associates (eds.), *Making a difference: Outcomes of a decade of assessment in higher education*, pp. 25–39. San Francisco: Jossey-Bass.

Cartwright Young, C., and W. J. Magruder. (1996). Juniot interview project on teaching and learning. In T. W. Banta, J. P. Lund, K. E. Black, and F. W. Oblander (eds.), *Assessment in practice: Putting principles to work on college campuses*, pp. 174–177. San Francisco: Jossey-Bass.

Case, R. (1996). Changing views of knowledge and their impact on educational research and practice. In D. R. Olson and N. Torrance (eds.), *Handbook of education and human development: New models of learning, teaching, and schooling*, pp. 75–84. Oxford, UK: Blackwell Publishers.

Cattell, R. B. (1963). Theory of fluid and crystallized intelligence: A critical experiment. *Journal of Educational Psychology* 54: 1–11.

Chun, M. (2002). Looking where the light is better: A review of the literature on assessing higher education quality. *peerReview* 4(2/3): 16–25.

Clark, B. R. (1983). *The higher education system*. Berkeley: The University of California Press.

Cohen, M. D., J. G. March, and J. P. Olson. (1972). A garbage can model of organizational choice. *Administrative Science Quarterly* 17(1): 1–25.

Colby, A., T. Ehrlich, E. Beaumont, and J. Stephens. (2003). *Educating citizens: Preparing America's undergraduates for lives of moral and civic responsibility*. San Francisco: Jossey-Bass.

Crissy, W. J. E., and D. G. Ryans. (1942). *The college sophomore appraises his curriculum: A report of the 1941 Sophomore Testing Program*. New York: American Council on Education.

Cronbach, L. J. (ed.). (2002). *Remaking the concept of aptitude: Extending the legacy of Richard E. Snow*. Mahwah, NJ: Erlbaum.

Crosier, D., L. Purser, and H. Smidt. (2007). *Trends V: Universities shaping the European higher education area*. Brussels: European University Association (www.eua.be/index .php?id=347).

Dill, D. D. (1997). Accreditation, assessment, anarchy? The evolution of academic quality assurance policies in the United States. In J. Brennan, P. de Vries, and R. Williams (eds.), *Standards and quality in higher education*, pp. 15–43. Higher Education Policy Series 37. London: Jessica Kingsley.

Dill, D. D. (2000a). Capacity building as an instrument of institutional reform: Improving the quality of higher education through academic audits in the UK, New Zealand, Sweden, and Hong Kong. *Journal of Comparative Policy Analysis: Research and Practice* 2: 211–234.

Dill, D. D. (2000b). Designing the academic audit: Lessons learned in Europe and Asia. *Quality in Higher Education* 6(3): 187–207.

Dill, D. D. (2000c). Is there an academic audit in your future? Reforming quality assurance in U. S. higher education. *Change* 6(1): 35–38.

Dill, D. D. (2001). The "marketization" of higher education: Changes in academic competition and implications for university autonomy and accountability. *Higher Education Policy* 14(1): 21–35.

Dill, D. D. (2003a). *The 'catch 22' of academic quality: Implications for universities and public policy* (www.unc.edu/ppaq).

Dill, D. D. (2003b). *The regulation of academic quality: An assessment of university evaluation systems with emphasis on the United States* (www.unc.edu/ppaq).

Dill, D. D., W. F. Massy, P. R. Williams, and C. M. Cook. (1996). Accreditation and academic quality assurance: Can we get there from here? *Change* 28(5): 17–24.

Diver, Colin. (2005). Is there life after rankings? *The Atlantic Online* (www.theatlantic .com/doc/200511/shunning-college-rankings).

Dunkel, H. B. (1947). *General education in the humanities*. Washington, DC: American Council on Education.

Dwyer, C. A., C. M. Millett, and D. G. Payne. (2006). *A culture of evidence: Postsecondary assessment and learning outcomes*. Princeton, NJ: Educational Testing Service.

Eaton, J. S. (2008). Attending to student learning. *Change* 40(4): 22–27.

Educational Testing Service. (1953). *The graduate record examinations institutional testing program: Summary statistics*. Princeton, NJ: Author.

Educational Testing Service. (1954). *Assessing the broad outcomes of education in the liberal arts*. Princeton, NJ: Author.

Educational Testing Service. (1966). *The graduate record examinations: Area tests*. Princeton, NJ: Educational Testing Service.

Educational Testing Service. (1993). *Tasks in critical thinking: A disclosed task and scoring guide*. Princeton, NJ: Author.

Ehrenberg, R. G. (2002). Reaching for the brass ring: The *U.S. News & World Report*. rankings and competition. *The Review of Higher Education* 26(2): 145–162.

El-Khawas, E., R. DePietro-Jurand and L. Holm-Nielsen. (1998). *Quality assurance in higher education: Recent progress, challenges ahead*. Education Paper Series No. 23. Washington, DC: The World Bank.

Erwin, T. D. (2000). *The NPEC sourcebook on assessment. Vol. 1, definitions and assessment methods for critical thinking, problem solving, and writing*. NCES 2000-195. For the Council of the National Postsecondary Education Cooperative Student Outcomes Pilot Working Group: Cognitive and Intellectual Development. Washington, DC: U.S. Department of Education, National Center for Education Statistics.

Erwin, T. D., and K. W. Sebrell. (2003). Assessment of critical thinking: ETS' Tasks in Critical Thinking. *Journal of General Education* 52(1): 50–70.

European Network for Quality Assurance. (2003). *Quality procedures in European higher education: An ENQA survey*. Helsinki: ENQA.

EVA. (2003). *Educational evaluation around the world*. Copenhagen: The Danish Evaluation Institute.

Ewell, P. T. (1991). To capture the ineffable: New forms of assessment in higher education. AAHE Assessment Forum, American Association for Higher Education. Also in *Review of Research in Education* 17: 75–126.

Ewell, P. T. (1993). Performance indicators: A new round of accountability. *Assessment Update* 5(3).

Ewell, P. T. (1997). *Accountability and assessment in a second decade: New looks or same old story?* Paper presented at the AAHEE Conference on Assessment and Quality.

Ewell, P. T. (1998a). National trends in assessing student learning. *Journal of Engineering Education*.

Ewell, P. (1998b). Statewide testing: The sequel. *Assessment Update* 10(5).

Ewell, P. (2001). Statewide testing in higher education. *Change* 33(2): 21–27.

Ewell, P. (2002). An emerging scholarship: A brief history of assessment. In T. W. Banta and Associates (eds.), *Building a scholarship of assessment*. San Francisco: Jossey-Bass.

Ewell, P., and P. Ries. (2000). *Assessing student learning outcomes: A supplement to Measuring up 2000*. San Jose, CA: National Center for Public Policy and Higher Education.

Executive Committee of the Cooperative Study in General Education. (1947). *Cooperation in general education*. Washington, DC: American Council on Education.

Feuerstein, R., Y. Rand, and M. Hoffman. (1979). *The dynamic assessment of retarded performers*. Baltimore: University Park Press.

Fishkin, M. W. (1978). *Federal reliance on educational accreditation: The scope of administrative discretion*. Washington, DC: Council on Postsecondary Accreditation.

Floud, R. (2006). The Bologna Process: Transforming European higher education. *Change* (July/August): 8–15.

French, N. J., W. F. Massy, P. K. Ko, H. F. H. Siu, and K. Young. (1999). *Research assessment in Hong Kong* (www.ugc.edu.hk/english/documents/papers/HKRAE_6.html).

French, N. J., W. F. Massy, and K. Young. (2001). Research assessment in Hong Kong. *Higher Education* 42(1) July.

Gardner, H. (1983). *Frames of mind*. New York: Basic Books.

Gentner, D., and A. L. Stevens (eds.). (1983). *Mental models*. Hillsdale, NJ: Erlbaum.

Goedegebuure, L., F. Kaiser, P. Maassen, L. Meek, F. van Vught, and F. de Weert (eds.). (1994). *Higher education policy: An international comparative perspective*. Oxford, UK: Pergamon Press.

Gormley, W. T. Jr., and D. L. Weimer. (1999). *Organizational report cards*. Cambridge, MA: Harvard University Press.

Graff, G., and C. Birkenstein. (2008). A progressive case for educational standardization. *Academe Online* (www.aaup.org/AAUP/pubsres/academe/2008/MJ/Feat/graf.htm?PF=1).

Graham, P. A., R. Lyman, and M. Trow. (1995). *Accountability of colleges and universities: An essay*. New York: Columbia University.

Grant, G., and W. Kohli. (1979). Contributing to learning by assessing student performance. In G. Grant and Associates (eds.), *On competence: A critical analysis of competence-based reforms in higher education*, pp. 138–159. San Francisco: Jossey-Bass.

Grant, G., and D. Riesman. (1978). *The perceptual dream: Reform and experiment in the American college*. Chicago: University of Chicago Press.

Gray, P. J. (2002). The roots of assessment: Tensions, solutions, and research directions. In T. W. Banta and Associates, *Building a scholarship of assessment*. San Francisco: Jossey-Bass.

Guilford, J. P. (1956). The structure of intellect. *Psychological Bulletin* 53(4): 267–293.

Guilford, J. P. (1971). *The nature of human intelligence*. New York: McGraw-Hill.

Gumport, P. J. (2000). Academic restructuring: Organizational change and institutional imperatives. *Higher Education* 39: 67–91.

Gustafsson, J-E., and J. O. Undheim. (1996). Individual differences in cognitive functions. In R. Calfee and D. Berliner (eds.), *Handbook of educational psychology*, pp. 186–242. New York: Macmillan.

Hardison, C. M., and A-M. Vilamovska. (2008). *Critical thinking performance tasks: Setting and applying standards for college-level performance*. PM-2487-CAE. Santa Monica, CA: Rand.

HEA. (2003). *The programme for research in third level institutions (PRTLI): Transforming the Irish research landscape*. Dublin: Higher Education Authority.

Henkel, M. (2000). *Academic identities and policy change in higher education*. London: Jessica Kingsley.

Hersh, R. H., and R. Benjamin. (2002). Assessing selected liberal education outcomes: A new approach. *peerReview* 4(2/3): 11–15.

Immerwahr, J. (2000). *Great expectations: How New Yorkers view higher education*. San Jose, CA: National Center for Public Policy and Higher Education.

Kandel, I. L. (1936). *Examinations and their substitutes in the United States*. Bulletin no. 28. NY: Carnegie Foundation for the Advancement of Teaching.

Klein, S. (2002a). Direct assessment of cumulative student learning. *peerReview* 4(2/3): 26–28.

Klein, S. (2002b). The educational effects of assessment policies: What the legal community is learning. *peerReview* 4(2/3): 29–33.

Klein, S., R. Benjamin, R. Shavelson, and R. Bolus. (2007). The collegiate learning assessment: Facts and fantasies. *Evaluation Review* 31(5): 415–439.

Klein, S., D. Freedman, R. Shavelson, and R. Bolus. (2008). Assessing school effectiveness. *Evaluation Review* 32: 511–525.

Klein, S. P., G. D. Kuh, M. Chun, L. Hamilton, and R. J. Shavelson. (2003). The search for "value-added": Assessing and validating selected higher education outcomes. Annual meeting of the American Educational Research Association, Chicago.

Klein, S. P., G. D. Kuh, M. Chun, L. Hamilton, and R. J. Shavelson. (2005). An approach to measuring cognitive outcomes across higher-education institutions. *Journal of Higher Education* 46(3): 251–276.

Klein, S. P., B. M. Stecher, R. J. Shavelson, D. McCaffrey, T. Ormseth, R. M. Bell, K. Comfort, and A. R. Othman. (1998). Analytic versus holistic scoring of science performance tasks. *Applied Measurement in Education* 11(2): 121–137.

Kohler, J. (2003). Quality assurance, accreditation, and recognition of qualifications as regulatory mechanisms in the European higher education area. *Higher Education in Europe* 28(3): 317–330.

Kristoffersen, D. (2003). Denmark. In *educational evaluation around the world. An international anthology*. Copenhagen: The Danish Evaluation Institute.

Kuh, G. D. (2001). Assessing what really matters to student learning: Inside the national survey of student engagement. *Change* 33(3): 10–17, 66.

Kuh, G. D. (2003). What we're learning about student engagement from NSSE: Benchmarks for effective educational practices. *Change* 35(2): 24–32.

Kuh, G. D. (2005). The scholarly assessment of student development. In T. W. Banta and Associates (eds.), *Building a scholarship of assessment.* San Francisco: Jossey-Bass.

Kuh, G. (2006). Director's message. In *Engaged learning: Fostering success for all students.* Bloomington, IN: National Survey of Student Engagement.

Kyllonen, P. C., and V. J. Shute. (1989). A taxonomy of learning skills. In P. L. Ackerman, R. J. Sternberg, and R. Glaser (eds.), *Learning and individual differences: Advances in theory and research*, pp. 117–163. New York: Freeman.

Lagemann, E. C. (1983). *Private power for the public good: a history of the Carnegie Foundation for the advancement of teaching.* Middleton, CT: Wesleyan University Press.

Lannholm, G. V., and W. B. Schrader. (1951.) *Predicting graduate school success: An evaluation of the effectiveness of the graduate record examinations.* Princeton, NJ: Educational Testing Service.

Learned, W. S., and B. D. Wood. (1938). *The student and his knowledge: A report to the Carnegie Foundation on the results of the high school and college examination of 1928, 1930, and 1932.* No. 29. Boston: Merrymount Press.

Lemann, N. (1999). *The big test: The secret history of the American meritocracy.* New York: Farrar, Straus, and Giroux.

Levi, A. W. (1948). *General education in the social studies.* Washington, DC: American Council on Education.

Lewis, R. (2004). Ten years of international quality assurance. In *Ten years on: Changing higher education in a changing world.* London: Center for Higher Education Research and Information, the Open University.

Lewis, R. (2005). External examiner system in the United Kingdom: Fresh challenges to an old system. Public Policy for Academic Quality Research Program. Chapel Hill: University of North Carolina (www.unc.edu).

Li, M. (2001). A framework for science achievement and its link to test items. Unpublished doctoral dissertation, Stanford University, Stanford, CA.

Li, M., M. A. Ruiz-Primo, and R. J. Shavelson. (2006). Towards a science achievement framework: The case of TIMSS 1999. In S. Howie and T. Plomp (eds.), *Contexts of learning mathematics and science: Lessons learned from TIMSS.* London: Routledge.

Li, M., and R. J. Shavelson. (2001). *Examining the links between science achievement and assessment.* Paper presented at the annual meeting of the American Educational Research Association, Seattle, WA, April.

Lingenfelter, P. E. (2003). Educational accountability: Setting standards, improving performance. *Change* 35(2): 24–23.

Lingenfelter, P. E. (2005). *The national commission on accountability in higher education.* Paper delivered at the American Council of Education, February.

Linn, R. L. (2000). Assessments and accountability. *Educational Researcher* 29(2): 4–16.

Loacker, G., and M. Mentkowski. (1993). Creating a culture where assessment improves learning. In T. W. Banta and Associates (eds.), *Making a difference: Outcomes of a decade of assessment in higher education*, pp. 5–24. San Francisco: Jossey-Bass.

Lubinescu, E. S., J. L. Ratcliff, and M. A. Gaffney. (2001). Two continuums collide: Accreditation and assessment. In J. L. Ratcliff, E. S. Lubinescu, and M. A. Gaffney (eds.), *New directions for higher education*, vol. 13, pp. 5–22. San Francisco: Jossey-Bass.

Lythcott, J. (1990). Problem solving and requisite knowledge of chemistry. *Journal of Chemical Education* 67: 248–252.

Magruder, W. J., and C. Cartwright Young. (1996a). Value-added talent development in general education. In T. W. Banta, J. P. Lund, K. E. Black, and F. W. Oblander (eds.), *Assessment in practice: Putting principles to work on college campuses*, pp. 169–171. San Francisco: Jossey-Bass.

Magruder, W. J., and C. Cartwright Young. (1996b). Portfolios: Assessment of liberal arts goals. In T. W. Banta, J. P. Lund, K. E. Black, and F. W. Oblander (eds.), *Assessment in practice. Putting principles to work on college campuses*, pp. 171–174. San Francisco: Jossey-Bass.

Mansbridge, J. (1998). On the contested nature of the public good. In W. W. Powell and E. S. Clemens (eds.), *Private action and the public good*, pp. 3–19. New Haven, CT: Yale University Press.

March, J. G. (1994). *A primer on decision making: How decisions happen.* New York: Free Press.

March, J. G., and J. P. Olsen. (1995). *Democratic governance.* New York: Free Press.

Martinez, M. E. (2000). *Education as the cultivation of intelligence.* Mahwah, NJ: Erlbaum.

Massaro, V. (1997). Institutional responses to quality assessment in Australia. In J. Brennan, P. de Vries and R. Williams (eds.), *Standards and quality in higher education.* London: Jessica Kingsley.

Massy, W. F. (1997). Teaching and learning quality-process review: The Hong Kong programme. *Quality in Higher Education* 3(3): 249–262.

Massy, W. F. (1999). *Energizing quality work: Higher education quality evaluation in Sweden and Denmark.* NCPI Technical Report no. 6-06. Stanford, CA: National Center for Postsecondary Improvement (www.stanford.edu/group/ncpi/documents/pdfs/6–06_swedendenmark.pdf).

Massy, W. F. (2003). *Honoring the trust: Quality and cost containment in higher education.* Bolton, MA: Anker Publishing Company, Inc.

Massy, W. F. (2005). Academic audit for accountability and improvement. In J. C. Burke and Associates (eds.), *Achieving accountability in higher education: Balancing public, academic, and market demands.* San Francisco: Jossey-Bass.

Massy, W. F., and R. Zemsky. (1994). Faculty discretionary time: Departments and the "academic ratchet." *Journal of Higher Education* 65(1): 1–22.

McClelland, D. C. 1973. Testing for competence rather than for "intelligence." *American Psychologist* 28(1): 1–14.

McDonough, P. M., A. L. Antonio, M. B. Walpole, and L. X. Perez. (1998). College rankings: Democratized knowledge for whom? *Research in Higher Education* 39: 513–538.

McLendon, M. K., J. C. Hearn, and R. Deaton. (2006). Called to account: Analyzing the origins and spread of state performance-accountability policies for higher education. *Educational Evaluation and Policy Analysis* 28(1): 1–24.

Messick, S. (1984). The psychology of educational measurement. *Journal of Educational Measurement* 21(3): 215–237.

Miller, M. A. (2006). *Assessing college-level learning.* Policy alert. San Jose, CA: National Center for Public Policy and Higher Education.

Ministry of Education. (2004). New economy research fund (http://myfrst.frst.govt.nz/ Public/ResearchReports/CD05/html/output/6.html).

National Center for Public Policy and Higher Education. (2000). *Measuring up 2000: The state-by-state report card for higher education.* San Jose, CA: Author (http://measuringup .highereducation.org/downloads/2000.cfm).

National Center for Public Policy and Higher Education. (2002). *Measuring up 2002: The state-by-state report card for higher education.* San Jose, CA: Author (http://measuringup .highereducation.org/downloads/2002.cfm).

National Center for Public Policy and Higher Education. (2004). *Measuring up 2004: The national report card on higher education.* San Jose, CA: Author (www.highereducation .org/reports/mu04/National%20Report1.pdf).

National Center for Public Policy and Higher Education. (2006). *Measuring up 2006: The national report card on higher education.* San Jose, CA: Author (http://measuringup .highereducation.org/_docs/2006/NationalReport_2006.pdf).

National Center for Public Policy and Higher Education. (2008). *Measuring up 2008: The national report card on higher education.* San Jose, CA: Author (http://measuringup2008 .highereducation.org/print/NCPPHEMUNationalRpt.pdf).

National Commission on Accountability in Higher Education. (2005). *Accountability for better results: A national imperative for higher education.* Boulder, CO: State Higher Education Executive Officers.

National Commission on Excellence in Education. (1983). *A nation at risk: The imperative for educational reform.* Washington, DC: U.S. Government Printing Office.

National Governors Association. (1991). *Time for results: The governors' 1991 report on education.* Washington, DC: Author.

National Research Council (NRC). (2001). *Knowing what people know: The science and design of educational assessment.* Washington, DC: National Academy Press.

Naughton, B. A. (2004). *The efficacy of state higher education accountability programs.* Unpublished doctoral dissertation, Stanford University, Stanford, CA.

Naughton, B. A., R. J. Shavelson, and A. Y. Suen. (2003). *Accountability for what? Understanding the learning objectives in state higher education accountability programs.* Paper presented at the annual meeting of the American Educational Research Association, Chicago, IL, April.

NCPI. (2002). Shopping for the right fit: Patterns of college choice in the postsecondary market. *Change* (March/April): 47–50.

Nettles, M., and J. Cole. (2001). A study in tension: State assessment and public colleges and universities. In D. E. Heller (ed.), *The states and public higher education policy: Affordability, access, and accountability,* pp. 198–218. Baltimore: Johns Hopkins University Press.

Nettles, M. T., J. J. K. Cole, and S. Sharp. (1997). *Assessment of teaching and learning in higher education and public accountability: State governing, coordinating board, and regional accreditation association policies and practices.* NCPI Technical Report no. 5-02. Stanford, CA: National Center for Postsecondary Improvement.

Newman, Frank. 2003. Higher education in the age of accountability. Testimony before the Committee on Education and Workforce, United States Congress, May 13, 2003, Washington, DC: The Futures Project (www.futuresproject.org/publications/Testimony.pdf).

Ohanian, S. (2005). Refrains of the school critics. *The School Administrator* (www.aasa.org/publications/saarticledetail.cfm?ItemNumber=2808andsnItemNumber=950andtnItemNumber=).

Pace, C. R. (1979). *Measuring outcomes of college: Fifty years of findings and recommendations for the future.* San Francisco: Jossey-Bass.

Pascarella, E. T., T. A. Seifert, and C. Blaich. (2008). *Validation of the NSSE benchmarks and deep approaches to learning.* Iowa City: University of Iowa, College of Education, Lindquist Center (also at www.liberalarts.wabash.edu).

Pascarella, E. T., and P. T. Terenzini. (2005). *How college affects students: A third decade of research.* San Francisco: Jossey-Bass.

Pellegrino, J. W., N. Chudowsky, and R. Glaser (eds.). (2001). *Knowing what students know: The science and design of educational assessment.* Washington, DC: National Academy Press.

Peterson, Marvin W., D. S. Vaughan, and T. E. Perorazio. (2001). *Student assessment in higher education: A comparative study of seven institutions.* Stanford, CA: Stanford University, National Center for Postsecondary Improvement (NCPI).

Pike, G. R. (1989). Overview of general education assessment instruments. *Assessment Update* 1(1).

Pike, G. R. (2002). Measurement issues in outcomes assessment. In T. W. Banta and Associates, *Building a scholarship of assessment.* San Francisco: Jossey-Bass.

Pike, G. R. (2008). Making accountability transparent: Next steps for the voluntary system of accountability. *Assessment Update* 20(2): 8–12.

Pini, G., J. Cardinet, and S. Johnson. (In press). *Applied G-theory: Measurements we can trust.* New York: Routledge/Psychology Press.

Present and Former Members of the Faculty. (1950). *The idea and practice of general education: An account of the College of the University of Chicago.* Chicago: University of Chicago Press.

Roberts, G. (2003). *Review of research assessment* (www.ra-review.ac.uk/reports/roberts .asp).

Robertson, S. L., X. Bonal, and R. Dale. (2002). GATS and the education service industry: The politics of Scale and global reterritorialization. *Comparative Education Review* 46: 472–496.

Romzek, B. S. (2000). Dynamics of public sector accountability in an era of reform. *International Review of Administrative Sciences* 66(1): 21–44.

Rose, P. (2003). *Education and the general agreement on trade in services: What does the future hold?* Report of the Fifteenth CCEM Preliminary Meeting. London: The Commonwealth Secretariat.

Ruiz-Primo, M. A., R. J. Shavelson, M. Li, and S. E. Schultz. (2001). On the validity of cognitive interpretations of scores from alternative concept-mapping techniques. *Educational Assessment* 7(2): 99–141.

Sackett, P. R., M. J. Borneman, and B. S. Connelly. (2008). High-stakes testing in higher education and employment. *American Psychologist* 63(4): 215–227.

Savage, H. J. (1953). *Fruit of an impulse: Forty-five years of the Carnegie Foundation.* New York: Harcourt, Brace and Company.

Sawyer, B. A. (1990). Concept learning versus problem solving: Revisited. *Journal of Chemical Education* 67: 253–255.

Shavelson, R. J. (1991). Generalizability of military performance measurements: I. Individual performance. In A. K. Wigdor and B. F. Green Jr. (eds.), *Performance assessment for the workplace (vol. 2): Technical issues,* pp. 207–257. Washington, DC: National Academy Press.

Shavelson, R. J. (2007a). Assessing student learning responsibly: From history to an audacious proposal. *Change* (January/February): 26–33.

Shavelson, R. J. (2007b). *A brief history of student learning: How we got where we are and a proposal for where to go next.* Washington, DC: Association of American Colleges and Universities' *The Academy in Transition.*

Shavelson, R. J. (2008a). The collegiate learning assessment. *Forum for the future of higher education: Ford policy forum,* pp. 18–24. Cambridge, MA.

Shavelson, R. J. (2008b). Reflections on quantitative reasoning: An assessment perspective. In B. L. Madison and L. A. Steen (eds.), *Calculation vs. context: Quantitative literacy and its implications for teacher education.* Washington, DC: Mathematical Association of America.

Shavelson, R. J. (2008c). The Spellings Commission report on the collegiate learning assessment. *Forum for the future of higher education*, pp. 35–38. Cambridge, MA.

Shavelson, R. J., G. P. Baxter, and J. Pine. (1992). Performance assessments: Political rhetoric and measurement reality. *Educational Researcher* 21(4): 22–27.

Shavelson, R.J., N. B. Carey, and N. M. Webb. (1990). Indicators of science achievement: Options for a powerful policy instrument. *Phi Delta Kappan* 71(9): 692–697.

Shavelson, R. J., and L. Huang. (2003). Responding responsibly to the frenzy to assess learning in higher education. *Change* 35(1): 10–19.

Shavelson, R. J., R. W. Roeser, H. Kupermintz, S. Lau, C. Ayala, A. Haydel, S. Schultz, G. Quihuis, and L. Gallagher. (2002). Richard E. Snow's remaking of the concept of aptitude and multidimensional test validity: Introduction to the special issue. *Educational Assessment* 8(2): 77–100.

Shavelson, R. J., and M. A. Ruiz-Primo. (2006). *Assessment of student learning in college: Rhetoric and promises*. Paper presented at the annual meeting of the National Council on Measurement in Education.

Shavelson, R. J., and J. L. Seminara. (1968). Effect of lunar gravity on man's performance of basic maintenance tasks. *Journal of Applied Psychology* 52: 177–183.

Shavelson, R. J., and N. M. Webb. (1991). *Generalizability theory: A primer.* Newbury Park, CA: Sage.

Shermis, M. D. (2008). The collegiate learning assessment: A critical perspective. *Assessment Update* 20(2): 10–12.

Shulman, L. S. (2007). Counting and recounting: Assessment and the quest for accountability. *Change* 39(1): 20–25.

Sidman, M. (1989). *Coercion and its fallout.* Boston: Authors Cooperative.

Sims, S. J. (1992). *Student outcomes assessment: A historical review and guide to program development.* New York: Greenwood Press.

Snow, R. E. (1994). Abilities in academic tasks. In R. J. Sternberg and R. K. Wagner (eds.), *Mind in context: Interactionist perspectives on human intelligence*, pp. 3–37. Cambridge, UK: Cambridge University Press.

Snow, R.E., and D. F. Lohman. (1984). Toward a theory of cognitive aptitude for learning from instruction. *Journal of Educational Psychology* 76(3): 347–376.

Stensaker, B. (1999a). External quality auditing in Sweden: Are departments affected? *Higher Education Quarterly* 53(4): 353–368.

Stensaker, B. (1999b). User surveys in external assessments: problems and prospects. *Quality in Higher Education* 5(3): 255–264.

Stensaker, B. (2003). Subject assessments for academic quality in Denmark: A review of purposes, processes and outcomes (www.unc.edu/ppaq).

Stensaker, B. (2004). Subject assessments for academic quality in Denmark: A review of purposes, processes and outcomes. *Public Policy for Academic Quality.* Chapel Hill, NC: The University of North Carolina Chapel Hill Department of Public Policy (www.unc.edu/ppaq).

Taylor, K. L., and J-P. Dionne. (2000). Accessing problem-solving strategy knowledge: The complementary use of concurrent verbal protocols and retrospective debriefing. *Journal of Educational Psychology* 92(3): 413–425.

Thelin, J. R. (2004). *A history of American higher education.* Baltimore: Johns Hopkins University Press.

University of Texas System Board of Regents. (2005–2006). *Accountability and performance report.* University of Texas Office of Institutional Planning and Accountability (www.utsystem.edu/ipa/Accountability.htm).

University of Texas System Board of Regents. (2006–2007). *Accountability and performance report.* University of Texas Office of Institutional Planning and Accountability (www.utsystem.edu/ipa/Accountability.htm).

U.S. Department of Education. (2006). *A test of leadership: Charting the future of U.S. higher education.* Washington, DC: Author.

Vygotsky, L. S. (1986–34). *Thought and language.* A. Kozulin (ed. and trans.) Cambridge, MA: Harvard University Press.

Wagner, R. B. (1989). *Accountability in education: A philosophical inquiry.* New York: Routledge.

Warren, J. R. (1978). *The measurement of academic competence.* Princeton, NJ: Educational Testing Service.

Wergin, J. F. (2004). Taking responsibility for student learning: The role of accreditation. *Change* 37(1): 30–33.

Wigdor, A. K., and B. F. Green Jr. (eds.). (1991). *Performance assessment for the workplace,* vol. 1. Washington, DC: National Academy Press.

Wilger, A. (1997). *Quality assurance in higher education: A literature review.* NCPI Technical Report no. 6-03. Stanford, CA: National Center for Postsecondary Improvement.

Yin, R. K. (2003). Case study research: Design and methods. Third edition. *Applied Social Research Methods Series,* vol. 5. Thousand Oaks, CA: Sage.

Zemsky, R. (2000). A new way to look at colleges: How to discover the reality behind the dream. *Peterson's Guide to Four Year Colleges.*

Zemsky, R., and W. F. Massy. (1990). Cost containment: Committing to a new economic reality. *Change* 22(6): 16–22.

Index

Academic audits: accountability and, 6–7, 125, 183; assessment and accountability, 206; international accountability systems and, 164, 166–169, 180, 181–182; proposed assessment programs and, 185, 198, 203–205

Academic domains, 62–63, 67, 189

Academic majors: campus assessment programs and, 76, 87; Collegiate Learning Assessment and, 46; domain-specific knowledge and reasoning, 14–15; grade-point average (GPA) and, 62; history of student learning assessment and, 41; learning outcomes and, 4, 185; proposed assessment programs and, 190–191; state accountability programs and, 153

Academic review process, 163–164, 167

Accountability: assessment and, 4–7, 183–185; assessment frameworks and, 18–19; the Bologna Process and, 178; complicating factors, 121, 124–131; defined, 121–123, 214n3; external accountability and, 31–38; history of higher-education accountability, 102–110; impacts of higher-education accountability, 123–124; information distribution and, 110–120; institutional improvements and, 39; learning outcomes and, 185–186; principles for, 192–196; prior proposals for, 196–200; proposal for, 200–205; Spellings Commission and, 1–2

"Accountability of Colleges and Universities" (Graham, Lyman, & Trow), 192–196

Accountability programs, international, 183; the Bologna Process and, 176–180;

mechanisms for quality assurance, 163–166; rise of, 161–163; types of quality assurance programs, 166–176

Accountability programs, state, 134–144, 158, 159, 160, 183

"Accountability triangle," 113–114, 119–120, 132, 155–157, 193, 195, 199

Accreditation, 5, 206; accountability and, 102–103, 104–105, 106, 118, 196; campus assessment programs and, 80, 94, 97; government authority and, 199; international accountability systems and, 161, 165, 177, 179; learning outcomes and, 154; proposals for, 184, 197–198, 200–201; Spellings Commission and, 2; state accountability programs and, 144, 156

Achievement, 11, 16, 19, 24, 39

ACT. See American College Testing Program (ACT)

Actions, responsibility for, 122, 124–125, 131

Administrative processes. See Operational procedures

Admissions tests, 110, 138, 152

Alverno College, 71, 72–75, 105, 189, 205

American Association of State Colleges and Universities (AASCU), 3, 33–34, 110

American College Testing Program (ACT), 22, 23, 29, 30–31, 32, 36–37

Analytic writing tasks, Collegiate Learning Assessment and, 47, 52, 53, 55–56

Assessment: accountability and, 4–7, 183–185, 198; defining learning and, 10–11, 10–11; direct and indirect measures, 9–10;

Assessment (*continued*)
   framework for, 8–9, 11–20; learning
   outcomes and, 192–193, 206; proposal for,
   184–185, 201–203. *See also* Student
   learning assessment, history of
Assessment and accountability, proposal for,
   200–205
Assessment-Centered University (ACU):
   assessment and, 79, 83, 84, 89, 91–92;
   culture of evidence and, 205;
   development processes and, 80, 82;
   operational procedures, 85–86, 87–88;
   program performance and, 86–87; quality
   assurance processes and, 90
Assessment frameworks, 11–14, 18–20;
   disciplinary and broad abilities, 15–17;
   domain-specific knowledge and
   reasoning, 14–15; state accountability
   programs and, 145; what to assess, 17–18
Assessment instruments, 90–92, 96, 149
Assessment offices, 84–85, 87–89, 95–96, 204
Assessment philosophy, 47–49, 64, 78, 81, 82–84,
   95, 97–98
Assessment program, proposed: academic
   majors and, 190–191; broad abilities and,
   189–190; learning outcomes and, 185–187,
   191–192; social responsibility outcomes,
   187–189
Assessment programs, campus: academic
   majors and, 190; audit programs and,
   6, 7; benchmark programs, 71–77;
   cross-campus comparisons, 80–94;
   exemplary programs, 70–71, 77–80, 94–101;
   learning outcomes and, 193; proposed
   assessment programs and, 201–203; state
   accountability programs and, 144–145
Association of American Colleges and
   Universities (AAC&U), 110, 111, 186
Associations. *See* Higher-education
   associations
Audit programs. *See* Academic audits

Benchmark campus learning assessment
   programs, 71, 71–72, 72–75, 75–77
Benchmarking, state accountability programs
   and, 135, 136, 151, 158
Benchmark institutional comparisons:
   academic majors and, 190–191;
   assessments and, 42–43, 70, 76, 184, 194,
   202; Collegiate Learning Assessment and,
   35–36, 45, 65, 67, 68–69; international
   accountability systems and, 179; learning

outcomes and, 189, 191. *See also*
   Cross-institutional comparisons
Bologna Process, 173, 176–180, 193
Broad abilities: assessment and, 18, 193;
   assessment frameworks and, 15–17, 19;
   Collegiate Learning Assessment and,
   48–49, 67–68; Graduate Record
   Examination (GRE) and, 29; history of
   student learning assessment and, 30–31,
   39–40; learning outcomes and, 186,
   191–192; proposed assessment programs
   and, 189–190; state accountability
   programs and, 149, 153
Burdens, on faculty, 92–93, 94, 98–99

Capstone courses, 76, 93, 190
Carnegie Foundation for the Advancement of
   Teaching, 21, 23, 27–28, 30, 39–40, 212n1
Case study sites, campus assessment programs
   and, 79–80, 99–100
Causality, accountability and, 122, 125–128, 132
Chicago College General Education
   assessment, 22, 26, 40
Closing the Gaps program (Texas), 149, 151
Cognitive demands, Collegiate Learning
   Assessment and, 63–64
Cognitive outcomes: assessment frameworks
   and, 12, 13, 19; history of student learning
   assessment and, 41; proposed assessment
   programs and, 189–190; state
   accountability programs and, 148, 149, 153
College Outcomes Measurement Project
   (COMP), 30–31
Collegiate Assessment of Academic
   Proficiency (CAAP): Collegiate Learning
   Assessment and, 47; disciplinary and
   broad abilities, 16; history of student
   learning assessment and, 30, 32, 34;
   learning outcomes and, 186, 189, 202;
   measurement of student learning and, 10
Collegiate Learning Assessment, 10, 110, 213n7
   (Ch. 4); analytic writing tasks and, 52,
   53; criticisms of, 65–69; development of,
   44–47; history of student learning
   assessment and, 33, 34–38; learning
   outcomes and, 186, 189, 202; performance
   tasks and, 50–52; reliability and validity,
   53–64; state accountability programs and,
   138, 147, 150, 151, 155; testing philosophy
   of, 47–49
Committee structures, campus assessment
   programs and, 87, 88, 93, 96

Consequences. *See* Impacts; Sanctions
Consistency, of scores. *See* Reliability
Consumers, of education: access to
  information and, 117–118, 132;
  accountability and, 102, 106, 111–112, 119;
  assessment and accountability, 4, 5,
  206–207; international accountability
  systems and, 168
Content knowledge. *See* Domain-specific
  knowledge and reasoning
Content representativeness, Collegiate
  Learning Assessment and, 57–58, 64
Cooperative Institutional Research Project
  (CIRP), 76
Cooperative Study of General Education, 22, 27
Coordination, campus assessment programs
  and, 88–89
Council for Aid to Education (CAE), 23, 32, 33,
  38, 45, 46
Credits, transferring, 179
Criterion sampling measurement approach,
  48–49, 64, 73–74, 95
Critical-thinking measurements, 62, 83–84,
  145, 186
Cross-institutional comparisons:
  accountability and, 105, 106, 109, 111–112,
  113, 119; attributing causality and, 127;
  campus assessment programs and, 81–82;
  diversity of outcomes and, 127–128;
  information asymmetry and, 195;
  proposed assessment programs and, 185;
  standardized assessments and, 4; state
  accountability programs and, 138–139, 145,
  147. *See also* Benchmark institutional
  comparisons
Cross-sectional measurements, 19, 25, 56–57
Crystallized intelligence, 14, 17
Cultural clashes, 111–114, 116, 119, 129–130,
  155–157, 201

Danish Evaluation Institute (EVA), 163, 170
Data sources: campus assessment programs
  and, 74, 98, 100–101; performance
  reporting and, 215n2 (Ch. 8); report cards
  and, 158, 159; state accountability
  programs and, 139–142, 146–147. *See also*
  Information distribution
Declarative knowledge and reasoning, 14, 23,
  24, 190
Democratic society, accountability and,
  121–122, 123, 131
Denmark, 163, 170, 172, 172–173, 215n2 (Ch. 9)

Development processes, campus assessment
  programs and, 78, 80, 81, 82, 94–95
Dill, D. D., 168, 197, 203
Direct measures of learning, 8–9, 9–10;
  accountability and, 19, 109, 119;
  achievement and, 11; assessments and, 184;
  learning outcomes and, 202, 214n2 (Ch. 6);
  social responsibility outcomes and, 187–188;
  state accountability programs and, 138,
  146, 147–148, 149, 152
Disciplinary abilities, 15–17, 191–192, 193
Discrepancy scores, 54, 56–57, 67
Domain-specific knowledge and reasoning:
  academic majors and, 190–191; assessment
  frameworks and, 13–14, 14–15; Graduate
  Record Examination (GRE) and, 28;
  history of student learning assessment
  and, 40; learning outcomes and, 185; state
  accountability programs and, 149, 153;
  what to assess and, 17–18

Educational capital, 146, 147
Educational Testing Service (ETS), 22, 23, 29,
  30, 31, 32, 187
Eight Year Study (Progressive Education
  Association), 212n1
Enrollments, learning indicators and, 142
ETS. *See* Educational Testing Service (ETS)
External accountability, 107–109, 113, 184;
  academic audits and, 167; campus
  assessment programs and, 94; history of
  student learning assessment and, 23, 31–38,
  42–43; international accountability
  systems and, 164, 168, 179–180; learning
  outcomes and, 105; organizational
  leadership and, 122; proposed assessment
  programs and, 197; subject assessments
  and, 169, 170; use of information and,
  114–115
External assessments, 76, 193, 202

Faculty participation: accountability and, 116;
  campus assessment programs and, 77,
  84–85, 85–86, 88, 89, 98; impacts of
  campus assessment programs and, 92–93,
  94; international accountability systems
  and, 169; social responsibility outcomes
  and, 187
Faculty perceptions, of performance tasks,
  58–59
Federal government, 103, 199. *See also*
  Government authority

Feedback: accountability and, 127; assessment and, 202–203; assessment instruments and, 91; assessment offices and, 89; campus assessment programs and, 84, 86, 93, 96, 98; proposed assessment programs and, 195, 203

Financial incentives, 75, 107–108, 128

Flexible University (FU): assessment instruments and, 92; assessment offices and, 89; assessment philosophy and, 83; campus assessment programs and, 79–80; impacts of campus assessment programs and, 93–94; quality assurance processes and, 90

Floud, R., 215n1 (Ch. 9)

Fluid intelligence, 14, 17

Formative function, of accountability, 114, 115, 116–117, 119, 120, 127; assessment and, 201, 202–203; cultural clashes and, 130, 194; international accountability systems and, 165; learning indicators and, 143

Functionality, campus assessment programs and, 92–94, 97

Funding, of higher education: international accountability systems and, 161–162, 171, 182; performance budgeting and, 107, 108, 134, 153; performance funding programs and, 107–108, 134, 153–154; Research Assessment Exercises (RAE), 174–175; research assessments and, 176

Gender correlations, 63–64

General ability (G), 13–14, 42, 149

General education: campus assessment programs and, 86–87; graduate education and, 22, 26–29; history of student learning assessment and, 26–27, 41; state accountability programs and, 138, 153

Globalization, international accountability systems and, 176–177, 178

Goals, of higher education, 12, 17–18, 125–126, 134, 147, 154–155, 162

Gormley, W. T., Jr., 8, 92, 101, 135, 157, 214n2 (Ch. 7)

Government authority, 115, 132, 193, 199, 201, 206–207; accountability and, 130, 183, 215n1 (Ch. 9); international accountability systems and, 162–163, 165, 172, 173, 182; state accountability programs and, 155, 156. See also Public policy

Grade-point average (GPA), 61–62

Graduate Record Examination (GRE): disciplinary and broad abilities, 16; history of student learning assessment and, 22, 27–29, 40; measurement of student learning and, 9; social responsibility outcomes and, 187; state accountability programs and, 147, 152

Graduation rates, 142, 143–144

Graham, Patricia, 192, 196–197

Higher-education accountability, history of, 102–104, 118–119; accreditation and, 104–105; report cards and, 109–110; states and, 106–109; student learning and, 105–106

Higher Education Act (1998), 105, 133

Higher-education associations, 3–4, 102–103, 104, 110, 118, 144, 191

Hiring decisions, campus assessment programs and, 86, 96, 98

Impacts: academic audits and, 168–169; campus assessment programs and, 78, 82, 92–94, 97; international accountability systems and, 165–166; Research Assessment Exercises (RAE), 174–176; subject assessments and, 171–172; unintended consequences, 128, 132

Incentives: accountability and, 128, 131–132; Collegiate Learning Assessment and, 68; financial incentives, 75, 107–108, 128; proposed assessment programs and, 203

Indirect measures, of student learning, 8–9; accountability and, 19, 109, 118–119; defining learning and, 10–11; learning outcomes and, 202, 214n2 (Ch. 6); state accountability programs and, 147–148, 151–152

Individual and social responsibility skills. See Social responsibility outcomes

Individual development, 10, 72, 73–74, 82, 95

Individual responses, accountability and, 130–131

Information distribution: academic audits and, 182; access to information and, 117–118, 119; accountability and, 110–120, 129–130, 132; attributing causality and, 127; information asymmetry, 156, 195; information overload, 157; information structures, 204–205

Information technology, Collegiate Learning Assessment and, 34–35

Input indicators, 141, 142, 143, 214n2 (Ch. 7)

Institutional improvements, 114, 127, 195; academic audits and, 166–167, 185, 205; accountability and, 39, 102, 111, 112, 113, 117, 119; campus assessment programs and, 70; Collegiate Learning Assessment and, 35–36, 38, 46, 65; international accountability systems and, 164–165, 165–166, 168, 171–172; Research Assessment Exercises (RAE), 175; state accountability programs and, 136, 151, 152, 157–158

Institutional responses, accountability and, 130–131

Institutional reviews, international accountability systems and, 164

Intelligence, 14, 17, 24, 149, 211n2

Internal accountability, 179, 197

Internal assessments. *See* Assessment programs, campus

International accountability systems: the Bologna Process and, 176–180; mechanisms for quality assurance, 163–166; rise of, 161–163; types of quality assurance programs, 166–176

Interviews, 76, 100–101

K-12 education, 107, 123–124, 125, 127, 128, 142

Knowledge and reasoning, 19, 24, 26, 39–40, 41–42. *See also* Domain-specific knowledge and reasoning

Leadership, organizational: academic audits and, 204; accountability and, 122, 124, 125, 131; campus assessment programs and, 85–87, 94, 96, 98; campus leadership support, 85–87; state accountability programs and, 156–157

Learned, William S., 21, 23, 25, 27, 40, 41, 214n1 (Ch. 6)

Learning. *See* Student learning

Learning assessments measures, 140, 144–145

Learning indicators: accountability and, 183; evolution of, 144–147; implications of, 151–153; international accountability systems and, 180; learning outcomes and, 193; performance reporting and, 147–151; state accountability programs and, 133–134, 141–155, 157, 158, 159

Learning outcomes: academic majors and, 4, 190–191; accountability and, 6, 105–106, 109–110, 122, 124–125, 131; accreditation

and, 104–105; assessment and, 192–193, 202, 206; assessment and accountability, 183–184; campus assessment programs and, 72–73, 75–76, 82–84, 95, 98; Collegiate Learning Assessment and, 58–59; defining learning and, 10–11; diversity of, 127–128; performance reporting and, 154–155; proposed assessment programs and, 185–187, 191–192; Spellings Commission and, 2; state accountability programs and, 134, 145, 148, 149–150, 152

Learning Outcomes University (LOU): assessment instruments and, 91; assessment philosophy and, 83; campus assessment programs and, 79; operational procedures and, 84–85, 87, 88–89; quality assurance processes and, 90

Legislation, state accountability programs and, 134–135

Licensure tests, 9, 110, 138, 147, 148, 152–153

Longitudinal measurements, 19, 25, 56

Lyman, Richard, 192, 196–197

Majors. *See* Academic majors

March, Jim, 116, 122, 124, 129

Market forces, accountability and, 106–107, 113–114, 115, 123, 162–163, 168, 182

McClain, Charles J., 75, 76, 77

Measurement: accountability and, 19, 106, 123, 126, 131; criterion sampling measurement approach and, 48–49; defining learning and, 10–11; direct and indirect measures, of student learning, 9–10; of individual and social responsibility skills, 20; learning assessments and, 8–9; learning outcomes and, 186–191; reliability and validity, 53–64; what to assess, 11–12. *See also* Scoring

Measure of Academic Proficiency and Progress (MAPP): Collegiate Learning Assessment and, 47; disciplinary and broad abilities, 16; history of student learning assessment and, 30, 32, 34; learning outcomes and, 186, 189, 202; measurement of student learning and, 10

Measuring Up 2000 (National Center for Public Policy and Higher Education), 109, 135–136, 146–147

Minority status, 63–64, 141

Missouri Experimental School Study, 21, 22, 23

Multiple-choice testing, 30, 32–33, 47, 49

National Assessment of Adult Literacy Survey
(NAALS), 110, 138, 147
National Assessment of Educational Progress
(NAEP), 146
National Association of Statue Universities
and Land-Grant Colleges (NASULGC),
3, 110
National Center for Postsecondary
Improvement (NCPI), 144
National Center for Public Policy and Higher
Education (NCPPHE): accountability
and, 103–104, 109–110; "learning model"
and, 139; learning outcomes and, 154; state
accountability programs and, 135–136, 137,
138, 146–147, 148–149, 157
National Education Goals (1990), 138
National Forum on College-Level Learning,
146
National Postsecondary Education
Cooperative, 145
National Survey of Student Engagement
(NSSE), 9, 91, 92, 202
New Jersey Basic Skills Assessment Program,
31
No Child Left Behind Act (2001), 123, 127, 128,
195

Open-ended assessments, 32–34, 34–38, 41–42
Operational procedures: access to
information and, 117; accountability and,
123; campus assessment programs and, 78,
81–82, 84–92, 95–96; responsibility for
actions and, 122, 124–125, 131. See also
Actions, responsibility for
Organizational processes, 126, 131, 166, 180,
204
Outcome indicators, 141, 142, 143
Outcomes. See Learning outcomes
Output indicators: accountability and, 126–127;
assessments and, 194; learning indicators
and, 143–144; state accountability programs
and, 134, 141, 142, 143, 147–148

Peer reviews, external, 167, 203
Pennsylvania Study, 22, 23–26, 39
Performance, measuring, 126–127, 128. See also
Assessment; Learning outcomes
Performance budgeting, 107, 108, 134, 153
Performance funding programs, 107–108, 134,
153–154
Performance reporting: academic audits and,
182, 203; accountability and, 107, 108,

193–194; accreditation and, 184, 197;
assessment and accountability, 206;
international accountability systems and,
164, 180; learning indicators and, 144–153;
learning outcomes and, 154–155, 193; state
accountability programs and, 134–144, 153,
157–158. See also Report cards
Performance tasks: assessment philosophy
and, 83; campus assessment programs
and, 73–74; Collegiate Learning
Assessment and, 37–38, 47, 48–49, 50–52,
55; validity and, 58–60
Personal Potential Index, 187
Philosophy. See Assessment philosophy
Political agendas, 111, 129–130, 132, 156, 184,
194
Portfolios, of performance assessments, 74, 76,
77, 91, 190
Prior learning, Collegiate Learning
Assessment and, 65–66
Procedural knowledge and reasoning, 14, 23,
24, 190
Process indicators: academic audits and, 166,
169, 198, 203; assessments and, 194;
international accountability systems and,
180; state accountability programs and,
141, 142, 143, 148
Professional authority, 162–163, 165–166, 182,
183, 193, 206–207
Professional qualifications, 177–178
Profile Tests, 28, 212n5
Program evaluations: assessment and, 202;
assessment instruments and, 91;
assessment philosophy and, 82, 84, 95;
campus assessment programs and, 86–87;
international accountability systems and,
164, 169–173; proposed assessment
programs and, 198; state accountability
programs and, 135
Progressive Education Association (PEA),
212n1
Progressivism, history of student learning
assessment and, 39–40
Publication, of assessment results. See
Performance reporting
Public goods, accountability and, 106–107
Public policy, 4–7, 113; access to information
and, 117–118; accountability and, 102, 106,
111, 115, 119, 131, 132; campus assessment
programs and, 80, 82, 94, 97; international
accountability systems and, 162; report
cards and, 134–135; Research Assessment

Exercises (RAE), 176; Spellings
Commission and, 1–4. *See also*
Government authority

Quality assurance processes: audit programs
and, 7; the Bologna Process and, 176–180;
campus assessment programs and, 96;
international accountability systems and,
161–163, 180–182; mechanisms for,
163–166; types of programs, 166–176
Question formats, 30, 32–34, 37t, 39, 47

Rankings, of colleges and universities, 157, 183.
See also Cross-institutional comparisions
Raw scores, Collegiate Learning Assessment
and, 54, 55–56
Real-life performance tasks. *See* Performance
tasks
Reasonableness, 92–94, 97, 98–99, 131
Reasoning processes, 15–16, 17
Regional agencies, accreditation and, 6, 113,
184, 201
Reliability, assessments and, 53–57, 65, 66–67,
90, 212n5
Report cards: accountability and, 107, 109–110,
118–119; audit reports and, 168; Collegiate
Learning Assessment and, 46; example of,
137; proposed assessment programs and,
195–196, 200–201; state accountability
programs and, 133, 134–139, 151, 157–158,
159, 160; subject assessments and, 170.
See also Performance reporting
Research: campus assessment programs and,
78–94, 99–101; Collegiate Learning
Assessment and, 46–47; external
accountability and, 181; by faculty
members, 86; research methods, 100–101
Research Assessment Exercises (RAE), 173–176,
181
Research assessments, 164, 173–176, 215–216n4
Retention rates, 142, 148

Sampling technology, 35–36
Sanctions: accountability and, 117, 123–124,
128, 131–132; assessments and, 125, 195,
211n1; K-12 education and, 127
Schematic knowledge and reasoning, 14–15, 190
Scholastic Aptitude Tests (SATs), 36–37, 42,
61, 66
Science area, 16, 62
Scoring: College Outcomes Measurement
Project (COMP), 31; Collegiate Learning

Assessment and, 35, 47, 50–52, 53–54, 67;
costs of, 212n4; free-response questions
and, 30; Graduate Record Examination
(GRE) and, 29; Research Assessment
Exercises (RAE), 176; Tasks in Critical
Thinking Assessment (New Jersey), 31
Self-evaluation, 163–164, 167, 170, 180, 203,
215n3 (Ch. 9)
Self-regulation: accountability and, 111, 112, 113,
118, 196–197; formative function, of
accountability, 116–117; proposed
assessment programs and, 198, 199
Self-reporting measurements, social
responsibility outcomes and, 186, 187
Shermis, M. D., 67–68
Signaling functions, 42, 94, 127, 138–139
Site selection, campus assessment research
and, 79–80, 99–100
Social control, accountability and, 130–131
Social responsibility outcomes: accountability
and, 6; assessment frameworks and, 18,
20; Collegiate Learning Assessment and,
46; history of student learning assessment
and, 26, 27, 41; learning outcomes and,
186, 211n3; proposed assessment programs
and, 187–189; state accountability programs
and, 148, 154–155
"Soft skills." *See* Social responsibility
outcomes
Spellings Commission on the Future of
Higher Education, 1–4, 8; accountability
and, 103, 108–109, 112, 113; accreditation
and, 196; learning outcomes and, 154;
proposed assessment programs and, 199
Staffing, campus assessment programs and,
84–85, 87–88
Stakeholders, 4–6, 121, 124, 151, 183, 211n1.
See also Consumers, of education;
Government authority; Professional
authority
Standardized assessments, 4, 8; domain-
specific knowledge and reasoning, 15;
history of student learning assessment
and, 21, 22, 23–26, 39; mandatory, 31–32;
sanctions and, 125; state accountability
programs and, 148, 154–155; test providers
and, 29–31
Standards, setting, 104, 107, 127, 135, 136, 199,
200–201
State governments: accountability and, 103,
106–109, 118–119, 133–134; cultural clashes
and, 155–157; external accountability and,

State governments (*continued*)
107–109; learning indicators and, 144–155;
report cards and, 8, 109–110, 157–160; state
accountability programs, 134–144
State Higher Education Executive Officers'
(SHEEO), 141–142
Stensaker, B., 172, 215n3 (Ch. 9)
Strategic knowledge and reasoning, 15, 18, 42,
190
Student-Centered Learning University
(SCLU): assessment and, 79, 83–84, 89, 91,
95; culture of evidence and, 205;
operational procedures and, 85, 87;
quality assurance processes and, 90
Student learning, 2, 4–6, 105–106, 136, 138. *See
also* Learning outcomes
Student learning assessment, history of:
external accountability and, 31–38; general
and graduate education, 26–29; origins of
standardized testing, 21, 23–26; summary,
22–23, 39–43; test providers and, 29–31.
See also Assessment
Student mobility, 176, 177
Student perceptions, of performance tasks,
59–60
Student performance, campus assessment
programs and, 72, 73
Subject assessments, 169–173, 180–181
Summative function, of accountability, 114–115,
119, 120, 127; assessment and, 202; cultural
clashes and, 130, 194; international
accountability systems and, 165; learning
indicators and, 143–144

Tasks in Critical Thinking Assessment (New
Jersey), 22, 30, 31
"Teaching to the test," 49
Testing philosophy. *See* Assessment
philosophy

Testing processes, campus assessment programs
and, 90–92
Test providers, 22, 29–31
Test technology, 24–25, 34, 39
Texas, state accountability programs and,
149–151, 154, 158, 215n6
"Think aloud" method, 57, 63–64
Thorndike MIT Engineers Study, 22, 23
Time required, for testing, 23, 24, 28, 29, 31
Total quality management. *See* Quality
assurance processes
Transparency. *See* Accountability
Trow, Martin, 192, 196–197
Truman State University, 71–72, 75–77

Undergraduate Assessment Program (UAP),
16–17, 30
United Kingdom, 171–172, 173, 174–175, 177
University of Texas, 149–150, 215n6
U.S. News and World Report college rankings,
135, 157, 183, 214n2 (Ch. 7)

Validity, of assessments, 65, 66–67, 187–188
Value-added models: accountability and, 125;
assessment instruments and, 92; campus
assessment programs and, 75; Collegiate
Learning Assessment and, 54, 56–57, 65, 67
Value-added performance, state
accountability programs and, 150, 151
Vision, campus assessment programs and, 80,
85–86, 88–89
Voluntary System of Accountability (VSA), 3,
110, 111

Washington Accord, 177–178
Watson, Thomas J., 212n4
Weimer, D. L., 8, 92, 101, 135, 157, 214n2 (Ch. 7)
Wood, Ben D., 23, 25, 40, 214n1 (Ch. 6)
Writing assessments, 37, 52, 53